REA

FRIENDS OF ACPL

Chasing Adonis
Gay Men and the Pursuit of Perfection

THE HAWORTH PRESS
Titles of Related Interest

Gay and Gray: The Older Homosexual Man, Second Edition by Raymond M. Berger

Against My Better Judgment: An Intimate Memoir of an Eminent Gay Psychologist by Roger Brown

Gay Men at Midlife: Age Before Beauty edited by Alan L. Ellis

Gay Men's Sexual Stories: Getting It! edited by Robert Reynolds and Gerard Sullivan

Gay Midlife and Maturity: Crises, Opportunities, and Fulfillment edited by John Alan Lee

Midlife and Aging in Gay America: Proceedings of the SAGE Conference 2000 edited by Douglas C. Kimmel and Dawn Lundy Martin

Social Services for Senior Gay Men and Lesbians edited by Jean K. Quam

Sociological Analysis of Aging: The Gay Male Perspective by J. Michael Cruz

When It's Time to Leave Your Lover: A Guide for Gay Men by Neil Kaminsky

The Mentor: A Memoir of Friendship and Gay Identity by Jay Quinn

Reeling in the Years: Gay Men's Perspectives on Age and Ageism by Tim Bergling

Chasing Adonis
Gay Men and the Pursuit of Perfection

Tim Bergling

Harrington Park Press®
The Trade Division of The Haworth Press, Inc.
New York • London • Oxford

For more information on this book or to order, visit
http://www.haworthpress.com/store/product.asp?sku=5745

or call 1-800-HAWORTH (800-429-6784) in the United States and Canada
or (607) 722-5857 outside the United States and Canada

or contact orders@HaworthPress.com

Published by

Harrington Park Press®, the trade division of The Haworth Press, Inc., 10 Alice Street, Binghamton, NY 13904-1580.

© 2007 by Tim Bergling. All rights reserved. No part of this work may be reproduced or utilized in any form or by any means, electronic or mechanical, including photocopying, microfilm, and recording, or by any information storage and retrieval system, without permission in writing from the publisher. Printed in the United States of America.

PUBLISHER'S NOTE
The development, preparation, and publication of this work has been undertaken with great care. However, the Publisher, employees, editors, and agents of The Haworth Press are not responsible for any errors contained herein or for consequences that may ensue from use of materials or information contained in this work. The Haworth Press is committed to the dissemination of ideas and information according to the highest standards of intellectual freedom and the free exchange of ideas. Statements made and opinions expressed in this publication do not necessarily reflect the views of the Publisher, Directors, management, or staff of The Haworth Press, Inc., or an endorsement by them.

Cover and interior illustrations by Joe Phillips.

Cover design by Karen Lowe.

Library of Congress Cataloging-in-Publication Data

Bergling, Tim.
    Chasing Adonis : gay men and the pursuit of perfection / Tim Bergling.
       p. cm.
    Includes bibliographical references.
    ISBN-13: 978-1-56023-508-8 (case 13 : alk. paper)
    ISBN-10: 1-56023-508-X (case 10 : alk. paper)
    ISBN-13: 978-1-56023-509-5 (soft 13 : alk. paper)
    ISBN-10: 1-56023-509-8 (soft 10 : alk. paper)
    1. Gay men. 2. Sexual attraction. I. Title.
HQ76.B493 2007
306.76'62—dc22

2006022965

For Dave Reynolds
1972-1995

I only wish I could have thanked you, Dave, for making all this possible, but you're with the angels now

"In between the moon and you, angels get a better view . . ."

ABOUT THE AUTHOR

Tim Bergling is the author of *Sissyphobia: Gay Men and Effeminate Behavior* (Harrington Park Press) and *Reeling in the Years: Gay Men's Perspectives on Age and Ageism* (Harrington Park Press). His work has appeared in *The Advocate, Genre, Out, Instinct,* and *HERO* magazines. A DC-area native, Bergling is a former U.S. Marine (1982-1990); he can be reached via his Web site: www.timbergling.com.

CONTENTS

Foreword *Greg Herren*	ix
Acknowledgments	xv
Introduction	1
Chapter 1. Eye of the Beholder	7
Chapter 2. The Rules of Attraction	29
Chapter 3. Beautiful Things	49
Chapter 4. Body Types	69
Chapter 5. Rejected!	115
Chapter 6. Dream Lovers	159
Chapter 7. Survey Says!	241
Afterword	265
References	277

NOTES FOR PROFESSIONAL LIBRARIANS AND LIBRARY USERS

This is an original book title published by Harrington Park Press®, the trade division of The Haworth Press, Inc. Unless otherwise noted in specific chapters with attribution, materials in this book have not been previously published elsewhere in any format or language.

CONSERVATION AND PRESERVATION NOTES

All books published by The Haworth Press, Inc., and its imprints are printed on certified pH neutral, acid-free book grade paper. This paper meets the minimum requirements of American National Standard for Information Sciences-Permanence of Paper for Printed Material, ANSI Z39.48-1984.

DIGITAL OBJECT IDENTIFIER (DOI) LINKING

The Haworth Press is participating in reference linking for elements of our original books. (For more information on reference linking initiatives, please consult the CrossRef Web site at www.crossref.org.) When citing an element of this book such as a chapter, include the element's Digital Object Identifier (DOI) as the last item of the reference. A Digital Object Identifier is a persistent, authoritative, and unique identifier that a publisher assigns to each element of a book. Because of its persistence, DOIs will enable The Haworth Press and other publishers to link to the element referenced, and the link will not break over time. This will be a great resource in scholarly research.

Foreword

Ah, the male body.

The past thirty years or so have seen a complete revolution in the way we as a society look at the masculine form. In 1965, the very notion of underwear ads showing models with rippling muscles and a rather prominent bulge beneath the fly would have been laughed off Madison Avenue. Yet little more than twenty years later, there was that massive billboard over Times Square advertising Calvin Klein Underwear. That billboard signaled a massive shift in what was then the dominant paradigm in American culture regarding the male body: the billboard was stating something that gay men had been aware of for years—that the masculine form *could* be a thing of beauty—and the definition of masculinity had been forever changed. Previously, the heavily muscled male body was out of vogue with the mainstream. It wasn't, after all, "masculine" for a man to be concerned with his appearance—particularly his physicality. If you were an athlete—Olympic, collegiate, or professional—your vigorous training resulted in a muscled physique that could be admired; otherwise, you were simply self-absorbed and vain.

As the 1980s played out, the objectification of the male body continued. Other clothing designers followed Calvin Klein's lead and began featuring homoerotic imagery of smooth, muscled young men in their advertising. As advertisers became more aware of gay men as consumers, the sexualization of the male form in their commercials and print ads continued, and their sales increased. Some gorgeous men even earned fifteen minutes of fame based solely on their appearance—remember the Diet Pepsi commercial with Lucky Vanous? Television and films soon picked up on this, and soon a muscled body was *de rigeur* for actors. And it was only a matter of time before the backlash began.

Michelangelo Signorile first examined this trend in his book *Life Outside* in 1996; Michael Bronski also talked about it in *The Pleasure*

Principle; Daniel Harris in *The Decline and Fall of Gay Culture;* it was debated in the pages of such hallowed publications as *Harvard Gay and Lesbian Review;* and even Tom Bianchi felt compelled to write a defense of his theory of art and photography called, aptly, *In Defense of Beauty.*

Few topics are as guaranteed to raise the blood pressure of gay men as the concept of beauty. *Everyone* has an opinion on this subject, and can argue their position as passionately as Ann Coulter defending why rich people shouldn't pay taxes. And while each person is as entitled to their opinion as the next, somehow it has become politically incorrect in intellectual circles to defend the notion of men working out their bodies. How many times have I been told "those arrogant muscle queens enjoy feeling superior" or have myself been described as a "body fascist" because I work out regularly and take some pride in my body? If I had a dollar for every time, I would be sipping margaritas on my own private Caribbean beach right now rather than writing this Foreword.

I used to write a syndicated health and fitness column for gay men. I was a certified personal trainer, and I was also certified to teach aerobics. In 1998, in response to a vicious article in *Harvard Gay and Lesbian Review* about muscular gay men and the self-esteem problems they were causing in "less perfect" members of the community, I wrote a column called "It's About Your Health." In this column, I wrote about the reasons *why* people should exercise, that it was about being healthier, improving your quality of life, and feeling better. I went on to say that the development of a muscular body should merely be seen as a pleasant side effect of exercise and that "people take better care of their cars then they do their bodies—and you can always get another car. You can't replace your body." It was the theory of exercise I had painstakingly developed over the years of battling my own self-esteem problems and working in the fitness industry. My clients never came in saying they wanted to be healthier; they always wanted to be more attractive. The health and fitness industry had been built up at that point into a multi-billion-dollar industry, yet more and more Americans were out of shape and overweight. I theorized that the marketing of fitness in America, by appealing to vanity, was actually doing more damage than good and was more concerned with profit than actually helping people lead healthier lives.

Within a day of that article being published, the flood of angry e-mails began. I was astonished, not only at the amount of emails I received, but at the levels of venom directed at me personally. Up until then, the e-mails I received about my columns primarily asked for advice with workouts or "how can I build my arms up?"—things of that nature. Within two days, I had received more e-mails than I had in the two years I'd been writing the column. Not one single e-mail agreed with the column; instead, they were out for my blood.

Obviously, I'd struck a nerve.

> "It's easy for you to say that it's about being healthier. . . . all one has to do is look at your picture and see how handsome you are. . . . you're the kind of person who only hangs out with other muscular men . . . you'd never even look twice at me in a bar. I'm sure your partner looks like he stepped out of an underwear ad."

> "Guys who work out are all the same. They think they're better than the rest of us."

> "If you think guys work out to be healthier, you're crazy. They work out so they can fuck better looking guys and to make the rest of us feel less worthy."

On and on, ad nauseum, ad infinitum.

At first, I was hurt and angry at the responses. But as I read through them all, I slowly realized that these angry readers were proving my point. They saw working out as an exercise in vanity, a desire to be "prettier," and not as a desirable tool to improve the quality of one's life. Why this angry response to the concept of exercise? Studies consistently showed that even a little bit of exercise improved one's health; that being overweight and out of shape increased one's chances for heart disease, kidney and liver problems, and even developing diabetes, among other health problems. They also failed to recognize, as I had often theorized, that they were making gross generalizations about other men solely based on their appearance, while complaining about how other men judged them on their own! They were certainly judging me by the photo that ran with my column—one, I might add, I thought singularly unflattering.

I answered each e-mail individually, pointing out these contradictions in their thinking, as well as how their comments actually proved the points I made in the column. Some of them responded in a positive, thoughtful way (once their initial anger had burned out, apparently), but the vast majority of them didn't. It was disappointing to not be able to break through the anger and hurt most of them felt, but I also felt that most of them weren't angry at me, but were angry because at some point in their lives they'd been made to feel unworthy, and by writing the column, I'd given their anger a focal point.

My own personal experiences with "body fascism" were torturous. I started working out, in 1994, for all the wrong reasons. I had always been attracted to muscular, fit men, and as an overweight, out-of-shape, ex-high-school jock who hadn't lifted a weight since the end of football season my senior year, I wasn't what the men I was attracted to wanted. I considered myself to be an intelligent, funny, kind, and generous man—the kind of man anyone would be pleased to have a relationship with—yet I didn't find men who looked like me attractive. Despite my own issues, I was very contemptuous of the muscle boys. Why can't they take the time to find out who I am, instead of just deciding I'm not good enough by the way I look? It wasn't until many years later that I realized I was just as guilty as they were. In 1994, I decided enough was enough—if you can't beat them, join them. I changed my eating habits and started exercising at home before bed every night—push-ups and the Abs of Steel tape. I figured if I could stick to the new diet and do the exercises three times a week minimum, on New Year's Day I would take the plunge and join a gym. I became obsessed with my physical appearance. I dropped thirty pounds in four months and joined a gym. By the following summer, I was down from 210 pounds to 155; from a 33 inch waist to a 28. Yet, at 5'11" and 155 pounds, I would look at myself in the mirror and think, "Hmmm, maybe another ten pounds and I'll be perfect." (Now, when I see pictures of myself from that summer, I want to scream "EAT SOMETHING!") And it was working. Every time I stepped into a bar I had my pick of several sexy men for the evening. Despite the vast changes in my appearance, and that I was now one of those sweaty and shirtless men on the dance floor I used to desire, I never felt like I belonged out there. I needed the attention and flattery of other men to validate myself, to feel like I was an object of desire.

One night I had the necessary breakthrough that shattered the glass through which I darkly viewed the world. I was standing by myself with bottled water, taking a break from the nonstop dancing, when a guy approached me. He was drunk and weaving a little, relatively attractive but out of shape, and he grinned at me and said, "You're hot and I want to fuck you." He slurred the words slightly, and some saliva flew. I smiled and said, "Thank you, aren't you sweet?" As I said, he was attractive in his own way, but he was also drunk. Unfortunately, my polite response apparently was interpreted as an invitation to grab me and try to stick his hands down my pants. For five minutes, I tried to get out of the situation gracefully without being rude, until finally I had no other option but to be rude. He stepped back, and his face contorted with rage as he spat out, "You muscle boys are all the same! You think you're too good for anyone else!" before storming off.

And memories flashed through my head—of me getting drunk in order to have the courage to approach some godlike being I'd been watching, of being rejected in just the same manner, and storming off humiliated, hurt, and angry. As I stood there, I realized that maybe, just maybe, the rejections I'd suffered might not have had anything to do with the way I looked, but because I'd been drunk.

I went home alone that night. All night long, I can remember thinking how I'd always vowed never to treat another man the way I'd been treated—without taking into consideration any other reason for the rejections I suffered other than the physical. I debated with myself whether what I was doing was healthy. I was obsessed with my weight, obsessed with my appearance, and obsessed with how I appeared to other people. And I realized, that night as I climbed into my bed alone on a Saturday night for the first time in months, that I wasn't going to give up lifting weights. I enjoyed it. It was fun. Being in shape made it easier for me to make it through my workday, made it easier for me to do things I couldn't do before (like move furniture), and I felt healthier than I ever had in my life. It wasn't about looking good; it was about feeling good. Essentially, I'd been wrong about everything.

That was the night I decided to become a personal trainer, in order to help other people feel better.

I still have issues with my body and my self-esteem. I don't think that is something I will ever get past. I always think I am too fat, that maybe if my chest and arms are bigger I'll be perfect, and so on. But I don't obsess over it anymore. If people find me attractive, fine. If they don't, it doesn't mean I am less of a person. There are no specific rules of attraction. People are attracted to what they are attracted to, whether it's smooth young boys with slim bodies, guys with huge muscles, Bears, daddies, whatever. Advertising and the entertainment industry notwithstanding, not everyone wants to fuck Ryan Phillippe or the porn star of the moment.

When Tim Bergling asked me to write the introduction to this book, it was almost serendipitous. I'd long felt this kind of a book was needed and had despaired that one would ever see print. I was already a fan of his work—Sissyphobia and Reeling in the Years addressed issues within the gay community that were certainly hot button topics yet never discussed in a public forum—and I was very curious to see what he found out through his interviews and surveys, to see what people were thinking out there about the issues of body image. Some of the responses are angry, others thoughtful, some provocative. But if the issues relating to body image are ever going to be worked out, it is only through thoughtful and intelligent dialogue rather than emotional tirades that answers can be found.

How this book will be received remains to be seen. Undoubtedly, there will be reviewers and columnists who will seize on its publication as an opportunity yet again to bash on muscle boys rather than putting thought into the issues raised and the responses found. I will, no doubt, be targeted once again as a "body fascist," as will Tim and his work—not recognizing or understanding that such attacks tell more about the attacker than the subject. I hope this book will be greeted as a starting place for open-minded discussion about body image rather than as an open invitation to get "revenge" for perceived personal slights.

The advice I used to give to my training clients was this: No one can make you feel bad about yourself unless you let them. Why allow someone else that kind of power over you?

Why, indeed?

Greg Herren
Author, *Jackson Square Jazz*
and *Murder in the Rue St. Ann*

Acknowledgments

I'm fortunate—this I truly know—in that I have a whole host of people who support and encourage me in my humble efforts to inform (and hopefully entertain) with the written word. As always, I have to thank the folks at The Haworth Press—Bill Cohen, Rebecca Browne, and the rest—for their ongoing confidence in me. I also have to tip my cap to my new buddy Greg Herren, for all he's done to shepherd this book to completion. Extra eyes and ears are always welcome, and his have been more valuable than most.

Thanks as always to the professionals who lent me their expertise and answered all my annoying inquiries, and the hundreds who took my surveys or submitted to more personal interviews . . . and the thousands of folks out there who took my online polls. This book could not exist without you; nor could it exist with all the fabulous folks at Earth Village Creations (www.earthvillage.com) for their wonderful efforts at helping me design and maintain the Web sites and data management systems to collect those hundreds of stories.

Finally, there's my undying gratitude to all my friends, whose forbearance, support, and patience as I put this book together were a wonder to behold. I don't know what I would do without all of you.

Introduction

I can still recall with crystal clarity, even after all these many years, the moment my body knew it was gay. Not my *mind,* mind you, but my *body.* It would be a couple of years yet before my brain was able to consciously wrap itself around the concept of gayness, and a few years more before I'd be mentally okay with the whole male-on-male love thing as it applied to me.

What I'm talking about is the moment my pure, *physical* self had its dawning awareness of impending fagdom. I was 12, and it was a sunny springtime afternoon not long before the final bell—if we even had a bell in sixth grade at Chestnut Hills Elementary, that I *don't* remember—and we were in PE class, getting ready to play kickball, one of the few team sports I ever excelled at. I'm not sure why I looked away as our teams lined up—I might have been tying my shoe or something—but when I looked back up it seems half the guys had decided, en masse, to doff their shirts in the warm sun.

Elementary school being what it was—the last academic era of my life when I would be considered anything close to popular: junior high school would be a living hell, and high school not much better—I was pretty much friends with everyone, at least the guys. (Girls I just never had much interest in. Go figure.) I'd known just about everyone on that field since the first grade, but oddly enough, this was the first time I'd seen most of them without shirts, bare-chested to the wind . . . certainly the first time I saw so many of them at the *same* time . . .

There was Steve, a study in shades of tan and brown—he was Italian, as I recall—and already solidly built at that young age, all pubescent chest and abs; there was Matt, slim and fair-haired, a half-naked angel come down from heaven to toy with my unnamed and unanticipated yearnings; Kenny was the tall gawky kid who lived up around the block from me, but now without a shirt on he was a vision, and it was *me* that was gawking at *him.*

Chasing Adonis
Published by The Haworth Press, Inc., 2007. All rights reserved.
doi:10.1300/5745_01

In the space of a few seconds I was sweating like a pedophile on a playground. Not surprising, since I was, in fact, *on* a playground—and hardly pedophilic, there's nothing perverse at all about ogling all those fine 12-year-old bodies, when the "ogler" is but a lad of 12 himself—still I was caught unawares by a sudden urgency I could not fathom. I'd played "games" with many of these same friends before in years past, of the time-honored "I'll show you mine if you show me yours" variety, but those had been much more innocent interludes, born more of a curiosity to see what the other 9- or-10-year-old was packing. (If you could consider the micro-johnsons we all possessed in those days something one might "pack.") Now this sight of so many fine shirtless boys strutting about and feeling their oats, coming as it did at the dawning of my sexual awareness, was nearly overwhelming; all that visual information was burrowing in through my eyes at the speed of light, and seemed to be passing right through my brain to be processed far south of my cerebral cortex, like somewhere in the general area of my prostate, if I'm remembering the sensation correctly. It was a singularly powerful experience, one felt completely on a physical, rather than a mental, level as my mind had literally no idea why I was perilously close to swooning.

It took a few more similar occurrences to realize there was a name for the sensation I'd encountered—*desire*—and I would feel its pangs thousands of times over the next several decades, in a thousand different manners and degrees. Sometimes it would be inspired by those I would become actively and romantically involved with, sometimes by those who never knew the slow burning flame I was hiding inside. It's something I still occasionally stumble on today—thank God—but rarely does it ever equal the mind-numbing and delightfully confusing intensity of its first appearance, on that sunny day in May of 1972.

It never ceases to amaze me just how powerful the *D* word can be, how it can take control of our lives and shut everything out, sometimes for just a few moments, sometimes for days or weeks at a time, depending on how badly we're smitten. Ask just about anybody, and they can likely pull up a story from their past—or their present—when they've done something incredibly stupid or ill-advised, or maybe just something completely out of character, in pursuit of their heart's desire. (We used to have a great term for it back in my Marine

Corps days: we called it "brain/dick interlock.") Sometimes the fixation isn't even on someone we actually know: I've talked to men who've become hopelessly obsessed with actors, models, singers, athletes, porn stars, even politicians ... or maybe just the hot guy they work out with at the gym, and never have the nerve to talk to.

And then of course there's the other kind of desire, the one turned inward, the flame that fires our need to be fitter, stronger, or better looking ... more successful at our art or business, to have the best, or be the best in everything we do. Not coincidentally, achieving even some of those goals to just a small degree can often open the door to getting the mates we seek, finding Mr. Right, or just—forgive me—Mr. Right *Now*.

In my first book, *Sissyphobia: Gay Men and Effeminate Behavior* (2001, Harrington Park Press), I took a look at what often seems to be a growing tension in the gay community, between men who consider themselves masculine and "straight acting," and those who have a tendency toward the effeminate or all-out flamboyant. In my second, *Reeling in the Years: Gay Men's Perspectives on Age and Ageism* (2004, Harrington Park Press), I examined how ageist behaviors come to bear in the way older and younger gay men relate, or fail to relate. I found some men who have no problem at all bridging the gap between generations, and others who can only sit beside the chasm, with little or no interest at all in what might be happening on the other side. I also tried to document the experiences of gay men through the lens of time, to take the pulse of gay teens, and gay seniors, and all those in between

In researching both books I encountered along the way hundreds of men who held forth at length about all they wanted to find in life—the personal, professional, and material—and all they were willing to do to get it. It's in the spirit of examining the intensity and depth of those differing yet often complementary brands of desire that I embarked on *Chasing Adonis: Gay Men and the Pursuit of Perfection*. I've become curious over the years, watching the behavior of gay men—and my own behavior—as we track down the people and things we think might make us satisfied, and then go off in search of something or someone else. I've come to ask myself, and others: *Why* do we want what we want? What do we seek in others, and in ourselves? What is it about some men that makes them an object of our deepest desires, while others hardly spike our interest? How far are some of us willing to go in pursuit of such men . . . and how far will we go to remake or maintain our own selves at various points of our lives, to become or remain that which others might seek?

After two years of talking with gay men about such things, I'm moved to ask if we simply demand too much of others, and sometimes ourselves, as we chase our specific ideal of perfection. But just how much *does* that concept of perfection vary, from individual to individual, and how much does it evolve and change within our own minds and hearts as years go by? Does the exterior package *always* outweigh that which may lie behind the face and body? Or does the so-called "person inside" matter more to us? And how much do our external and internal selves influence and reflect upon each other?

Those are just some of the areas I've been looking into, as I tried to get a handle on gay men's attitudes and opinions for this book. I've also tried to address some other issues that directly relate upon what some have called gay men's "naked obsession" with beauty, such as the topic of rejection. How do you bounce back when your intended tells you that you don't measure up to his standards? How do you let someone down lightly, or turn away someone who's not getting the message? How do you handle the frightening prospect of being stalked? And just what the hell is going on *inside* the mind of a stalker?

Then there are those who make a living—or maybe merely a hobby—out of our fixation on fabulous looks. What's it like to be an exotic dancer in a go-go bar, the star of a porn video, or the main attraction on an X-rated webcam site? How does it feel to be objectified so, and what effects, positive and negative, does it have on the relationships and the self-esteem of those in the spotlight trying to earn a buck—or $2.95 a minute? What about those of us who still find that our idea of perfection lies on the other side of the orientation divide, either in the straight men we seek for companionship, or in the "straight-acting" identity that we try to create for ourselves? And speaking of identity . . . what the hell is going on with the men who try to meet or talk with other men online or in personal ads by creating a fantasy about themselves, even to the point of sending out or posting other people's photographs and personal stories, and making them their own, even when they intend to meet up *in person*?

As in my other books I've thrown quite a lot on the plate, but once you're finished digesting it all I hope you'll find it was a satisfying trip to the buffet table. It was certainly something of a challenge to write, when you consider that so many of the men I interviewed had contradictory views when it came to the notions of beauty and desire; some stated unequivocally that they would *never* be so shallow as to reject someone solely for their looks, only to then relate tales when they did *precisely* that. And long before this book made its way into your hands, I was getting nasty e-mails from people who saw the survey online and castigated me for posing questions they saw as inherently insulting to anyone whose beauty isn't typical of an Abercrombie & Fitch or Calvin Klein ad—i.e., Bears and other large men. "I think you need to come off your gym bunny high horse and realize that not everyone can be a smooth young twinkie," wrote one fellow. "Nor should anyone think they have to."

Yet I also received an equal number of angry missives and comments from folks who thought my questions on the Web site were somehow denigrating them for the hours they choose to spend in the gym, out on a running or bike path, or simply watching what they eat. "I think your survey showed a bias, and I found it particularly offensive," wrote one angry man. "The undertone was clearly that fit and attractive people are shallow and arrogant, and good people are fat and intellectually superior . . . I didn't appreciate that line of thinking." (Geez, Louise . . . the book wasn't even in stores yet, and I was already pissing people off.) I can only guess that in trying carefully to compose my survey to include all viewpoints I managed to step on everyone's toes equally. That was not my intent, but if it helps me give you, the reader, a balanced snapshot of gay men's feelings about beauty and desire, maybe I've done the job right.

Economist John Kenneth Galbraith once noted, "There is certainly no absolute standard of beauty. That precisely is what makes its pursuit so interesting." Yet "interesting" does not come close to describing what it was like getting into so many gay men's heads over the past two years—hopefully once you closed the last of these pages, I'll have given you a little something to think about.

Chapter 1

Eye of the Beholder

We all want something beautiful . . . man, I wish I was beautiful.

"Mr. Jones"
Counting Crows

It is said that from the day of his very birth he was loved, admired, and desired, as he was the most beautiful of young men. He was fought over, murdered by one jealous of his beauty and the affections he inspired in others, then brought back to life by the pleadings of the gods themselves. His appearance in spring and summer was said to make the land grow warm and fertile, but his departure to the underworld in autumn and winter each year brought coldness and death.

That's the Adonis myth of ancient times, and it's one that scholars say had strong resonance in cultures throughout the Mediterranean. And in many ways the myth still holds true, its echoes carrying forth even to these crazed modern days we live in. Haven't we all seen beautiful young men fought over, and have not many of us noted how others, jealous of their beauty, wished them nothing but ill fortune? I know I have.

But the Adonis I will speak of in this book isn't a beautiful mythical boy in the classic sense; rather, he's an ideal, a goal, or a concept. At times I use the word Adonis to represent the near-unattainable standard many gay men set for themselves as they embark upon a new fitness regimen or a major change of life; most often, I use it to refer to that man, or that kind of man, that we all find ourselves pursuing—or dearly wish might pursue us. He comes in many different forms, ages, stations in life, even sexual orientations. When he makes his appearance it's always remarkable and, for gay men in particular it seems, invariably memorable.

Chasing Adonis
Published by The Haworth Press, Inc., 2007. All rights reserved.
doi:10.1300/5745_02

"He was the lifeguard at the beach where my family used to go on summer day trips," remembers Johnny, a 28-year-old office worker in Chicago. "I'd actually started hating to go, because I was in that mid-teens rebellious stage, and as soon as we'd get there I'd just start walking down the sand to get away from my parents, be alone. Then the summer I was 15, I saw him up there on his chair. I've always wished I could have gotten a picture of him, but I really don't need one, I can remember pretty much exactly what he looked like . . . he had a great face, light brown hair cut really short like he was a Marine or something, nice muscles. (Well, hot, actually.) I was already pretty sure I was gay, even though I had a girlfriend at the time. This guy really confirmed it for me. I only saw him three or four times the rest of the summer, but he was in my dreams for years, just my idea of the perfect guy."

"This may sound weird, but I was only eight years old at the time," says Jeff, a 16-year-old high school student in Richmond, Virginia. "My family was getting construction done on our house and there was this one construction worker who was in his 20's . . . he was very tan from working out in the sun all the time and had light brown hair, he seemed to be very strong, and he had a great build . . . everyday I would watch him from my porch because I thought he was gorgeous. Then on their last day on the job the crew took me and my brother for a ride in the cherry picker, and I can still remember it, being close to that guy and getting really excited."

"I never believed in that whole 'love at first sight' thing, until the moment I saw Jerry for the first time," recalls Pat, a 30-year-old attorney in Boston. "It was college, early 90's, and I was out with some friends at a pub just off campus. In walks this guy, the epitome of tall, dark and handsome, and I was absolutely stunned. As it turns out he happened to know one of the girls in our group, and he came right over, sat down in front of me, looked up in my direction, and smiled. My heart just melted. Eventually we started meeting at that pub alone, and we even ended up dating for a couple of years. We run into each other some these days, we're still friendly . . . but that first day, seeing Jerry walk in . . . I have never forgotten that sight, and I don't think I ever will."

Who among us *doesn't* remember those times he's found himself arrested by such a sight, the moment he suddenly came face to face with a guy who could fire up his fantasies and give him fodder for dreams on end? For two years I've been quizzing men about their encounters with and concepts and attitudes on beauty; even though they differ greatly according to the individual, I found the reactions to it are largely shared.

For some men it's all about the eyes: deep dark brown and luminous, or glowing blue like a warm summer sky, glancing in their direction with an unexpected fire and intensity that takes their breath away. Others speak of dazzling smiles that could light up darkened rooms, or take the gloom off the drabbest winter day. Some talk of the face as a whole, a compendium of features that create the rugged good looks like a cowboy of old, or perhaps the fresh-scrubbed appearance of the sweetest boy-next-door. There's the cut of the clothes, a stylish swagger that nearly shouts of confidence and success, or a simple display of pure contentment. Often it's the form *beneath* those clothes that sparks the greatest interest, be it a fit and muscular body attesting to youth or one that shows off many years of effort and maintenance. Sometimes it's the softer shape that appeals most, one that carries its own telling brand of self-assurance, announcing to the world that "I am just happy being me."

Whatever creates that spark, there's a strong commonality in the way the flame burns inside, and in the words gay men choose to describe it. "I was 15, and there was this other guy on my swim team, he was a bit older than me," says Xavier, a 22-year-old computer science student from South Carolina. "He was much better built than your average high school student, and he had a great smile and lots of self-confidence. Of course he became the object of lots of fantasies, from the purely sexual to the all-out romantic. I think I'm still attracted to that type today, someone better built and bigger than I am, with a square jaw and killer smile. Someone that makes me feel safe when they're holding me."

"I was probably a freshman in high school when I began to notice some of the 'heavier' wrestlers at my school," says Mike, a 20-year-old theater student in New Jersey. "I always liked guys that were average. Not insanely muscular, but average, kind of 'couch potato.' Anyway, in high school there was this one guy, a soccer player who was average-looking, but had an amazing ass . . . I would find reasons to be late for class just to see him walk down the hallway."

David is a 25-year-old graphic design student on Long Island; it wasn't a fellow student or lifeguard that first caught his eye, but rather pictures from an ad campaign that many gay men still remember rather fondly. "I was around 13 or 14, and I became fascinated with those Calvin Klein ads with Mark Wahlberg, who was then known as 'Marky Mark.' It was the fine muscled look of his, and the really sexual poses that I reacted to . . . then I started noticing I was having the same reactions to any man I saw shirtless, or had a sexy pose."

For Paul, a 36-year-old construction foreman in Kansas City, it was a music video that made one of the strongest impressions on him. "You're gonna just shoot me for this, but it was that Billy Ray Cyrus, singing 'Achy Breaky Heart.' I'd heard that stupid song for weeks on the radio, just hated it, then I saw him singin' and dancin' on TV, and fell in love with him. After that I kinda fell in love with the song, too. Isn't that just awful? Not such a big fan of the song anymore, but he's still hot."

A "real live boy" blew Justin away about ten years ago, but just like a model in an ad, or the singer in a music video, he turned out to be inaccessible. "I was in the Air Force, stationed near DC, and we all went down to this bar called Tracks, which isn't there anymore." [Tell me about it, Justin, I *still* miss the place.] "From time to time back then they would have exotic dancers up on boxes by the dance floor, and on that particular night there was this kid, maybe 19, 20 tops, up on the box by the main floor. Jesus Christ, I wish you could have seen him, he had to have had the most perfect face, the hottest body, I have ever seen, and all he was wearing was a g-string . . . then somehow, without showing all the goods, he somehow slipped that thing off and just held it in front of him. There he was, pretty much naked, in this room with a thousand guys, pumping and grinding to the music . . . I just stared and stared and stared, he had me locked there in place for the hour or so it felt like he was up there. Then the lights go out, and he's gone. I searched that bar for hours, trying to find him, I just wanted to say something to him to express my sheer appreciation for his beauty, corny as that sounds. But I never found him. It's been ten years, and I remember every detail of him like I just saw him last night."

BEAUTY THAT REMAINS

Keats said that "a thing of beauty is a joy forever: Its loveliness increases; it will never pass into nothingness." From all that the men

I've talked with tell me of their first or most memorable encounters with their own visions of Adonis, nothing could be more true. Certainly I find I have lots in common with their tales; hell, I can still remember that May day back in 1972, relatively chaste as it was. But there would be other, less chaste vistas I would soon behold. Like the time back in tenth grade, in the school gym locker room, when I saw a fully realized, near-adult male form naked for the very first time in person. His name was Jose, and he was this tall muscular kid in my class; he had a ripped, V-shaped midsection and well-rounded pecs, along with a killer face and smile, and he was just taking his time getting dressed after taking a shower, not acting shy or self-conscious in the least. To see him like that, a live nude kid just a few feet away from me, was so powerful for my 15-year-old libido that I nearly passed out. You have to remember, the mid-1970s were a vastly different, even innocent time, especially for a suburban teenager. There was no MTV bombarding us with taut male bodies getting busy in a beach house or in some music video; there were no videos or DVDs to rent easily or borrow from a friend; and there was *absolutely* no Internet to scan for porn or hot pictures, no precocious lads acting out their horniness on a webcam. For a gay boy to stumble upon a vision like that was akin to Columbus stubbing his toe on the Bahamas on his way to find India. Talk about a whole new world; Jose's body was literally *all* I could think about, for the rest of the school day, all the way home, and up into my bedroom where there was suddenly some serious pressure that needed to be released . . .

As it turns out Jose was built very much like the young man that I would happen to fall head over heels in love with just a year later—his name was Billy, someone I've spoken of before in other books and someone I'll speak more of here and there as we go along—and I've always wondered if such early and frequent exposure to that particular body type, smack dab in the middle of puberty, didn't have something to do with how I formed my own sense of desire and of male perfection, much of which lasts to the present day. As I started to research this project, I became curious to find out what the experience of other gay men might be, what kind of man first sparked their interest, and what manner of man they *now* find attractive. Knowing some of the boneheaded things I've done in my time to spend some time with (or simply get a glimpse of) an Adonis or two, I wanted to find out what similar tales *other* men had to tell . . . and not just those men who tend to pursue what some might call "classic" or "typical" beauty. What beauty there is comes in all forms and sizes, all ages, races, and places. I wanted to get the broadest possible cross section of experience that I could.

So I created a survey that quizzed men about their lives and their loves, requited or otherwise. I also created a much longer list of true/false/multiple-choice poll questions, and put the whole shebang up online, where it stayed for a year. A couple of hundred people took the survey, and a thousand or so took the poll. Along the way while the Web site was patiently gathering all that information for me, I interviewed scores more men in person, people I knew from the Internet or ran into in bars, on the beach, at work, at the gym, or in the grocery store, pretty much anyone who crossed my path in my various travels who seemed like he might have a story to tell. Many other men came to me on their own, having heard of the project through mutual contacts.

It's the sum total of those hundreds of stories that form the overwhelming bulk of this book. Those men and their tales are the "stars" of this show. But I also found the occasional need for a little "professional" analysis. So I spoke with scientists and psychologists, counselors and sociologists, fitness trainers and photographers, artists and film producers, anyone at all I could think of who might have something interesting to say about *why* we like *what* we like, what it is that men find beautiful in other men, and how they try to achieve it in a mate or create a certain sense of beauty within themselves.

As always, there are caveats and disclaimers. Anyone who took the polls or surveys or submitted to interviews obviously *wanted* to do so; no one was contacted at random and bullied for responses when he was trying to eat dinner or watch *Desperate Housewives* . . . so I will not claim that the results reflected within these pages pass "scientific" muster, whatever the hell that is. I'll share the occasional poll result from time to time as we go along here; the full poll questions and results are included in the final chapter, along with some choice quotes I hope you'll find as illuminating or entertaining as I did.

As for the surveys that elicited the longer, more in-depth responses and anecdotes, as far as possible I tried to word the questions as neutrally as I could, not so much as to avoid offending anyone—though that's a neat trick when one can actually pull it off—but rather to not prejudice anyone's reply; any journalist, cop, or lawyer can attest to the fact that people often tell you what they *think* you want to hear. As I noted in the Introduction, some people took issue with what they saw in my questions as a bias toward the fit and pretty; others thought I was putting exactly those same people *down,* in favor of men whose beauty is less mainstream or conventional. So I'm guessing I did in fact achieve a certain "middle of the road" quality.

But in the interests of full disclosure—can't tell I'm from Washington, DC, can you?—I suppose I *should* from the outset give you an idea of the biases that I *do* have, what kind of men I find most compelling, at least from the purely physical aspect. And that's pretty simple to relate, since it's not too different from young Jose three decades ago. (If you want a more modern equivalent, just look at one of those impossibly beautiful Abercrombie & Fitch ads, or the body on the boy you find on a box of chic underwear; I'm all about that smooth, chiseled chest and six-to-eight-pack ab thing.) I've been attracted as well to guys with a little less muscle, as long as the build remained firm and athletic; thin and slim can be also be quite hot, as long as it doesn't stray over too close to emaciation.

Is that the *only* kind of guy I've ever dated, or pursued, or maybe just ended up taking a tumble with on a long lazy afternoon? Hell no, not at all; "looks" are only about half the package that appeals to me. Like a lot of men whose stories you'll see soon, for me a pretty face or hot body with nothing going on upstairs gets rather boring, and rather quickly. Often there's the oddest flicker and flash in the way a guy talks, or the way he carries himself, something ephemeral that can go miles toward compensating for any immediately perceived "lack" of beauty or athleticism. (It's always fun to look back at guys I've dated or even obsessed over, to take a glance at a photo that can't possibly capture that intangible sizzle you get only in sound and motion, and ask myself with the distance that only time can provide, *What the hell was I thinking?*)

Perhaps the biggest factor these days—as I hear my own bio clock tick-tick-ticking away—is youthfulness. *Actual* age really doesn't matter; my guy can be anywhere from a teenager to middle aged for all I give a hoot about. I talked about that in *Reeling in the Years,* and I probably put it as succinctly then as I could now: how I seek a youthful outlook and enthusiasm, "that open and wide-eyed view of life, a lack of jadedness and 'been there, done that' . . . along with the energy and willingness and daring I like to believe I still have" (Bergling, 2004, p. 153).

I fully realize that while many gay men will likely share my tastes, many others will not, and that's a wonderful thing, variety being the spice of life and all that. You won't find *me* trashing anyone in these pages for the way they look, or for the men they'd like to share their intimate moments with. I won't bash them for the time they spend working on their bodies, or for the hours they like to sit in front of the television, munching down chili dogs. More power to you, and whatever makes you happy. But many of the men I've interviewed *do* take others to task in these pages for their life habits, so be warned that some of what you read here may be offensive to you, wherever you fall in the "looks" or "fitness" spectrum.

I just want you to know right from the get-go where *I'm* coming from. Whether it's up close—and very personal—with a guy I'm dating, or when I'm glancing from afar—checking out an ad or a music video, watching a good-looking guy dance at a club or scoping out the hotties on the beach—I have to admit to a certain kind of addiction to beauty. I literally cannot get enough of it. It will nearly always stop me in my tracks. That makes me either exactly the wrong person to complete this project or absolutely the correct one.

Like they say on FOX, I'll report, you decide.

"SKIN DEEP, AND VERY SHALLOW"

"I will just say it: If you're not cute, don't even try." That's Greg, an 18-year-old sales associate in Lake Ridge, Virginia. He describes himself as a "small-framed guy with defined muscles from gymnastics and tumbling. I consider myself thin and gangly, but others tell me differently."

I want to know what's going on in his head when he's looking for a guy. He's not very shy about expressing his view: "I know I sound like such a horrible person, that I would just look on the outside before I will even get to know 'the person within.' So sue me. I think that me being with a guy who is cute is going to make me 'cuter by association.' And everyone will remember us."

Lest you simply ascribe Greg's view to the immaturity or inexperience of a callow youth, consider Chuck, a 39-year-old human resources recruiter in Miami. "I think physical attractiveness is Number 1," he tells me. "If I'm not physically attracted to someone, I've tried to make it work and it just doesn't. It all comes down to the sex in the end. If you're not having great sex, you're not going to stay faithful, and it's not going to work, no matter how hard you work at it . . . I've tried everything and it just keeps coming back to that."

"Not to sound like a bitch or anything, but the man of my dreams has to be exactly that," says Jimmy, a 28-year-old day spa manager in St. Louis. "I've waited 28 years to find perfection, and I am not about to settle now."

Those kinds of views weren't something universal among the men I surveyed and interviewed, but they *were* very common. In my polling, 65 percent of gay men say they've rejected someone else, based *solely* on their physical appearance, and a little more than half of those queried say *they* have been rejected for the very same reason. "Look, there are ugly people everywhere, people getting fatter, not taking care of themselves or their skin, and wearing just hideous clothes," says Seth, a 28-year-old retail worker in Santa Barbara, California. "If I am going to make the effort to make myself the best I can be, to be stunning for my man (whoever he may be) then *he* damn well better be stunning, too. Ugly you get for free, pretty takes work, and that's what I am after, just the best looking guy I can land. Call me skin deep, call me very shallow, I am just being honest."

Other men, of course, find that attitude to be just precisely that: Shallow. "I think physical attraction is important, but it's not everything," says Cameron, a 21-year-old office manager in Washington, DC. "My husband Rob isn't a Titanmedia porn star, he's not six-feet tall and muscle bound, just turning heads wherever we go. But I guess that's the kind of guy some think he *should* be . . . I introduce them and some are like 'that's your man?' At first it bothered me, why *shouldn't* he be my man? So what if he's shorter than I am, and doesn't have the most amazing body in the world? They can only see the outer shell. I know he has amazing green/blue eyes, a wonderful smile, can sing like an angel—and by the way, the best cock I've ever known—but it's the *emotional* part of our bond that I value the most."

Phillip, a 30-year-old physician's assistant in Minneapolis, says he was a lot like Seth, and started out "extremely shallow" in the way he looked at other guys: "I was always pretty popular, and I guess someone considered pretty well above average in the looks/body department. When I was first coming out and starting to date in college, I wouldn't even think of hooking up or even going out with someone if he didn't knock my socks off. But then I started growing up a little, I guess, seeing the way that interiors can outweigh exteriors, and vice versa . . . like you can have the best face, the most rockin' bod, but if you're an asshole, why would I be interested for more than the five minutes it's going to take for me to find that out?"

"Gay men have always been the sort that values the wrapping paper more than the present inside," says Barry, a 50-year-old stock broker who hails from London. "And I think I have been every bit as guilty as the next chap, looking past the plain fellow who might have been the love of my life, just so I could focus on the fair-haired bloke who seemed to have a spotlight following him all over the place. The fair-haired man was often good for the one-night stand . . . but the plain fellow might have cooked me breakfast in the morning, and seen me off to work properly. It's really only now that I'm starting to see those 'average Joes' in a new light."

Nationally syndicated columnist and author Michael Alvear took on the topic in one of his commentaries. He tells the story of a fellow named "Ted," about whom he loved everything—except his body.

> I tried to do the chick thing. You know, screw the guy even though you're not physically attracted to them because they're kind and smart and loving and that's what you want in your life so what's a few minutes of terror. Well it didn't take. I tried but I just couldn't do it . . . I don't know how women do it, but if I'm not attracted to a guy physically, I can't have sex with them no matter how attracted to them I am emotionally. I'm not the only one. Most gay men I know are like that . . . I've never overheard anyone say "Look at the morals on that stud. I bet he's loyal as shit." (Alvear, 2003, p. 40)

It's an undeniable stereotype that gay men are more naturally attuned to aesthetics—*Queer Eye,* anyone?—and like many stereotypes, this one appears to have a rather firm grounding in fact. "I think since men are more visually-oriented than women (we're hunters versus nesters) we place more importance on what we can actually see," says Andrew Gottlieb, a clinical social worker for the past 22 years, now living in Brooklyn, New York. He says men in general—and gay men in particular—tend to focus on the face and the body, even to the point of sectionalizing the body down to its parts. "So it would only follow that what we can see, what's on the surface, would be more important to us."

Someone who knows a thing or two about that "surface" male beauty is the popular cartoonist Joe Phillips, the artist behind several illustrated books such as *Adventures of a Joe Boy* and *Boys Will Be Boys*—you can check them out on his Web site, www.joephillips.com—and the creator of several calendars over the past several years, all featuring scores of great-looking guys of all races and ages at play or in love. (I'm proud to say he is the illustrator of all my books so far.) The one thing virtually all his creations have in common? They're jaw-dropping hot. The guy knows how to grab your eye, because he's figured out what lots of men want to see, what makes them tick.

"Our addiction to the aesthetic goes far beyond our choices of who we date," he tells me. "It's our clothes and homes and cars too. Not to sound glib . . . but who wants a fixer upper?" As for men who tend toward what some call shallow, who value the curve of the ass perhaps more than the shape of the heart, Joe is rather understanding. "Inner beauty is a thing that few can gauge at first meeting. It takes time to build up to that. It's as if we were all books and the better our cover looks, the more likely we are to be picked up to be read. I personally have a great sense of humor and fantastic personality. I also don't have a size 32" waist . . . so the dating pool I'm in is considerably smaller."

"It's totally understandable to believe that, unless someone puts your hormones in an uproar, that certain spark is not there," says Michael Shernoff. He's been a psychotherapist since 1977 in Manhattan's Chelsea neighborhood. "Yet I have also heard numerous men say that initially there was not a spark for them, but after a while it began to grow due to how interesting or sweet a person was."

San Francisco's Michael Bettinger has been a relationship counselor and psychotherapist for some 33 years; he suggests that there's a lot more going on inside when men size up other men visually—much more than they actually realize—and that they're seeing a lot more than the bright blue eyes or big broad shoulders they admire. Bettinger also submits that we all tend to size people up differently, according to whether we're looking for short-term or long-term companionship. "What anyone sees as 'hot' is a combination of conscious and unconscious perceptions about the other," Bettinger says. "We are perceiving much more than the exterior . . . we are also perceiving a lot of non-verbal information about that person, how confident they look, how secure they are with themselves, their level of dominance or submissiveness, etc. All this goes into what makes a person desirable. What we want in a date, and what we want in a mate, are somewhat different . . . and what a person says they want, and what happens in practice, are two different things, they're generally not the same."

Giorgio is a 30-year-old self-described "fashionista" in New York City. He tells me he doesn't believe in a concept of "exteriors" or "interiors" when it comes to looks . . . for him it's one in the same. "I don't believe you can separate the way you look from the way you act. Just look at how differently people behave when they put on a suit, as opposed to wearing jeans and a tee shirt. People assume a role—my God, it's just like drag, isn't it?—and play to it. One is very straight-laced and business-like, the other relaxed.

"So I think that over time people's looks become just like the clothes, except they're harder to change or manipulate. If you feel ugly, you will 'act' ugly, you will not be as outgoing, you will be reserved, and people with see you as withdrawn, and treat you like an outsider. That in turn will make you feel even more isolated, and it just creates this self-perpetuating cycle of ugliness. It's so sad."

Andy, a 64-year-old military retiree living near Phoenix, agrees wholeheartedly with those sentiments; he says he should know, because he's been "ugly as home-made sin" for most of his life. "Well, not really ugly," he says. "But I have never been anyone's pretty boy. The funny thing is, I never really *cared* what people thought about my looks. It must have been the way my parents brought me up, I don't have a clue. One thing I have always been, though, is extremely confident. My parents again, probably, especially my father. And my military background . . . that's a world where you're judged by your skill and ingenuity, no one gives a good goddam what you look like. I came into the gay game rather late, but I never had any trouble wooing a man when it came down to it. The people who rejected me lost out. The people who were taken by my personality, they found the swan under the ugly duckling."

"If I sat being around angry about the fact that I wasn't handsome, well-built or sexy in most people's eyes I really wouldn't have much of a life," says Steve, a 33-year-old office worker in Lexington, Kentucky. "I haven't lost much sleep knowing I'll never be on the cover of a magazine or be the belle of the ball whenever I go out." He compares being born beautiful or achieving a certain amount of physical attractiveness over time to other random occurrences in life. "It would be like sitting around pissed off because I didn't win the lottery, or that I wasn't born into a wealthy family. But rich people have problems too, some of them have some really fucked-up personal lives. So I'm sure pretty people have their issues . . . just don't ask me what they are!" Still, Steve tells me that it's easy to understand why other men might very well grow resentful: "Gay men are so harsh, so judgmental when it comes to looks, you'd think we know better after all we've been through, being judged by society just for being gay."

And sure enough, other gay men who've spent a lifetime being rejected or ignored by others based on their appearance—and that kind of rejection is a topic we'll take a look at in much more depth later—tell me that being judged is something they're still bitter about. "I learned a long time ago that life wasn't going to be fair when it came to my looks," says Aaron, a 34-year-old bank employee who lives in Houston. "I had bad acne all the way through middle and high school, and my build was always rather stoop-shouldered, with a chest that's almost concave. I never felt good-looking one day in my life, so you'd think I'd 'know my place,' right? Nah . . . I still get angry when I go out to places where there are hot men around, which I rarely do, because it's like a club I will never be a member of. I wouldn't even think of walking up to a guy and introducing myself, because I know he's either going to (1) recoil in horror and reject me to my face, or (2) try to be nice and let me down easy. But either way, he's not going to be interested, even though if he took the time to know me he'd see I could offer him a good heart and stability. It's so maddening!"

SPLITTING THE DIFFERENCE

Harry tells me about the night he had last week in a "small cowboy town out West." He's mid-40s, a rancher, very few folks happen to know he's gay, and he's fine about that. "But once in awhile you feel the need, as they say, and when you do, there's a little hole-in-the-wall joint you can go to here, tip your cap the right way, kinda make yourself known."

Harry says on the night in question, he spotted a much younger man already in the place sitting down when he got there, a man who spotted him and smiled a kind of "come hither" smile; not long after that, the young man got up and made his way to the restroom, nodding at Harry as he went by. "I have to tell you, the way those jeans just stuck to him, and the way his shirt was half open and I could see how muscular his chest was, was awful arousing. Truth be told I wanted to jump his bones right there, follow him into the men's room and have at it."

Instead Harry says he waited for the fellow to get back, offered to buy him a drink, and kicked off a conversation. "I already knew I liked his looks, a lot. Wanted to see if there was anything about his personality that would kill the deal, like if he turned out to be too femme for me." Harry says the youngster was in fact very butch, but the conversation was "a painful" ordeal for him. "First off there was politics . . . he was a young Republican, and I'm a Democrat . . . didn't tell him that, of course, since Democrats out here are just about as rare as queers. More important was just how stuck on himself he was, and how he kept trying to impress me with all the things he'd done, all the places he'd been to." The longer they talked, Harry explains, they more he found himself wishing he'd just smiled at the boy and left it at that.

"Then a funny thing happened. He leaned over, and the lighting was just right so I could see all the way down inside his shirt, past that beautiful chest and down to his tight stomach, it was Grade A six-pack down there. Then he says 'let's get out of here.' I'll just say we didn't waste any time, I didn't even finish my drink."

Mike is a 37-year-old attorney in Manhattan, recalling a night last year when he went home with a "young frat boy-type" he met at a bar in Chelsea. "We didn't make a lot of small talk in the club, and I guess we didn't feel like we had to. There really seemed to be a lot of electricity in the air, a lot of non-verbal communication. I got him back to my place, and non-verbal is exactly what he was. It wasn't that he didn't like to chat, more like he just didn't know how. There were lots of nods, grunts, and pointless smiles. Then just when I was thinking maybe this was a big mistake, he stood up and stripped off his t-shirt, and my jaw just about hit the floor. I have never been one of those 'body worship' guys, but holy hell and a half, this kid was incredible.

I just pulled that youngster into my bedroom, and gave him the time of his life. Mine too."

In his "Letter from the Editor" in the July 2003 "Hot" issue of *Out Magazine,* Brendan Lemon talked about the splitting of a personality from an otherwise otherworldly physique, something he maintained he just would not do.

> Don't get me wrong . . . if Antonio Sabato Jr. walked past me in his underwear he would get my undivided attention. But if he and I had a conversation and there was nothing to enhance his physical attributes—if he told me, say, that George. W. Bush was the greatest president that America has ever had—then I wouldn't want to sleep with him. (p. 19)

But with all due respect to Mr. Lemon, lots of other gay men *would.* If not Antonio specifically, then certainly some other Adonis; a full 69 percent of the men I heard from—and you have to like *that* percentage—admitted they would be happy to consider having sex with a man whose personality wasn't up to par, or was just "so-so," as long as he had a killer build and a handsome face. Not necessarily date the guy, or even have a relationship that lasted more than a date or two; just a question of pure sexual attraction, for purely recreational purposes. (I would note here that dozens of men I spoke with are scandalized by the notion of sex as recreation, but let's face it, folks. We have lots of hound dogs and tomcats and lord-knows-what other kinds of frisky animals in our midst. It's just reality.)

Jeff is a 44-year-old assistant English professor at Virginia Tech in Blacksburg, Virginia. He's fascinated by the thought processes that go on when people separate the physicality of a guy from what might be going on inside. In fact, it's something he says he's done himself. "I was single for so long that, in order to have any sex at all, I was forced by circumstance to focus on the physical. In short-term or anonymous sex, the interior isn't really relevant since it isn't likely to be experienced. That is, I didn't have time to get to know the interiors of my sex partners, or they didn't want to be known in any way deeper than the flesh . . . as a friend of mine likes to say, when he drools over some guy who's sexy but probably not smart, 'Honey, I don't want to suck his brains.' That is, the body's priority is other bodies. Fuck the sexy ones; talk to the smart ones. You're lucky if you get both in one package. And some of us, including me, for some perverse reason are not sexually attracted to men who are emotionally or intellectually good for us."

"Normally I like my men to have some years under their belts, and some experience in the bedroom if I'm going to play with them," says Jonathan, a 35-year-old salesman in Dallas. "I met this guy about a month ago that didn't have either. His name was Lance, or Justin, or one of those boyband names, and he couldn't have been more than 22 or 23. Really a 'pretty' guy, too, all curly blonde hair and bright blue eyes, perfect skin and teeth, a really nice athletic build. I met him at a party where he was hugging the wall, and I couldn't believe it when he told me he was a virgin. I don't get off on that at all, like some guys do, I like the other guy to take control of the situation. And besides his inexperience, he was painfully shy, to the point of being almost inarticulate." Jonathan tells me that's the kind of thing that will usually make him take a walk. "I'm not all dirty talk and verbal in bed, but it's fun to actually communicate while you're 'doing it,' at least it is for me."

But something made him invite the boy home. "He was just so angelic looking, and flawless if you forgot all the other stuff. So I did. It was actually kind of fun, just having that perfect body to play with. I don't know, maybe that's just his way of getting guys into bed, but he sure didn't seem to be acting."

Gary is a 56-year-old "early retiree" living in Palm Springs. "I was in a long-term relationship that ended after 15 years, and I wasn't expecting to be tossed back in the dating pool at this age," he tells me. "Back when I was younger I used to have a litmus test for the guys I would date or just have sex with. They had to have similar or least complementary values and experiences, not just have a handsome face or a hunky body. These days I am not that picky about the personalities, I just look for someone that turns me on somehow. If I find a hot guy that has more inside, that's great, he may be my next husband. If he's just hot outside, and he wants to spend some bedroom time with me, well, that's okay, too."

But lest you go thinking that more than two-thirds of gay men are total body/face whores when it comes to sex, think again. The very next poll question turned up an interesting result: When asked if they'd consider have sex with a fellow whose body and face are just "so-so," but who has a great personality, more than three-quarters—or 76 percent—said yes. "I can get really turned on by a laugh, or a smile, even if the guy isn't that all that attractive from a looks standpoint," says Dave, a 25-year-old student in Texas. "I've 'hooked up' with lots of great looking guys, sure, and that's always fun. But I've also had some great sex with guys I guess a lot of other guys wouldn't look twice at. They just had something else going for them, it's hard to put your finger on."

"It's not something we would brag about to our buddies, the way we might say 'I did it with this guy last night who was so hot, fabulous body, huge dick, etc.'," suggests Chris, a 37-year-old mechanic in western Pennsylvania. "But I bet a lot of us get taken by dudes who have nice eyes, or a warm smile, or just have a special way of moving or talking without being 'all that' to look at . . . especially if he's someone that we've come to know a little over time."

Tom, a 42-year-old private pilot, agrees. "If you're talking about that instant, set-your-pants-on-fire kind of attraction, that's going to be primarily physical, sure. I know I've had some flings with guys like that, and their personalities weren't that important. But once in awhile you do find yourself attracted to someone who just kind of bowls you over with who he is, not so much what he looks like."

"There's the adage that less good looking guys tend to be better sex partners, because it's less about them and they're more into pleasing you," says Rory, a 43-year-old furniture maker in South Carolina. "The joke about the hot guys is yeah, they're gorgeous but a boring lay. The converse is also true, about the guys who aren't an Adonis, but they really know how to suck a dick. As for a boyfriend, I want both, looks and personality, not to mention brains . . . Once you get past the physicality of the guy there has to be some connection that's deeper or you just end up with a one night stand."

PARTS IS PARTS

"I don't like men who don't have a visible ass," says Mike, the couch potato lover from New Jersey we heard from earlier. "If his ass is flat as a pancake, it's no-go. Bubble butts are just, well, they're great. But eyes—eyes can take me over. I'm currently ogling this guy who is 8 years older than me but has these deep brown eyes that I just feel I'm not staring into his eyes, I'm staring into *him* as a person, and eyes like those make me cream."

Mike is among the many gay men I've interviewed who talk about how they find themselves not only separating faces and bodies from personalities at times, but sometimes even the disparate body parts from each other, giving some more weight than others when it comes to attraction. "I've been with guys who had a killer body, but should have gone through life with a paper bag over their head," he says. "The face is important to me when it would come to a relationship. I need a face I can look at and feel comfortable being with. But if it's just a quick piece of ass—who cares? I mean, within reason. If they have messed up teeth, nose hair galore and major skin problems, no way it's getting up."

In my polling I found more people valued a "good face" over a "good body"; a quarter of those surveyed said they could stomach a bad bod if the face was outstanding, as opposed to 18 percent who contended that what lies below the neck is more important. What was more intriguing was the number of folks who talked about the individual parts they found most compelling; for Howard, a 31-year-old grocery store manager in Seattle, a hot chest can make up for a "multitude of sins" when it comes to catching his eye. "I don't know what it is, exactly, about a chest that makes me crazy, but it does. It doesn't have to be a real smooth hairless chest (but those are my favorite!) It can have a little fuzz on it, or even more thicker hair—as long as we're not talking Tom Selleck from his *Magnum PI* days. But if I see a guy with a great chest at my gym, or someone like that on the beach, I am just stuck on him. I'm convinced that if I was straight I'd probably be all about tits on chicks."

"I'm embarrassed to admit it a little, but it's feet," says Joey, a 17-year-old high school student in Warwick, Rhode Island. "I just like guys that have nice feet. Even if the guy is really hot, if he has feet that are ugly it will totally turn me off . . . on the other hand, if a guy has really nice feet but he's kind of homely otherwise, I'll still find myself talking to him."

Liking feet doesn't make you crazy, Joey—you'll find lots of Web sites devoted to feet on the Internet, of both the homo and hetero variety—but it does put you in the minority as reflected in my polling. (Feet scored only 1 percent out of all the men who answered.) Howard, on the other hand, has lots of company: Chests were the favorite male body part of all, coming in at 18 percent, followed closely by eyes at 17 percent, and a smile at 16 percent. Not everybody who took the poll or survey singled out the quality of one specific body part as an absolute necessity, but lots of men *did;* Kevin, a 42-year-old lawyer in Fort Lauderdale, even admits he should know better than to buy into the practice, but calls a "nice smile" something he just cannot do without. "I'm not saying he has to have perfect teeth, like he just wrapped on a tooth paste commercial. But all teeth must be present, and fairly white. And the smile has to come easily and naturally, without being in any way forced. I have learned that people who don't smile just don't do it for me, no matter how well-built they are or are 'otherwise endowed.'"

That leads me to report that, despite my suspicions when I first composed the poll, a large "endowment" got surprisingly short shrift; only 7 percent singled out a guy's penis as their favorite feature. Make no mistake, now, big johnsons certainly have their fans. "There definitely has to be some meat down there, trust me," says Mark, a 27-year-old grad student in Connecticut. "Sure I'd like him to be sweet, have a nice face, a good body, all that stuff. But if we get into it and his dick is like the size of my pinky, then I'm probably not going to see him again." Mark says he's not some kind of "needy bottom boy" or anything, that he's "usually the top" when it comes to full-on getting-it-on. "But even if I'm going to be poking him from behind there has to be a handful to reach around and grab."

"It's not a size thing with me at all, it's more of a shape thing," says Cory, a 30-year-old "starving artist" in LA. "The guy's cock doesn't have to be huge, but I am very much into oral sex, so I like it to be 'pretty,' not one of those ding-dongs that look like a half-eaten hot dog."

Other men told me they simply have to have men with penises that are "huge," or "thick and long, like a porn star." [Good luck with that, guys.] But more typical were comments like those from Dave, a 28-year-old computer store worker in Arizona. "I have never understood the gay male fascination with dicks, as if we didn't all have them. If I like a guy enough, then I'm sure I am going to like his equipment, unless he's deformed down there or something."

Rory the furniture maker freely admits he goes overboard at times, not just assessing the "parts," but comparing them to each other. "Every one I see gets broken down into sections," he tells me. "It's like 'great eyes but really needs to do something 'bout that bulge in the middle,' or the man is gorgeous from the waist up but needs to spend more time at the gym on his legs and less on his chest . . . I'm very much a leg and ass man, a great pair of legs and a firm, furry, little butt will get my attention very fast . . . but I've gotten so bad at dissecting men's features and body parts that I take note of everything from the hair on his head, or lack thereof, to the shape and condition of his feet. Chest hair pattern, eyebrows, hands and forearms, belly buttons, you name it, I analyze it."

None of the experts I spoke with could really answer the question why some of us look at other men as a collection of individual parts rather than a whole, other than to suggest it has a lot to do with our evolution as hunter/gatherers, the way our brains are wired to sort through a checklist of likes and dislikes. But that doesn't stop some from using the "S" word, as in "shallow," if people take it too far. "For some who can only see a checklist of ideal external characteristics to be fulfilled, they may indeed be very shallow people, or perhaps just simply seduced by the American marketing machine of a perfect type," says psychotherapist Michael Shernoff. "It is also a way of keeping yourself from experiencing a true intimacy, by not allowing other traits to influence what does get you turned on."

But sometimes that impulse is something that occurs on an unconscious level; we may not even know we're doing it. Indeed, many of the men interviewed tell me they never really realized that they valued some body features more than others, until I asked them to think about it. "I didn't know I placed such a premium on a firm round butt until I sat down and took the poll and survey," writes Bill in an e-mail. He's a 30-year-old office worker in Georgia. (Butts, by the way, tied with penises at 7 percent.) "Ever since I took them I have been catching myself whenever I spot a guy walking past me, and my eyes go right to the seat of his pants. How funny is that?"

Chapter 2

The Rules of Attraction

Beauty's where you find it.

"Vogue"
Madonna

Picture, if you will, an urban park in any city with a sizeable gay population; if you live in or have visited such a place, you know the kind of location I'm talking about. It might be one of those public squares or circles, sometimes dominated by a fountain or a statue, or maybe it's just a grassy area near a popular gay bar or hangout, but whichever it is, it's probably not too far from the tony neighborhood that lots of gay men like to call home; consequently, on sunny days it's become a gathering place of sorts, for men of all ages to meet and greet, walk a dog, or just sit and grab some rays, all the while keeping an eager eye open for the next hottie who might happen by.

Suddenly there appears a runner, a tall and finely physiqued young specimen out pounding the pavement in the late-morning sun, longish hair streaming behind him. As he circles the crowd he seems outwardly oblivious to the reactions he's getting . . . there's one fellow, staring with an all-out, mouth-wide-open gawk . . . a few steps on there's a small group of friends chattering on delightedly, quite impressed by his passage . . . and here and there others look up to appraise him with more subtlety, wearing stone-faced expressions, eyes hidden behind dark or mirrored sunglasses, yet no less taken by his beauty.

The runner allows himself just the trace of a smile as he trudges on—he knows *exactly* how people are reacting, and he's enjoying it immensely—and he moves off, directly past another man strolling in the opposite direction; this man is much older, bulkier, head shaved to the skin, with a salt and pepper beard adorning his rugged face. The older man hardly even notices the runner as he passes, and he gets few stares from the onlookers still checking out the vanishing youngster's ample rear end, but some *are* staring, make no mistake; they're taken by his apparent strength and near-military bearing, his obvious comfort with himself as stakes out a spot near the end of a bench, opens a newspaper, and sips his coffee.

Just a few yards behind him there's a trio of young 20-somethings, stripped to the waist and tossing around a Frisbee; though rail thin and a bit pale in the bright sunshine—they usually get their exercise when the sun is long gone, or not yet quite up—they're also getting their share of looks from the crowd, and doing a little looking of their own. In particular they're focused on a couple of studs with "circuit boy" bodies, who seem rather intent on each other and aren't much noticing anyone else. But maybe they're too focused; an errant toss sends their Frisbee wide of its mark, and it sails just above the head of a shy-looking, bookish fellow, who is perhaps a little overdressed for the warmish weather—he would never even *think* about taking *his* shirt off in public—but even as he himself might be surprised to discover, a few of the folks here in the park have noted his presence as well among the guys scattered about in the park. Either as individuals or clustered into smaller groups, all are representatives of just about every subset among us, every age, race, and ethnic group, and just about everyone here is looking around at somebody else at some point, and thinking "he's hot."

Now all that may sound a little idyllic, but it's a scene I myself have observed countless times in gay neighborhoods from Chelsea to West Hollywood. There's always a little something for everyone's tastes and desires to be found when gay men turn out en masse. And such scenes don't just happen in sun-splashed parks; you can observe the same kind of goings on at a beach, a bar, even in the virtual reality afforded by some Internet chat rooms—but they all have the same kind of things in common. This is where you'll find confident men of all ages, secure in the knowledge that whatever "it" is, they definitely have it going on; the men who are perhaps no less confident, but who are usually more content less to strut about than to watch those strutting; the guys who just like to "boy watch" without any desire to share the limelight, drawn by the promise of a pretty face or body, and the improbable—but not impossible—chance they might meet someone approaching their heart's desire. Or maybe just get a smile out of him as he goes by.

Certainly we all chase Adonis in our own ways. But as often as I've found myself in the middle of such boy-watching scenes, I've been inspired to ask what it is that forms that image of Adonis in our minds, or more simply: *Why* do we like what we like? What might drive us to look past the smooth young runner and notice only that older fellow with his coffee? Or perhaps notice neither, and place our sights on that bookish guy with a squeamishness for showing skin, or the twinkie Frisbee tossers, or that pair of circuit-boy hunks?

Assuming, as this book will, that despite some still lingering controversies our same-sex orientation is something formed deep within our own biology, where do we come by our sense of physical perfection or attraction in others? Could it be something that's ingrained just as deeply as our sexual orientation is itself, as if wrapped around the double helix of our very DNA there's a little banner that might read "SGM seeks tall dark Latino with a nice build, dashing smile," or "Big Loving Bear w/salt & pepper hair, ISO same"?

Perhaps it's a case of "imprinting," as if the first guys that we found ourselves attracted to have so much resonance in our lives that they become the same kind of fellows we find ourselves returning to time and again, with some allowance for variation as time goes by; maybe in a lot of ways we're seeking reminders of our fathers, or a beloved brother, a classmate, teacher, or coach who may have been the object of our first crush. Or perhaps there's a kind of obverse logic at work, that we find ourselves avoiding certain "types," because they dredge up unpleasant reminders of the kids who picked on us at school, or a father who was distant or abusive.

Maybe we simply take each new person as he comes, using a whole list of unconscious criteria by which to judge him to be appealing to us, criteria as ever changing and shifting as the variety of new people coming in and out of our lives; we may have "types," or a certain set of types we find "hot or not," but perhaps they're never set in stone. We could be looking for someone who in some odd way reminds us of us. Or we might be seeking to find the truth in the old adage that opposites may, in fact, attract.

DESIGNER GENES, OR FIRST IMPRESSIONS?

"From my earliest memories, I felt an attraction to tall guys, with nice muscles, and broad shoulders," says Cal, a 50-year-old postal worker in Milwaukee. "Never really did understand where that came from, since no one in my family ever looked like that, and no one I ever knew as a child or growing up remotely resembled that type, if you don't count the GI Joes I played with, or the action heroes I saw on television or at the movies."

But Cal says he doesn't think his childish playthings or cinematic crushes had much to do with his sense of male beauty, or his inner desires. "I have always thought 'my type' is something that came with the gay package, along with my aesthetic sensibilities . . . I can still remember the first time I saw a nearly nude male art figure in a book, the kind of guy I am describing to you now . . . it was just so exciting and titillating. It wasn't just that I was a horny teenager, there was just a 'rightness' to liking that sort of build for me. There were other pictures in the book with men in them, but I only gravitated to the tall, muscular ones, those were the only ones that got me excited. So that kind of man has always been my ideal, both in art and in real life."

Other men have similar tales of desire that dawned at a very early age. "I was just a kid, 'cause I was still at the age when I was reading Dr. Seuss books," says John, a 30-year-old paramedic in Los Angeles. "On the cover of one of his books was a cartoon guy, holding up several other cartoon boys and girls. As he held them above his head, he had a nice V taper and biceps, and I remember going back to that tiny drawing over and over and not knowing why." John says he can also remember being incredibly drawn to the pictures of "hot boys" on posters that were aimed at the female, teeny-bopper crowd, pictures he would sneak a glance at whenever he was out shopping with his mother. Now as an adult gay man he says he still finds athletic and strong bodies devastatingly attractive, and he thinks he knows why. "I believe it goes back to the same biological reasons that females find any male attractive: The virility, ability to propagate—if only by appearance—and the ability to protect. It's all subconscious thought."

Greg is a 34-year-old sales rep in Jersey City, New Jersey. He says he's always believed he was "programmed to like certain types" of people and thinks it comes from something other than just his life experience. "I'm sure the people I've met have had some effect on the kind of guy I'm attracted to, but probably not all that much, just like I would have been gay no matter where I grew up or how." Greg likens the experience of meeting the "right" guy, the kind he's "supposed" to be with, to what a "bird would feel like if it was cooped up" then finally allowed to fly. "When you meet the guys who match that inner programming, it's like freedom and magic, and things really click. I think where we run into problems is when we try and make things work with guys who aren't really compatible with what we like inside, just like it doesn't work when gay guys try to make it work playing it straight. You can't fight what's right for you."

Over the years a number of researchers have conducted studies to find out just how much any supposed "inner programming" might have to do with what men find attractive, but the overwhelming majority have focused on heterosexual males. Results that seem to indicate cross-cultural preferences for a certain kind of woman—with desired traits such as ample breasts, wide hips, and other features that might denote fertility, as John suggested previously—have often been controversial, and blasted as sexist and patriarchal. Speaking for myself, it's not at all hard to believe that some features that could help perpetuate the species might in fact become "hardwired" into our genetic code; that's how nature and evolution work, after all . . . but how could that hardwiring cross the line into our neighborhood, and crash our little same-sex party?

Dean Hamer is a microbiologist at the National Institutes of Health in Bethesda, Maryland; he's also the author of *The God Gene: How Faith Is Hardwired into Our Genes* (2004) and co-author of *Living with Our Genes: Why They Matter More Than You Think* (Hamer and Copeland, 1999). Both books go to great lengths to describe how the same genetic principles which give us our eye color or right- or left-handedness also affect our very behaviors. But although Hamer calls the formation of our sexual ideals—i.e., the kind of person we think would make a perfect sexual partner—one of science's "greatest mysteries," he's not afraid to advance some ideas about it. If you want to know why some gay men find other types of men attractive, he suggests looking first toward heterosexual women.

"Gay men have a lot in common with straight females, in that they have pretty similar male archetypes that they come to desire," he says. And just like those females, Hamer says, most gay men tend to gravitate toward "healthy, symmetrical, fertile, masculine men." But when it comes to what exact variety of man they seek out, several different factors begin to manifest themselves.

"I think that every person's ideas about what's attractive are a mix of genetic hardwiring, and past life experience. We know for example that babies are able to distinguish other humans from animals, and are drawn to them. That must be hardwired. But there's also a strong environmental factor, because that baby learns to love its own mother, and not another woman. Likewise we are all probably in part hardwired to be attracted to certain types, but our life experience comes into play as well. I would compare sexual orientation to height, in that it is mostly hardwired in our genes. Your sense of sexual attraction, however, is something more akin to weight; there's a genetic component, but it's likely something that will change over time, depending on your circumstances."

Still, from what many tell me their tastes as formed early in their lives haven't changed all that much, especially if their first brush with male-on-male attraction was powerful. "I was about 15 and I had a crush on the captain of the track team that I ran on in high school," says Ed, a 24-year-old college student at the University of Connecticut. "He pretty much defined what my type was, and still is. He was very mature for his age, straight and athletic, and he already had 5 o'clock shadow, and some hair on his chest. He was so muscular and lean, with these great blue eyes and perfect brown hair—he had one of those hairlines that went straight across his forehead—with strong facial features, a square jaw and broad chin. And besides that great upper body he had huge muscular legs . . . yeah, that was the first guy that I ever felt a sexual attraction to. These days my tastes have broadened somewhat, but that type is still what I go for." [Jesus, Ed . . . if you ever find him again, send him my way!]

Tony, a 23-year-old college student in Boston, tells me he wasn't "turned on by men at all" until he was about 18 or so; that's when he and his best friend at the time progressed from being "just friends" to something else. "I think we were attracted most by each other's personalities, but he was a good looking guy, tall, dark, and handsome." Now five years later, Tony tells me that "nothing has changed, I am still mostly attracted to that type of man."

Bob, a 51-year-old personal trainer in Rancho Mirage, California, tells me he was always attracted to strong men, even as a child watching superheroes on television. That attraction easily transferred itself outside the confines of the small screen. "I was always turned on by muscular men of any age, but specifically remember a next door neighbor when I was five . . . I once saw him in a T-shirt working in the yard. He had baseball biceps that fascinated me. I'd watch him for hours out my bedroom window."

Bob says that to this day, his tastes have not changed. "I still go after that muscularity, a sense of physical power, but not the bulky powerlifter look . . . it's the sense of strength I find most appealing. And I can only imagine that the initial appeal is rooted in a sense of security, someone powerful to protect me, perhaps."

Jeff, the college professor at Virginia Tech, says he's convinced our sense of beauty and attraction has much to do with the men we found ourselves surrounded by as children. "I grew up in southern West Virginia, around a lot of beefy, hairy, bearded, butch guys who wore boots, jeans, T-shirts, wife-beaters, and flannel shirts. Thus, not only do I find that 'country-boy' look most attractive, but I have patterned my own look after that."

Doug, a 37-year-old creative consultant who doesn't tell me where he's from, says his first male crush had a profound effect on him. "I saw my gym teacher (Mr. Gibson) naked when I was 14 . . . it was kind of strange because I'd lost my virginity with a girl about two weeks before. It was good with the girl, I really loved it . . . so I was dumbstruck with the realization that as good as it felt with her, and I wanted *him* to ravage me so bad that my heartbeat almost exploded out of my head. He was the picture of what I had never imagined: Pure masculinity offsetting my boyish exterior . . . six-foot-one, 200 pounds of slightly hairy, muscular Italian man!"

Doug says in "a line-up of a hundred guys," he'll still find himself lustily checking out the ones that resemble Mr. Gibson first before anyone else. "I believe 'types' develop from the first initial neural pathways to pleasure," he tells me. "They 'pave the road,' so to speak, for the neural signals to get to [our deepest desires] and since they are the first, they are the 'road most traveled,' and therefore the easiest and quickest receptors."

Probably about two-thirds of the men I contacted had stories like those, and most firmly believe that their current sense of beauty and attractiveness, even as it may have changed some around the edges over the years, has strong roots in their very first male-on-male desire. Dean Hamer concurs with that assessment. Despite whatever programming our genes might start us out with, he says the exact type we come to like frequently corresponds with the males we grew up with, met at different points of our lives, and were around at that point we were becoming sexually aware. "One could call it imprinting, because it tends to happen about the same time that some people are forming their religious convictions," he says. "It's that time in your life when you're reaching out and forging social connections as well. Most people's sexual fantasies involve people that they grew up with, so that's the simplest theory when it comes to how we come to find certain types of people attractive."

If you've ever trolled the aisles of a bookstore, looking for books that display some of the most "attractive" male physiques to be found, then you likely know the work of artist/photographer Tom Bianchi. The artist behind eleven published works of exquisite nude art—including *Out of the Studio* (1991), *In Defense of Beauty* (1995), and *On the Couch* (2002/2004)—Bianchi has a somewhat intimate understanding of what it is one man often finds the most compelling in another and his own beliefs about what forms that attraction. "In a deep part of our brain we are looking for the nurturing we did not get as children. We are looking for our idealized parent," he suggests. "People who resemble that image will be seen as knockouts to us. This image may include the boy we couldn't love—my lover, Fil, for example, has the idealized body of a college athlete. I can't imagine a more potent attraction for me—he looks like the guy I was in love with from the 3rd grade through college . . . Fil finally allows me to complete that love affair."

Like Dean Hamer, Bianchi says the second piece of the puzzle is found in our evolution. "It is simple. We find beautiful that which ensures our survival. Can her hips produce children and her breasts produce milk? Can he chase down an antelope, and carry it home? So we value strength expressed in the human form to do what it is designed to do. Of course for us this is mostly metaphor now; we dance, we have sport, we make love. We want to look good, agile, and strong enough to do these things . . . we are attracted to people who realize their potential."

Psychotherapist Michael Bettinger tells me he also believes that there's some nature and some nurture at work here. "I believe some of [who we find attractive] is inherent in who we are, and it's probably coded in our genetic makeup. And particular types that attract people are generally because of experiences in life . . . what one's father looked like, what the ethnic group into which one was born looked like . . . how rebellious a person is, i.e., liking what others do not consider good looking." Bettinger says as much as genetic factors affect the "look" we as individuals admire, there has to be a strong environmental component as well.

Bettinger's Manhattan colleague Michael Shernoff agrees. "Some men find themselves attracted to men who remind them of their father or a first boy they had a crush on," he tells me. "For others it is hard-wired to like blonds, men of color, or tall dark and hairy men. In some respects it is like what food we find ourselves craving . . . or in other words, it's all very complex and not always predictable."

Even to the point of being perversely attracted to the sort of fellows that once made our lives difficult. Jerry tells me he grew up in a "small, backwater town in North Carolina, just to the east of Outer Bumblefuck," where he was "constantly and continuously" picked on by the larger, meaner boys he grew up with. Now 28, and working in retail in Atlanta, he says he sometimes finds himself drawn to the same sort of fellows. "I'm not out looking to be bashed or anything," he says. "I don't go looking for trouble in straight biker bars. But if I'm out in a gay club, and I see somebody that reminds me of one of those hoodlums, I can get very interested in them."

Edwin, a 33-year-old video news photographer in Arlington, Virginia, grew up in Vienna, West Virginia. He can remember being attracted to "a neighborhood boy who threatened to beat me up," even though he was only 8 years old at the time and didn't realize yet he was gay . . . not until a just a few years later, at any rate. "That same kid who used to beat me up? Eventually we got to be friends, and started sucking each other off all the time . . . and I still find that kind of man attractive. I like the strong, rugged type of guy."

For Michael, a 41-year-old psychology professor at a "large Midwestern college best left nameless," it was a kid in his high school class that intrigued him then, and in some ways haunts him still. "His name was Bobby, and he was just beautiful, with tanned skin and long hair, with a very large arms and a strong solid build. Even though I knew he was something of a bully I was fascinated by him. He was my very first teenage crush. I didn't really mind it when he picked on me because I enjoyed the fact he was noticing me at all. And it's rather curious how I think back now, and on some level I think Bobby knew I liked him 'that way,' because he was never as brutal with me as he was with some of my other classmates."

Michael says he still finds men who have a "strong physical presence that borders on arrogance" to be the most captivating, and he's sure that it all started with Bobby more than 20 years ago. "I should probably do some sort of research project on this one day, I am sure it's fertile ground for study, so many gay men have had the same sort of experience."

But other gay men tell me that, if anything, they *avoid* the type of guy that might have once made them a victim of bullying or harassment. "I never liked bullies, not then, not now," says Aaron, a 44-year-old insurance executive in Newark, Delaware. "Like a lot of gay guys I had my share of run ins with them, and couldn't wait to get out of school. Years later at a high school reunion—with my non-bullying partner by my side—I hoped to see some of them again, and have them see me, about 50-pounds of muscle heavier. And I did spot a few of them, they were all fat and bald with their shrew-like wives towing them around. I always though they were pathetic inside, even when they were big and bulky and strong. It was nice to see how pathetic they'd grown on the outside as well."

"I've heard some guys say they were attracted to the rough 'straight boy' types they knew in school, but that sounds like some kind of post-traumatic battered spouse syndrome kind of thing to me," says Chet, a 30-year-old accountant in Baton Rouge, Louisiana. "I'm no shrink, but it sounds like they're working out some issues, trying to re-write their pasts and give the stories a better ending. If anything I like exactly the opposite of those guys, and I was probably picked on as much as anyone. Nowadays I like 'em strong, but they better be sweet, too."

And what about dear old Dad? How many gay men are looking for their fathers in the men they now find attractive, or still running like hell to get away from the old man? That's hard to say; many men I spoke with tell me the idea of finding something sexually attractive in their fathers, whether they got on well or not, makes them feel rather odd and uncomfortable, even as they admit it's probably a fundamental aspect of their formative years. "My Dad fought in Vietnam, but it wasn't something he talked a lot about," says David, a 38-year-old teacher in Maine. "He died a few years ago from cancer, and while my sisters and I were going through his things I found his photo album, and I was kind of floored. You have to understand we were never really close, especially after I came out, and he wasn't really a big part of my life for the last 15, 20 years or so. So when I saw the pictures of him as a really young guy barely out of his teens, how good-looking and virile he was in that Army uniform, hanging all over his buddies with cigarettes hanging out of their mouths, I was shocked. I also couldn't help but notice how much he looked like a few of the guys I've dated. Talk about creepy."

"I don't know if I've ever done it consciously, but I have to admit a lot of the guys I've pursued over the course of my life do look a lot like my father, says Bill, a 57-year-old restaurant manager in Springfield, Massachusetts. "What's more, they rather act like he did, too, very gentle and very kind. We got along quite well (he never knew I was gay before he passed, though I don't think he would have cared) and yes, he was a pretty good-looking guy. I suppose it could be a coincidence, but there's probably something to the idea."

"I personally believe gay men fall in love with their fathers to a large degree," says Michael Bettinger, and he adds that love might be expressed by being attracted to men who either look like their fathers or act like their fathers. "But this is not universal," he cautions. "There is an element of both parents in all our lovers, and we can also be programmed to want someone the opposite of our parents if there was a particularly bad relationship with one or both parents."

Which is exactly the case with Jeremy and his father; in fact, at 22 he tells me he's still smarting from the day two years ago when his father asked him to leave their home in Northern California, if he "insisted on pursuing a gay lifestyle," as he put it. Now a coffee shop worker in San Francisco, Jeremy tells me to "feel free" to shoot him if he ever hooks up with anyone who "even in the slightest way" resembles his dad. "He's a total bastard, so I am working real hard to avoid the 'total bastard type,' however they look on the outside. So, yeah, my Dad had an influence on me. I'll go after people who don't remind me of him, and if someone I'm dating starts acting like he does, I am history."

THE MAN IN THE MIRROR

Damon is telling me about the time he and one of his female friends were hanging out at their gym, checking out the good-looking guys who were pounding weight or sweating it out on the treadmills. "She pointed at one guy, and said 'Oh, he is so your type.' I asked her why she thought that, and she said 'Because he looks just like you.'" That surprised the 21-year-old Illinois college student a little, and made him think about his past relationships. "It was weird, but I realized that every guy I had dated or pursued had exactly the same features I have."

"I have always had a weakness for younger guys who have a certain 'look' about them," says Drew, a 40-year-old real estate broker in Minnesota. "When I say 'look,' I mean a certain build—kind of athletic, but not too big or bulky—with dark hair, dark eyes, a handsome but not exactly pretty face. Young rugged types, like a soccer player perhaps, or a really toned swimmer/diver . . . anyway, what often happens is when we go out someone will ask 'Is this your son?' or 'Is this your little brother?' and it's occasionally been a little embarrassing. Not too long ago, my current boyfriend—he's 23—saw some old pictures of me from college, and he said he was a little freaked out. I asked him why, and he was surprised I didn't see it immediately, how much he looked now like I looked then. I guess a lot of people would call that narcissistic, but I try not to psychoanalyze it too much. I just like who I like."

Damon and Drew weren't alone in relating such tales. "I'm a young guy, but I've already developed what I would call a very healthy sense of self-esteem," says Troy, a 20-year-old college student in Ann Arbor, Michigan. "When I first realized I was gay, I also realized that there was nothing wrong with it. I am only going to go after guys who feel the same way . . . and as for how I look, well, I am not what you'd call bad looking. I know this will piss people off to read it, but I'm actually very hot, tall, lean, and pretty nice muscles, and people are always telling me I could be a model." [Troy sends along a link—and no, I won't share it—that sends me to his pictures on one of those "rate my body" Web sites. If those are in fact his pictures, he is indeed very attractive—one might even say "hot" without fear of contradiction.] And Troy says he finds himself looking at and wanting to date guys who look a lot like him. "I know people will say

I only do it because I'm stuck on myself, but I don't really care what people think."

Probably as many as a fifth of the men I interviewed or surveyed said they always or often dated or chased after men who strongly resembled the guy they looked at in the mirror every morning. And just under half of those who took the *Chasing Adonis* poll said that they preferred guys who looked a *lot* like they do. "I think you'll find that's pretty common," says Bart, a 37-year-old personal trainer in San Diego. "At least when it comes to the way guys are built, if we're talking about guys who have spent a long time weight training and shaping their bodies. A lot of us find certain body types to be sexy and appealing, and we work on creating that physique in ourselves. If someone else has the same kind of body, why wouldn't we find it appealing as well?"

"A lot of men, myself included, like to stay close to the familiar," says Sergio, a 29-year-old club deejay in New York. "Sure it's fun to try different things, for a slim, dark-haired guy like me to see what it's like to hang out with a big buffed-out and blue-eyed Swede. [But] I will almost always find myself going back 'to the 'hood,' especially if I am looking for more of a boyfriend-type thing, and for me that means guys who have the same kind of build, the same general facial features, it's just [my] comfort level."

Lots of other gay men of course have exactly the opposite viewpoint. "Oh good lord, no," says James, a 31-year-old writer in Salem, Massachusetts, when asked if he's attracted to men he resembles. "Don't get me wrong, I have no problems with self image, and I happen to think I am a pretty good catch when it comes to a face and a body." But James tells me he's always been attracted to "men of color, and strong ethnic features" as opposed to that "American 'boy next door' image." Wayne, a 47-year-old lab technician in Baltimore, says he's not at all surprised to hear so many gay men suggesting a preference for men like themselves. "This has to be the most narcissistic community in the history of the world, so why should anyone doubt that people who look alike will pair up like animals ready to get on Noah's Ark?"

Is it narcissism, or is it more like Sergio suggests, something as simple as seeking a "comfort level," that drives some men to look for the familiar in the men they go after? I put the question to a psychologist and relationship counselor I know, who asks me not to use his name for concern any of his clients might assume he was talking about them and be offended. "I would be loathe to ever pathologize someone's personal preferences, if that word 'preferences' even makes sense when it comes to the often unconscious desires we all have," he says. "Are some men falling victim to narcissistic impulses when they only date others who look like themselves? Perhaps, though true narcissism can be a dangerous and insidious condition which can be very difficult to treat, and simply choosing mates who closely reflect our own looks or personality doesn't necessarily fit the profile. A true narcissist has a lot more issues than that.

"If someone likes to date or simply socialize with others he resembles, in whatever form that resemblance takes, that is not necessarily narcissism at all, and it could be just that 'comfort level' you speak of. That person might simply enjoy the company of 'the familiar,' and that could extend all the way to preferring to have sexual relations solely with people he or she looks like physically. A diagnosis of narcissism usually implies all sorts of other issues, like the need for constant validation, attention, even adulation, with elements of abuse, and manipulation and domination present as well. A slim-bodied youth with light brown hair, who only likes other slim-bodied youths with light brown hair, doesn't necessarily have a problem. He might just need to get out more."

OPPOSITES ATTRACT?

"I almost always choose men that are the opposite of me," says Luke, a 21-year-old information tech student in Philadelphia. "I'm a twink, and I think twinks are kind of gross. I go for the muscular, well-built guys." Across the state there's Phil, a 17-year-old high school student in Pittsburgh, who tells me he only goes for older muscular men as well. "I just wouldn't be attracted to someone who looks like me," he says. "My hands give me enough love as it is, so why would I need another set just like them touching me? I would never even think about being with another guy like myself."

"All my mates are my opposites," says Dave, a 34-year-old personal trainer in Washington, DC. "I am hairy, they are smooth. I am in great shape, they are in medium shape." And Stuart, a 30-year-old flight attendant who lives in Atlanta, takes it even further than the mere physical. "I'm tall and thin, blonde & blue, and a little on the 'femme' side if you want to get the full mental image. What do I like? Short, heavy, husky men, preferably from the darker side of town, with those marvelously swarthy features. And they must be very, very butch." I ask Stuart how successful he is at finding such men, and whether they return his admiration. "Are you kidding me? I have to turn men down all the time, because my social calendar gets booked up real fast."

Earlier I alluded to the *Chasing Adonis* poll results, where just under half of the men who responded agreed that they preferred men much like themselves; however, many men didn't answer the question at all, and of those who did slightly more than 40 percent said they tended *not* to like men who look a lot like they do. Many of those men tell me that beyond physical differences, they find themselves seeking out or coupling with men vastly different from themselves in a number of ways, including ethnicity and social station. "I don't know why it is, but I never much cared for people like the folks I grew up around," says Demetrius, a 27-year-old restaurant worker originally from Alabama. "My friends from home say it was like I was always looking somewhere else, and I guess they were right. I live with my current boyfriend in Philadelphia, and he's not at all like them ... he's quiet (they were loud) he's smart (they're not dumb, but not geniuses either) and he's very ambitious (they're still living in Alabama, ok?) We're very different, but the difference is the thing I like the most about him, and I think he would tell you the same thing."

"I happen to like myself just fine, thanks. No problems with self love at all, here," says Ben, a 34-year-old office worker in Cincinnati, who describes himself as a "medium white guy, with a medium build," and a "propensity" to be shy and quiet. Yet Ben tells me his boyfriend is anything but. "He's a total jock, completely outgoing, and he's into all sorts of crazy things like skydiving and rock climbing, you name it. It sounds very trite I know to say that we 'complete' each other, but that's exactly what it feels like."

It's those sorts of contradictions that Dean Hamer refers to, when he calls the phenomenon of human sexual attraction such a "mystery"; though he makes a good case for the theory that genetic coding and life experience largely form our desires, he himself admits there are some holes to account for. "There are so many exceptions—the white man who finds himself attracted to a person of color, the upper class guy who is drawn to working class men—that it's a hard theory to apply across the board."

"The idea that we all have some kind of 'type' we're supposed to like is really limiting if you ask me, but it is amazing how many friends of mine seem to live or die by it," says Craig, a 29-year-old software designer in Athens, Georgia. "I don't have any one kind of visual template in my head, I am all about variety. I like Asian guys, Latino guys, and regular old white bread guys, guys with muscles and guys who are thin and just really toned. The only thing that matters to me is that we hit it off, that he likes me the same ways I might be into him."

Steve is a 22-year-old student at the University of Maryland in College Park. "I honestly have no idea why I'm attracted to the types of guys I am," he says. "I think some people are attracted to who they think they should be, and I think others take what they can get. Some go for types they've been around, and others go for someone totally opposite, and that may be because they don't like who they are, and the guy is like someone they wish they could be. Personally, I'm attracted to someone I enjoy being around, and that I can make laugh, just someone I have that 'connection with,' as corny as that sounds."

Comments like those come from the several men I've spoken with, who tell me the reasons they find certain men attractive isn't something they'd really given much thought to—they simply take each new guy in their lives on his own terms—and they suggest people find one another attractive for a whole host of reasons. Like Craig, many of them also say they don't much believe in the "type" concept, or have so many types that the very concept is rather meaningless. "Ask me what kind of food I like, I might say pizza," says Cory, a 23-year-old college student in Austin, Texas. "Or if I think about it a little differently, I might say Chinese food, or Mexican. But the honest answer is I like them all, just like I have found myself really attracted to a little buff bodybuilder type one day, and the next I thought this skinny little nerdy boy was just the cutest guy I had ever seen. And they had absolutely nothing in common, except the fact I happened to think they were both sexy. So let's say I like my men in all sorts of flavors, and leave it at that." Fabio, a 20-year-old college student in Sao Paulo, Brazil, says he may start off with a certain ideal in mind for the kind of guy he finds most compelling, but he's quite prepared to be flexible. "I'm usually turned on by older men, the hairy, manly-man type, someone I can see some maturity in, but I don't take the idea of 'types' very seriously. 'Sparkles' can show up, even if the guy is not my 'perfect' guy . . . and if they do, then something more can happen."

Other men are equally eager to ditch the whole analysis of the situation; they're just hoping to find a "good guy" to be around, like Joe, a 27-year-old auto repair shop worker in Ohio. "I never spent much time wondering why I was gay, I just am, so I guess I've also never really wondered why I like the types of guys I do. I think what really matters is finding someone you like, and go from there."

But even when they *do* find someone they like, some men still question their good fortune. "You know that old Groucho Marx line, about how I would never belong to a club that would have me as a member? That's sometimes been my approach to guys I find attractive," says Terry, a 39-year-old computer technician in Spokane, Washington. "I was very fat as a child, and even though I dropped that weight ages ago I still have a very poor self-image. So even when I am really attracted to someone, if he starts returning my attention I become convinced there has to be something wrong with him." Bill, a 27-year-old retail employee in Allentown, Pennsylvania, is equally suspicious when his "would-be beaus" begin to reciprocate his attentions. "Most of my friends are women, and sometimes I think I've picked up some of their worst habits, like talking about people behind their backs, and being 'beyond critical' when it comes to how people dress . . . but probably the worst thing I do is start dissing the same guys I once thought were hot, because they start to pay attention to me. Don't ask me to make sense of it, because I know there's no way I can justify it. It's just how I am."

Joel Perry writes an often-amusing advice column in *Instinct Magazine* called "Man to Man," and in the September 2004 issue he found himself confronting this question:

> I'm 23-years old, 220 pounds, 6'3"—not fat but a large guy. I recently met a guy who is 28, 5'10", tan, athletic build, great ass, and I feel self-conscious about my size. He's so good looking, I feel like he's Jane and I'm King Kong. I don't know why he's into me.

The fellow went on to suggest he was worried about climbing that metaphorical Empire State Building, that he feared getting shot down "if somebody better looking comes along" (Perry, 2004a, p. 92).

Perry's response was typical, and pithy, pointing out that this odd universe we live in often creates the most unlikely couplings, and whatever facets there are to our persons or personalities, even those things we don't much like in ourselves, there's probably somebody out there looking for exactly that feature. "That's why you'll see a twinkie with a bear, a gym rat with a nerd, Ben Affleck with Matt Damon," he wrote (p. 92). Perry also pointed out that those who question why someone finds them attractive have to get past their own self-esteem issues first. "You might learn what really attracted him could have been your humor, your personality, or maybe that big, hard, throbbing muscle—your heart" (p. 92).

Those kinds of "self-esteem issues" are something we'll talk more about later, since they were a recurrent theme among many of the men I talked to, and a constant barrier in their quest to find companionship. Speaking for myself, I've never had anything but an *excess* of self-esteem, which carries its own peculiar little bundle of woes with it—you tend to make a lot of enemies, some you're never even aware of, because they somehow find you threatening—but other than that, I can see a lot of myself in all the comments related in this chapter. Those tales that men have that suggest their specific desires and attractions have a strong biological basis? I can remember being a boy of 13 or 14 and stumbling on pages torn out of some old porn magazine, and becoming totally riveted on the images of fit and muscular nude males, while other kinds of naked guys did so little for me I barely noticed them. Feeling what seemed to be such an innate sense of desire for that kind of guy, it's not that hard to believe there might be something genetic behind it all.

But then I remember the beautiful boys of my own youth, and I recall the absolutely powerful effect their physiques had on me; I have to wonder if that didn't also have a certain "imprinting" effect, as many of the gay men I've talked with suggest. It seems rather likely, as all of my experts propose, that nature and nurture combined to create a rather potent hankering for certain body types. While I can also see in myself some commonality with those who simply have no idea why they feel the way they do—they're happy to just "go with the flow"—I've been happiest and most satisfied when I hewed closer to the men who happen to approach what my mind—or my body—sees as its "ideal."

And when I take out my old box of photographs, or pull my old junior and high school yearbooks off the shelf, something interesting happens. I'll comb through the pictures of guys I remember finding most compelling, and though I find that occasional anomaly, I more often spot a lot of common traits among the guys that used to set my heart all aflutter . . . starting with that tough kid back in the seventh grade who used to like to jack me up against the wall after gym class, just because he could—he was a brute, but damn, what a *fine*-looking brute—through the rest of my high school days, almost eight years in the Marine Corps, and all the way up to the guys I've met and slobbered over just within the past decade and a half. There's a real observable resemblance in the facial features, the set of their eyes, their body shapes and musculature . . . even, if I recall correctly, the way they moved and spoke. It's almost as if, in many ways, I've fallen for or simply been infatuated with the same guy, over and over, despite the wide span of years and geographical distances involved.

Is that imprinting, or an inborn trait, or just pure coincidence? It's hard to say, precisely. But one thing I do know, and I think Greg from New Jersey says it exactly right: When you do stumble on "that guy," wherever you meet him and for whatever reason it happens, it is very much like magic.

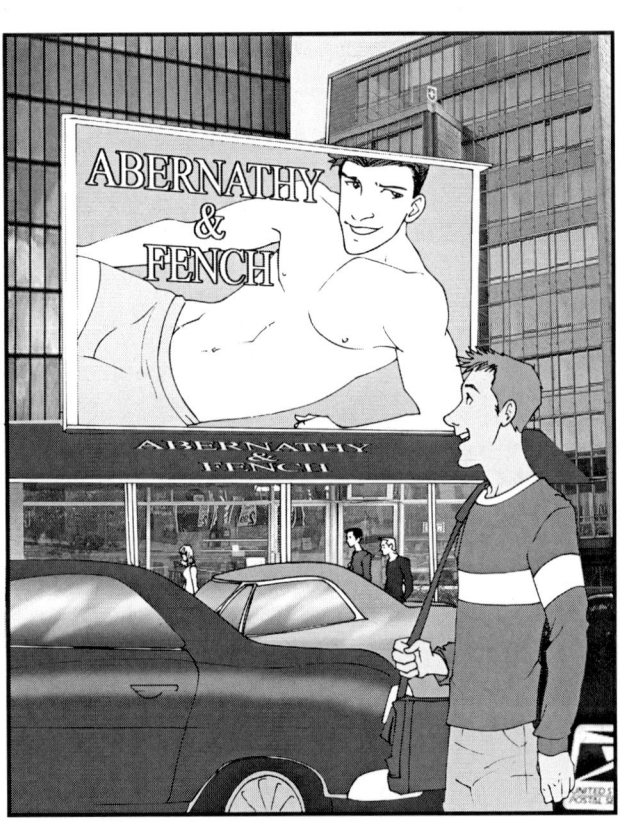

Chapter 3

Beautiful Things

> The beauty of the world has two edges,
> one of laughter, one of anguish, cutting the heart asunder.
>
> Virginia Woolf

He's a wide-eyed, smiling image of youthful innocence and all-American perfection. His gaze is fixed on some unseen object or person down the beach from where he's standing, posed with one hand in his pocket, the other resting inside the unbuttoned waistband of his water-soaked jeans. His shirt is open to the sea breeze, revealing smooth skin, tanned and toned; looking on, you can surely feel the heat radiating from that tropical sun above, not to mention the heat radiating from that flawless, oh-so-touchable body. . . .

A sigh of appreciation escapes your lips, but he'll never hear it. That beach is hundreds if not thousands of miles away, and the object of your admiration is nothing more than a handsome boy in a photograph, smiling in a sun-splashed moment captured in time some months before. Still you linger for a moment, mentally placing yourself in that photo; now there's sand between your toes, ocean wind in your hair . . . and for just that instant, the boy is smiling at you.

I wrote those words in 1999, in an article for the fourth issue of the late *HERO Magazine* (p. 18), and I was talking about the peculiar love affair lots of gay men were having at the time with the relatively new Abercrombie & Fitch *A&F Quarterly*. It was more than just a clothing catalog and collection of music, book, and travel reviews;

with its bold yet classy Bruce Weber photos of gorgeous young men often entwined in innocent yet intriguing poses, the *Quarterly* quickly became a must-have coffee table item for anyone who considered himself an admirer of youthful male beauty.

The *A&F Quarterly* wasn't the first advertising vehicle to transcend its original mission—sending you off to the mall with credit card in hand—to become a virtual objet d'art; it was preceded by the classic International Male and Undergear catalogs, and who-knows-how-many other Calvin Klein or Versace ad campaign photos lovingly snipped from countless magazines and newspaper inserts, some finding their way into frames, others simply tacked up on a bedroom wall. Still, Abercrombie & Fitch is famous—some might say infamous—for depicting male bonding gone wild; as I wrote in that *HERO* article about the late *Quarterly* (which was, ironically, discontinued in 2003 after numerous complaints about depictions of heterosexual couplings run amuck), one could

> open up the book up almost anywhere you wish, and there's a good chance you'll encounter a horde of smiling boxer-clad boys in a massive tangle of biceps, pecs, and abs ... turn another page and there's a pretty pair wrestling shirtless on the grass ... there's a single young man, looking past the camera over your shoulder, his bright eyes and smile a flawless, sepia-toned study ... turn again and those boxer boys are back. (Except this time they've removed the boxers on the way to some kind of mass skinny dip.) It doesn't seem to matter whether it's Spring or Summer, Fall or Winter; those Abercrombie & Fitch boys just don't seem to be able to keep their buttons buttoned or their zippers zipped for long, and they certainly don't mind touching each other in a more-than-brotherly fashion. (Bergling, 1999, p. 19)

Abercrombie will not say specifically that they target a gay audience; when I speak to company representatives they make it clear they market their products to anyone who wants to pony up his cash. Still, it's no surprise that so many gay men would fall in love—at least figuratively—with the handsome faces and hunky bodies found in such ads, nor is it in the least shocking that advertisers, even nominally straight ones, would take advantage of a typical gay man's propensity to go all weak in the knees when he turns a page and sees a stud; sex sells quite well, thank you, and we gay men are usually more than happy to pay the freight.

"The men in the ads you talk about just make me want to take a few moments, go off and enjoy myself," says Bob, a 26-year-old bank employee in Roanoke, Virginia. "I love the way they look. . . . it's almost like you can feel the smoothness of their skin and the muscles they have underneath. I can't afford to buy many of the things they're wearing on my salary, but I really enjoy looking at them." Chase, a 40-year-old horse trainer who doesn't give me his hometown, may not be quite that enthusiastic but still admits he's something of a fan. "It's not like I'm going to go beat off to them, but they do make me somewhat sexually aroused. And they actually do inspire me to keep working out and stay in shape."

"I have a kind of complex reaction when I see a really hot man in an ad on a billboard or a clothing store or in a magazine," says Drew, a 19-year-old college student in New Haven, Connecticut. "It's a very positive reaction, but complex. My first impression is, 'wow, he's hot!' and I picture what it would be like going to bed with a guy who looked like that, waking up to him the next morning, then spending a long lazy day in bed with him just exploring every part of that perfect body. . . . the second reaction is like, 'wow, what would it be like to be that guy?' I'm often told I am cute, so it's not like I don't get attention or anything, but to look like that, like an Adonis, to have so many people wanting you and wanting to be like you . . . that must be pretty powerful."

In Chapter 2 we talked about how genetic programming and the life experiences we have come to shape what it is we find attractive in other men; what also intrigues me—and many of the men I interviewed for this book—is the effect that media imagery might have in that process. From all those static ads with their parade of perfect physiques, to calendars and art books that feature a wide range of hunks of all ages and varieties of male beauty . . . from network television programming (some actually aimed these days at gay audiences) that's increasingly filled with just as many "hot" men as "hot" women, to all the erotic pictures and videos one encounters (if one so chooses) on the Internet, we are simply bombarded by suggestions of the near-impossible level of perfection that the male figure and face can attain. How much of what we like, and don't like, might turn on the choices made in some Madison Avenue ad agency or in some anonymous network producer's office? Do these ads create such a high level of expectation in some men that they'll forever be searching for such perfection in the everyday people that they meet? And what effect do all those images of sheer perfection have on the self-esteem of the regular joes out there who don't have a matinee idol's eyes or teeth, or who, try as they might, cannot square their rounded shoulders or turn a keg into a six-pack?

LET'S HEAR IT FOR THE BOYS

"I think I first realized I was gay when I started noticing the pictures in the department store advertisements you get in the Sunday paper," says Brian, a 34-year-old health care worker in San Francisco. "I was probably 14 or so, and it was springtime, so there were all the pictures of cute boys my own age wearing swimsuits, and young men a little older. They were very innocent pictures, but they gave me a huge erection all the same, so that's when I started figuring there was something different about me. (Years later when I started seeing all those A&F ads, I thought it was hysterical that I was having the same kind of reaction.) Looking back it makes me think that the kind of guy I have always wanted, and still want to find, is just like the guys in the pictures: He's in-shape, all-American boy next door, with a great face, and he looks totally killer just wearing a bathing suit . . . or nothing at all."

Few of the experts I spoke with tell me they see such ads having any kind of fundamental effect on the sort of man we'll find ourselves drawn to. "I don't put much stock in advertising to create images that we ultimately find attractive," says social worker Andrew Gottlieb. "What we find attractive is already 'set' in some ways, based on our early relationships with our parents, and early environmental factors. Advertising may play on, or strengthen what's 'there' to begin with, but it doesn't shape it from scratch." Dean Hamer is more a scientist than social critic, but he's got his own theory when it comes to what power media images might have on "shaping" our deepest desires. "There is a two-way interaction when it comes to what we want, and how the media portrays what it is we want. For instance, the media doesn't generally show us short, asymmetrical, ugly people. . . . it shows us beautiful people, the kind we tend to find attractive. And in so doing the media drives that archetype of a perfect male even deeper into our psyches. There's nothing innately attractive in a smooth, well-muscled look, it's purely a cultural taste like shorter skirts that go in and out of style. It's also a look that's easily duplicated for many gay men, and right now it's pretty much the 'in' look. It wasn't always that way. One used to see hairy chests everywhere. Now they're very hard to find, at least on gay men."

But Kevin, a 19-year-old college student in Michigan, is totally convinced that media ads have everything to do with what he finds "hot" or not. "They were the first examples of good-looking guys I saw when I was just coming out to myself," he explains. "They defined my expectations of what a hot studly guy is supposed to be. I know a lot of other people say those kinds of bodies and faces aren't 'realistic,' but apparently they haven't seen the kind of guys I see on campus all the time, or talk to online. There are thousands of hot guys like that around, and I think that's because a lot of them have modeled the way they want to look on A&F or Gap ads. . . . they work out to get those bodies, they get their hair cut that way, they wear those clothes. I guess some people find it superficial, but damn it, if a guy is attractive to me, why should I care about all that? Hot is hot." Jeff, the 16-year-old high school student in Richmond we heard from in Chapter 2, puts it more succinctly. "Oh my God, they are all so fucking hot, I'd bone every single one of them if I could."

As it turns out, opinions like those are pretty well represented; a full three-quarters of the men who took my poll say they enjoy seeing good-looking, sexy men as presented in catalog or magazine ads, and the lengthier answers in my survey show that many gay men see the models depicted therein as icons to be admired, desired, and imitated. "I know it's just a way to try and sell me something," says Ernie, a 27-year-old law student in Texas. "But that doesn't mean I can't appreciate it solely on 'face value,' so to speak. When I travel around the country and go to various gay clubs in New York, DC, or Florida, they all have ads showing hot young muscle studs to promote their events in the local gay paper. (Sometimes they even use the same models in different cities.) I find them very hot, and often titillating. Maybe they'll make me pick one club over another on a given night, which is exactly what they're trying to do. I know I've taken home some of the hotter ads from time to time as souvenirs."

Tim, a 21-year-old college student in Azusa, California, describes himself at "6-feet tall, 155 pounds," so he believes most clothing ads, especially A&F ads, are aimed squarely at him. "I like to use them as a standard of what I am always trying to achieve." Mark, a 26-year-old cook in Passaic, New Jersey, says he used the *A&F Quarterly* as an inspiration a few years back when he decided to slice off a few pounds. "There was this one great photo of a guy standing on a beach, pouring water down his body. . . . his muscles were so smooth and tight that the water barely made a ripple, and I started thinking 'this guy isn't a god, he just looks like one, there is NO reason at all that I can't have the same physique if I just start taking care of myself.' By about two years later I have to tell you I didn't just have a body like his, it was actually better."

That was a common theme I found running among a small subset of my surveys, from folks who look at hot guys in ads and think "Why can't that be me?" Like this response from Larry, a 31-year-old physician's assistant in Buffalo, New York. "They definitely get me going," he says. "They show me what the potential can be for your body if you eat right, get off your ass and get in the gym. Most of the ads you see show men with too little body hair for my tastes, but a nice face and well-maintained body are always a plus in my book. It's hard to see how some people can be offended by that, though I'm sure plenty of people are. As for me whenever I feel a little sluggish and want to skip a workout, I just flip through some hot pics, and it's not long before I'm inspired."

CAUSE AND EFFECT?

Larry is certainly right about some people taking offense; though the poll results and most survey responses are positive or at least neutral when it comes to godlike models used in advertising and most male art books, I found a sizeable undercurrent of resentment, outright disdain, or cool apathy about them, along with an extremely vocal and highly critical minority who strongly object to such imagery. And even many who say they find the images personally appealing worry about the effect they might have on gay men's self-esteem and sense of expectations.

Rutledge is a 24-year-old sixth-grade teacher in Los Angeles. "I can appreciate the beauty of the guys in the mainstream ads, but they don't really turn me on, they are too 'perfect,' and by that I don't mean they are the pinnacle or ideal, but that they are too 'clipped' and trained. They are far too vanilla and sanitized for me, and they do not look like real life men, whom I find far more attractive. But all that being said, I work very, very, very hard to attain that kind of body . . . and so I must, on some level, accept them as the ideal."

"I find those A&F/Calvin Klein models far too boyish for my tastes," says Peter, a 41-year-old consultant in Washington, DC. "I'm only interested in real men. How those boys are built and the prevailing 'gay image' of beauty has nothing to do at all with my self-image, it's all just propaganda. Mostly when I see those types of ads, I want to give the models a sandwich."

"I am simply not attracted to mainstream gay culture," says Dakota, a 37-year-old writer/administrator from London. "And that includes Abercrombie & Fitch/Calvin Klein/2-xist culture, unless they use an older or mature model, who looks 'real' like the guy you'd actually see at work, instead of spending three hours a day in the gym. Bless them, but what a waste of time. I think it is rather cruel that the same bullshit perpetrated on women has now found a home in gay culture, and advertisers have gotten fat off yet another group's insecurities."

In my polling, 24 percent of the men who responded agree that looking at "hot guys in ads" makes them feel bad about themselves. Men like Jeff, a 23-year-old retail worker in Wisconsin, who tells me that he's struggled his whole life trying to keep away "those extra pounds," and that the perfect young men displayed in fashion ads bring him anything but joy. "They often make me feel terrible that I have let myself go to waste," he says. "It's pretty depressing." Chuck, the 39-year-old human resources recruiter from Miami that we heard from earlier, tells me that as much as he enjoys looking at high fashion ads with great looking guys in them, they've made life problematic. "It's like the print media have destroyed my perception of a normal man's build. I'm not bragging, but I could be one of those underwear models, and I can totally relate to having that kind of body. But all those ads and the gay community's perceptions of a great physique have just about fucked up my eating habits. I am Italian and used to eat pasta all the time . . . now I eat it once a year if I'm lucky. I don't want to lose that chiseled look when I'm in a gay club with my shirt off." Rutledge from LA says the ads have no effect on his self-esteem, but he's convinced their overall impact is pretty negative. "I see them ravaging the gay community and our collective psyche in the same way advertising has manipulated women and girls to believe they are never good enough. It is hard to be barraged with these (unattainable) images and not internalize them; all men are highly visual . . . it is how we take in information from the world. Gay men seem especially stuck on physical image because it is an area of our lives we can control, and it has become socially acceptable . . . we've become obsessed with the quest for physical beauty and youth, and have created tremendous pressure, unattainable ideals, and general frustration and dissatisfaction."

Even those who work in the industry itself say they find themselves having conflicted views. Joshua, a 23-year-old sociology student in Houston, toils part-time at an Abercrombie & Fitch store, the veritable belly of the beast. "I work around those A&F ads all day, and it's a daily reminder of what I am not. Sometimes I can use it as motivation, but I don't gain muscle mass very easily . . . I have to tell you, some days it's a real pain in the ass." Jesus, a 23-year-old ad agency employee from Miami, has similar issues when he sees "hot boys" in ads. "At first I think 'hot damn, they're beautiful,' and sometimes I'll even get a woody," he admits. "Hell, I've jerked off to a few ads. But mostly I feel horrible because I want to look like that, and I can't. [Jesus explains that he's 5'10", 125 pounds, and cannot gain weight or muscle no matter how hard he works.] Ads, unfortunately, set the standards in society for what's acceptable and what's not. That's why I entered the industry, I hope to one day grow enough in the field to revolutionize advertising and change that. Every average joe is beautiful in his own way, and average joes make up most of our world. That's what should be portrayed."

That was a common theme among those men who told me that they have serious issues with "mainstream gay culture"—whatever that's supposed to mean—and its apparent obsession with youthful, muscular, and smooth models in its art and advertising. "There just aren't enough 'normal' people in magazines or posters in stores," laments Lars, a 41-year-old insurance salesman in Cleveland. "By 'normal' people, I mean folks that look like the people you see in everyday life, the guys whose hair isn't always perfect, whose teeth aren't bleach-white and razor straight, who don't always have bodies that look like they've been chiseled from marble. It's really hard for me to relate to buying clothes or products from someone who's just not a real person."

"You want to know my reaction when I see those ads? No, you really don't, because they just piss me off to no end," says Ken, a 48-year-old repair shop manager in Charlotte, North Carolina. "I don't see myself or anyone else I know who lives a real life. I don't see body hair, and I never see gray hair, which is really scandalous when you think about how our population is gradually growing older. Most people I know are getting on a little in years, and putting on a few pounds, we're not perfect, but we're real. And I think what those ads tell you, whether they mean to or not, is that 'unless you're smooth young and pretty we just have no place for you, and we don't care what you think.'"

THE IDEAL MAN

David Gilmore is the host and executive producer of Public Radio International's "Outright Radio"; he's also a filmmaker working on a project called "Ideal Man." As he explains it, the film explores "the personal experiences of gay male body image obsession, and also take[s] a look at how corporate America has programmed us into feeling insecure about our bodies by portraying the gay male body in unrealistic ways."

Gilmore suggests you have go back a lot further than last year's runway shows in Milan to understand the typical ad exec's strategy. "I believe it starts with art. Man has been making art of the human body since time began. It is to be admired. We like to make images of ourselves. But something happens to us when we see the representation of a body. We're either attracted or repulsed, or some feeling is elicited in us. Artists are well-aware of this. It is the attraction to those bodies that has fueled their creative process in the first place and when you stand in the Galleria dell'Accademia in Florence and gaze up at Michelangelo's David, you're going to feel something. When you see it at the end of the hall, it takes your breath away. That's why his foot is soiled. You're going to want to touch it, too. You want to possess that beauty, take it home, make it yours."

As Gilmore sees it, that power has not been lost on corporate America as it looks to penetrate the gay market. "Madison Avenue is full of smart homosexuals who recognize that power of attraction. And, in a perverse way, they use it to ensure the success of their products. Hence, you'll find our modern extrapolations of that statue of David selling you everything from deodorant to underwear.... If you think about who will be sitting at the conference room table of Abercrombie & Fitch, we're not talking men with beards, or overweight guys with hair coming out of their ears. We're talking [about] men and women who are very highly-styled and coiffed who are making decisions to use skin to sell their product. And they do sell. But they're not just selling their clothes, they're selling a look, an ideal. It's an ideal set high above us; who really looks like an Abercrombie ad?"

Gilmore points out that many of the ads that are ostensibly meant to market clothing often feature models who are nearly or completely nude. What's that all about? "Brand loyalty affixed to flesh," Gilmore says. "And so their ads, like art, elicit a feeling in us. But it's a feeling that's used to get you to the cash register; it's a feeling of craving, longing."

As to what exactly we're longing for, Gilmore says that's what "Ideal Man" sets out to explore. "The answer is attention, and belonging. We want to belong. We want to be noticed. What gay man hasn't looked at an Abercrombie catalog and thought wistfully about those idyllic golden-pond scenes. Who wouldn't want to be included in that scene? And worse, who would want to be left out? That is the fear message that is sparked from these ads. Fear of being left behind, left out, unwanted. So you'd better get those clothes, work off that extra fat, remove that unwanted hair and dry up those unsightly armpits."

If that is indeed the case, it is perhaps not surprising that most of the negative comments I logged from my surveys and interviews came from men who resent the pressure to maintain looks they already have, who fear that no matter how hard they try they can never measure up, or who are so far outside the narrow realm of what is often considered beautiful that they feel marginalized, if not actually ostracized. But what would happen if the world suddenly shifted on its axis, and those A&F and Calvin Klein boys went the way of the dinosaurs? What might happen if all of a sudden every ad just looked like you and me?

"I think it would royally suck if people stopped making those ads," says Kyle, a 24-year-old undergrad student in Columbus, Ohio. "I don't look like a model, but I really enjoy looking at them. I hate the idea that just because some people have such fragile self-esteem, we're going to have to start to 'ugly up' everything just to make them feel better about themselves."

Kyle's statement may sound a little extreme, but I know where he's coming from. A few months back I was browsing with a friend at Lambda Rising—DC's main gay bookstore—and was showing him one of Joe Phillips's books of perfectly illustrated, perfect young men. "I don't like those kinds of things at all," he confided to me. "I think it's just obscene to raise up that kind of beauty so high. It's just so unrealistic and unfair to most of us."

As it happens, I mention that little episode to the Artist himself. "I think that just shows his level of self esteem, which is obviously low," Joe says in response. "Art has always been used to record and show our dreams; through art you can show what we strive for better than any camera, as by its nature it is free from any limitation. My views on male beauty are reflected in my art; with that being said I don't happen to have a body like any of the guys I draw . . . but it sure is nice to think that maybe someone out there does."

Rest assured it's not just the "prevailing" variety of slim muscular youths—which are Joe's specialty—that has the power to both draw in and repel. "There are many men I find hot as hell, usually the beefy, hairy, goateed kind, in real life or in photos or porn movies, that make me feel entirely inadequate," says Virginia Tech's Jeff. "As if their beauty only highlights my lack of it. It's odd, yes, how beauty can be disturbing. It's like 'God, he's hot, and there's no way I can have him,' and 'God, he's hot, and any looks of mine pale in comparison.'" Jonathan, a 31-year-old nurse in Seattle, is likewise a big fan of the "big and burly" sort of fellow, but since he's by his own description "a bit of a wraith," he tells me his admiration thus far has been from a distance. "I've had a thing for the macho leather types since I saw my first Tom of Finland cartoon in my teens, but no matter how much I try I can't look like that. Leather looks pretty stupid on a pale skinny guy, so it's given me some issues to address. Maybe one day I will."

But whether they have "issues" or not, what many men tell me is how important they think it is to find a sense of balance, leavened with a little common sense. "All this bitching about good-looking models is really rather idiotic," says Louis, a 42-year-old computer specialist in Rhode Island. "I'm a heavy guy, and no one would mistake me for an underwear model, unless the underwear in question is really, really big. I see people all the time complaining about hot guys in magazines, and I just want to scream 'Get real!' No one wants to plop down his money to buy a magazine filled with ugly people, or even plain people. If I am going to part with my hard-earned cash, I'm looking for a little fantasy. The last thing I want to see is someone who looks just like me staring back at me."

"If it's ok to admire beauty, and I think most people would say it is, then why wouldn't it be ok to like a beautiful man's face or body, even when it's used to sell a product?" asks Stewart, a 29-year-old writer in New York. "Yes, you can get upset if you feel that someone is trying to shove his ideal of beauty down your throat, but that only has the power to piss you off if you allow it to. You can only feel inadequate or belittled if you buy into the whole concept they're trying to sell you. No one is forcing you to. So lighten up, already."

SMOOTH OPERATORS

Robert is a 47-year-old warehouse manager in Vancouver, British Columbia, and as someone who grew up and "came of age, gay-wise" in the mid-1970s he's been around long enough to have seen a lot of changes when it comes to what many gay men seem to find beautiful. "That was a time when you found more hairy and fuzzy men in advertisements and erotic magazines," he tells me. "And I know, because I still have a few of my very first magazines squirreled away somewhere." (Robert says people who come out these days just can't imagine what a chore it was sometimes to get your hands on a decent skin mag. "You had to make your way to the seedy part of town where they kept the adult book stores, and if you were young like I was then, you always had to watch your back because of all the perverts around. These days it's all just a mouse click or two away.")

As Robert recalls, one could spot some good-looking muscular men in the mold of today's models—"they'd fit right in real well," he says—but most were far from the godlike studs one tumbles on these days. "You never saw this sheer volume of smooth great bodies like you do now, with faces that have classical beauty like a Greek statue. There were lots of slimmer guys, and guys with great builds, but most of them were hairy with mustaches or beards, and a lot of them were really rather plain in the face."

"If you look at any of the ads or models from 'classic' gay magazines or art books you'll see a big difference from what you see these days," says Larry, a 50-year-old office worker in San Francisco who's been a collector of such items for years. He says he has them all "lovingly wrapped in plastic," and stored safely away from humidity. "They're like relics from another time, when we had different ideas about what constitutes 'beauty.' And what a hairy version of beauty we had!"

Certainly those long ago days had icons of their own to admire, the über-buff men of Finnish artist Touko Laaksonen—aka the aforementioned "Tom of Finland"—likely being the best known and most popular. As my friend Michael Alvear put in a piece he wrote for the online magazine *Salon,* Tom's "pornographic drawings of hunky, fuck-booted, bubble-butted beefcakes banging the booty in door-busting swells of charcoals, pencil and ink, watercolors and gouaches leave you—depending on which team you bat for—scratching your head, rolling your eyes or rubbing your crotch" (April 2000). Good ol' Tom of F.'s drawings did something that no one had really done before. They connected homosexuality and masculinity in such a sexually aggressive manner that even the gentle folk somewhat put off by the display couldn't help but feel a little empowered; as Alvear noted, the "gay characters in Tom of Finland's art are so masculine they make straight men look like girlie-boys."

"There was a time when a lot of men had that look," says Gregory, a 53-year-old art director who lives in South Beach. "That was what we called 'The Clone Look' back then. . . . it was sort of this hyper-masculine, heterosexually-based collection of flannel, jeans, and boots, almost taken to a ridiculous extreme, if you ask me. It had its sexy aspects, but it was also rather silly to see lawyers and doctors squeezing their frequently hairy chests and backs into the uniform before they'd go out on the prowl. It started fading away a bit in the '80s, and I remember that was when I started seeing lots of middle-aged yet hairless guys out on the beach and at the gym."

"I rather miss those old 'clones,'" confides Michael, a "50-ish" lawyer in Providence, Rhode Island. "That was the look I aspired to myself when I was first coming out, and it didn't demand that much of you. I can't imagine how I would ever get noticed these days, since the young people I see appear to be coming mass-produced from some beautiful smooth twinkie factory, and only want the company of other beautiful smooth twinkies. I always enjoyed the company of a real 'macho' man when I was younger, and we seem to have strayed quite a bit from that aesthetic."

From all I gather from the men surveyed and polled for this book, a general affection for that variety of "macho man" has indeed been largely superseded by a cultural taste shift. Make no mistake: You can still drop in at any gathering of the Leather folk among us and find living breathing examples of fuzzy beefcaked studliness that would make the late Laaksonen feel right at home. (He passed away in 1991.) You can also find younger men who are somewhat put off by the members of their own A&F/American Eagle generation, and look back at those halcyon days wishing they would have been born a few decades earlier, when "men weren't so prettified, and were more rugged and real," as a 20-something buddy of mine puts it.

Yet those would seem to be exceptions, if my data mean anything at all. Sixty-three percent of those I polled say they prefer men these days with "little or no" body hair; in other words, we're right back in the pages of the *A&F Quarterly* or the summer fashion spreads in *Out, Instinct,* or *Genre,* the gay men's news and lifestyle publications with the largest national circulations. These days your typical underwear-wearing ad boy, no matter how old he is, is smooth as a baby's butt, and so are most of the boys in the bar.

Just what causes our tastes to change so? Like any culture shift, it's probably impossible to answer the question with any certainty or pin it down to any single event. But theories do abound. "Having come out in the 1970's, I, too, am old enough to recall when hairy guys were 'all the rage,'" says Andrew Gottlieb, who suggests there are probably several levels to consider. "While we never know why tastes change, we might be able to trace the shift from hairy to smooth to the onset of AIDS. The smooth look seems 'pure,' perhaps a defense against looking/feeling/being diseased; and second, on a deeper level, since 'smooth' is the way our bodies were in childhood, remaining so may be connected to an unconscious wish to be children. How often we do refer to ourselves as 'boys'?"

Some trace the beginning of the shift to the 1980s underwear ad campaigns of Calvin Klein and his famous New York billboards, and the work of fashion and art photographers such as the late Herb Ritts and Bruce Weber (also of Abercrombie fame) who shot the early 1990s spread featuring a young "Marky Mark" Wahlberg in all his smooth and well-muscled glory. "I definitely remember that shift," says Tommy, himself an amateur photographer. Now 44 years old and living in San Francisco, he remembers how it seemed that "well-groomed and six-packed packing" models were suddenly becoming a hot commodity. "I don't want this to sound in any way sexist, because it's not meant to, but there was a certain 'feminization' in the look. Almost all the hot guys you would see in fashion ads and bar advertising—even in porn—were much more boyish, and less 'manly' than the guys you saw in the 70's and early 80's. I also started seeing a lot of guys in clubs and bars imitating that look."

Joe Phillips agrees. "I think the look of the modern-male archetype is a bit more polished, with slight feminine traits like attention to grooming. Clear blemish free skin and tidy hygiene marks our current ideal of the modern man. In the past rugged hairy 'outdoors' type of men were the rage for their own reasons. Just take a look at the new 'Brawny Towel' guy and you can see what I mean . . . before he was hairy with a mustache, now he's cuter, buffer and younger, and he looks sensitive, too."

Photographer Tom Bianchi suggests to me that the so-called shift toward a younger, smoother, more athletic physique is not so much a "shift" at all, as it is a throwback, across several hundred if not thousands of years. "Personally I like bodies that look like they can MOVE! Love dancers and gymnasts and divers . . . the abs and ass thing. My tastes are ultra mainstream. I'm right in there with the Greeks, Romans and Italian painters. My name is Bianchi; how could my head not be in that tradition? Some artists just got it right, centuries ago. They described perfectly—and in a broad spectrum if you look carefully—what the psychic and biological union of beauty looks like." As for the men who admire that look they see in art and advertising, and try to duplicate it in their living selves, Bianchi is cautionary. "A lot of guys get hung up in the young statue look. Hairless. For me that is just one type, and if you try to produce that look and make stubble instead, you are in aesthetic purgatory. I like the natural thing; make what YOU are the ideal of beauty. Project that, and plenty of guys will respond to the authenticity of that. It's much easier than trying to be something you are not, like 25 when you are really 45."

Of course, countless gay men try and do exactly that, up to and including spending all those hours in the gym pumping iron. In fact, the gym culture that exploded in the 1980s and 1990s—something we'll talk more about in just a bit—created legions of Hulk-sized homos, and for them it seems that all that body hair just gets in the way of other men seeing how big their chest is or how ripped their abs are; as Michelangelo Signorile put it in his 1997 book *Life Outside,* the "pumped and hairless" build was everywhere in those days. In New York, he wrote, it was "nearly impossible to escape the glossy little publications like *Next* or *Homo XTra,* stacks of which abound everywhere in the ghetto and even beyond, their covers, not to mention pages and pages of ads, promoting huge biceps, cut abs, perfect pecs, and bubble butts" (p. 25). As Signorile saw it then, virtually every American city with any gay population to speak of had at least one—and sometimes more—"bar rags filled with images of perfect gay men, the ideals that set the standard" (p. 25).

Nearly a decade later that smooth aesthetic is still the "standard" in the sort of "bar rags" Signorile cites, not to mention for the men that leaf through their pages; in the past year my own travels have taken me all along the American East Coast, quite literally from New England to Florida, and remiss I'd be of course not to stop in at the occasional gay watering hole to rub elbows with the queer folk. I can personally attest that it doesn't matter much whether one is pubbing in Provincetown, rolling through Rehoboth, or frolicking in Fort Lauderdale, there's nary a chest hair in sight in any of the thousands of images you find in any of the local mags. And the overwhelming majority of the men partying late into the wee hours at any of those local clubs have exactly the same look, if my bourbon-soaked recollections can be trusted. (Hey, it can't be all about work.)

I also took my own spot survey of the "adult entertainment section" furnished by my favorite gay paper—and one I've written for occasionally—the *Washington Blade.* It's a saucy little insert called *eclipse,* so saucy in fact that most out gay men who take the paper to work with them have to make sure they don't leave their *eclipse* lying around and accidentally frighten the straight people. (While it does offer location maps to and event calendars from the city's 40-odd gay bars and nightclubs, it also contains dozens of ads that offer up a variety of "services" and adult "get togethers" that one might not want to have to explain to clueless co-workers in the coffee room.) In any case, those services and gatherings usually have sexy photos of hot guys in their ads, with faces and bodies calculated to grab your eye and draw you in; by my count the average number of men shown in the section over a six-month period was about 41. The number of smooth or nearly hairless men? That averaged 39 per issue.

One can also do a similar if not scientific survey using a typical gay paper's coverage of the largest men's gatherings of the year, i.e., the annual Pride Day celebrations held from April to September in virtually every city with a gay population. Popping up the photo links available in any of their online editions, one can scan the crowds that turned out on those festive days and observe wave upon wave of men in their late teens into their fifties and beyond, and note the utter absence of body hair. (A friend of mine once suggested that the Pride Day mornings in Gay Town USA must see an inordinately high number of hair-clogged shower drains, as so many men have their razors and clippers flying all over their bodies.)

Scanning those pictures only convinces me even further that the smooth look is well entrenched, but it does beg a perhaps unanswerable question: How much of advertising is simply reflecting the reality it sees around us, and how much is that imagery actually influencing or shaping that very reality? I can give you my own take, from my own personal history. I can recall seeing all those "smoothies" popping up all over the place back in the mid-1980s, and having been given a certain amount of body fuzz by my genetics, that happened to be the time of my life—mid-twenties—when the hair growth on my chest started getting a bit thick, just as all those hours in the gym and out on the running track were really starting to pay off; in other words, just as my pecs were reaching their full potential and I'd started getting some serious abs, nature was seeing fit to cover the whole shebang with lots of definition-obscuring overgrowth. We were not amused.

Since my own tastes in men had always run to the smooth and muscular, that was a look I wanted to duplicate for my own body; I was also a U.S. Marine at the time and constantly surrounded by hordes of young muscular guys whose genetics for some reason weren't particularly inclined to be fuzzy. Between the barracks and bars, it was a virtual "smooth-o-rama," and I didn't like being left out. So I looked into some of the best methods available at the time, things like electrolysis and waxing. The latter just sounded too painful, and the former was wicked expensive. (laser hair removal wouldn't be invented for a few years yet, and it remains ridiculously costly as well.) After a few electrolysis sessions had cleared only a 50-cent size patch on my chest—which regrew in just a few months—I turned to my razor. That certainly worked . . . for a little while. Then the stubble broke out, creating that aesthetic nightmare Tom Bianchi mentions; what he doesn't mention is razor bumps and in-grown hairs. (My tweezers were awful busy at times, trying to pluck those nasty fuckers out.)

Eventually I just gave up and let it all grow out, until that happy day it occurred to me that a compromise was possible, courtesy of a small beard and mustache trimmer. These days I simply trim it down and keep it under control; it's not a "smooth" look precisely, but one that I can live with. It also has the advantage of a relatively "natural" appearance, one a friend of mine likes to call "well groomed but not obsessive." More and more I meet the occasional guy who tells me I should just let it all grow out again, and one wonders whether we're on the cusp of another shift back to more body hair for the masses.

But for right now, the smooth look still appears to be dominant. I don't think I'm under the thrall of an ad executive when I find the look attractive, nor do I remember feeling much in the way of "peer pressure," even when I was lying back in a chair getting zapped follicle by follicle. It was simply a look I happened to like, on myself and others. I will say that seeing so many others going hairless—both in media imagery and out in the real world—made it easier to put up with all the effort, as did getting the random compliments that my smoother look inspired. Most men I talked with saw something similar at work, like Paul, a 32-year-old personal trainer in Miami. "A lot of guys do it because they figure it must be the hot thing, they like how it looks on them, and their friends say they it looks hot on them. All the companies that make clothes and fragrances, and that want to send you on a gay cruise somewhere, see all these smooth guys, and make an ad tailored for them. It's just a cycle like that."

"There's nothing sinister about it," says Robert from Vancouver. "The guys in ads look the way they do, because that's what the people who want to sell you things think you like. If they thought you liked green-haired fat men, and that green-haired fat men would get you to buy what they're selling, you'd see green-haired fat men all over the place."

Filmmaker David Gilmore's take is somewhat more ominous. "Someday we may see radical faeries [in advertising] or anyone 'off target' from the typical California bleach-blond twinkie in an Abercrombie ad, just as we did recently on an episode of *Queer As Folk*.

But you can rest assured that if it happens, it was highly considered first for its marketability potential. Diverse is only cool when Madison Avenue says so. The skinny, clean-shaved with shaggy blond hair look only comes to us because media executives have deemed it suitable for this year's line. So when Coco Chanel says the hairy man is back, you better start looking for hair."

Chapter 4

Body Types

*I don't hate it that I don't look like a twink,
but I do hate it that I look like I ate one*

"Bitch Session"
Washington Blade

"A few years back when I lived in Boston I had this really large neighbor, had to be at least 100-150 pounds overweight," Stan is telling me. He's a 40-year-old banker, who describes himself as having an "above average build" from lifting weights and running/biking/aerobics, and a face that looks about 15 years younger. ("All I can say is 'moisturize, moisturize, moisturize'!" he confides.) Stan says he never saw his neighbor out and about much, though he would nod and smile at him on those rare occasions they passed on the street. "I felt sorry for him, because he was pretty obviously gay, and I know how brutal gay men are when it comes to how they treat anybody who isn't trim and slim."

Stan says one day he was planning a social gathering at his house, and in a moment of what he calls "make yourself feel good about yourself" compassion, he looked up his neighbor to invite him to drop by. "I honestly thought this guy had no social outlets, and because I hadn't seen him out, that he sat home alone all day feeling ostracized." Stan's big surprise came when his neighbor opened the door, to reveal a condo filled with people, all celebrating their host's birthday. "There were a lot of similarly large guys in there, a handful of women, and some thinner guys, mostly younger, all buzzing about." As Stan explains it, he went ahead and gave his invitation—"he was surprised, but gracious in accepting it"—and the two men got to know each other fairly well before Stan's job sent him south to North

Carolina. He tells me his neighbor turned out to have a rather extensive network of friends, who mainly got together at each other's homes, and largely communicated via their e-mail and instant messaging correspondence. Says Stan, "I was really arrogant in assuming just because he was fat he was also sad and lonely, and I couldn't have been more wrong. Once we got to know each other a little and he started opening up to me, I found out his sex life was just as active as mine was at the time. Okay, that's a lie. His was actually better, and the guys he was meeting were higher quality, and a lot less flaky."

It's one of those trite but true observations, that you never know another man until you've "walked a mile in his moccasins." But as I pored over the hundreds of life stories and interviews collected for this book, I was constantly struck by the fact that many gay men were quite happy to cast judgments without making a single lap around the track, let alone walk the whole mile. Intent on pursuing their own concepts of perfection—or content to be the objects of pursuit by a coterie of admirers—they are often completely lacking in either understanding or empathy for those whose lives exist outside their own sometimes narrow orbits. I think about Stan's story and give him due credit for wanting to reach out, but he's the first to admit his own arrogance at making assumptions about someone based solely on his physical appearance.

I discovered similar trends while researching *Sissyphobia,* where so-called straight-acting men swore by the many assumptions and judgments they'd made about effeminate or flamboyant men, most of them quite wrong, or at least misguided; in *Reeling in the Years,* I was constantly shocked about the ageist myths young gay men had bought into when it came to older men, and the wholly erroneous misconceptions older gay men had when it came to men much younger than themselves. I don't know why I should be surprised—one would think I'd lose the capacity, yet still I am—as I find out what a lot of "in shape" men think about men they consider overweight or obese, what body-builder types think about thinner men—and vice versa—and what smooth guys such as the ones we talked about in Chapter 3 think about "Bears," or large hairy gay men.

It's in that spirit that I've singled out some of the basic body types you find within our fractious little "community"—boy, does that word seem more and more like an oxymoron—to take a look at some of their experiences when it comes to chasing their own Adonises, and to give people not of that particular type a look inside a world they may not know much about. As we go along here you may find some of your long-held beliefs debunked, or perhaps confirmed; either way, here come those moccasins. If they don't fit, I'm sure I can find a lovely pair in the back.

WHERE'S THE BEEF?

Meet "Chad," a 25-year-old bartender in West Hollywood. (Chad is not his real name; he's disguised for reasons which will become clear in just a bit.) "Tending bar is what I do to pay my bills," he tells me. "But if you really want to list my 'occupation,' you should probably call me a body builder, since that's really what occupies most of my time."

And Chad isn't kidding, not if he's holding true to the regimen he sends me in an e-mail after we speak on the phone. Besides the hours every day he spends in the gym, which are considerable and punishing, his diet is one so disciplined and planned out that it would do a military strategist proud. "I eat constantly, every three hours on the dot, and hardly any of it contains any fat at all, just the kind you can't avoid if you're eating all the chicken, fish, and beef I put down. I haven't touched a slice of bread or a grain of white rice in ages, because I'm totally opposed to any kind of unnecessary carbs . . . a dietician friend of mind told me I need to eat a lot more than I do, but then again she isn't looking at the mirror every day like I am, looking at where I can carve out one more ripple."

He has always been a "big boy," as he puts it, even going back to junior high school. "My gym teachers were always amazed at how much muscle mass I had at 14 and 15, and they were the ones who first encouraged me to get into a gym and start banging away at weights. The first time I ever tried a bench press I put up more weight than anyone in the school had ever lifted, so that's when I knew I was home." He played football for a while, and liked it a lot, though he says it was always the training he preferred over the actual games. "I wasn't good enough to play at the college level, so school for me was just a local community college, which was okay, because it gave me more time to just lift weights for the sake of body building." Now he's 5'11" and weighs 225 pounds, and favors clothes that show off every gain he makes. "What's the point of having a body like mine, if the world isn't going to see it?" he asks me rhetorically.

I wouldn't call Chad's story "typical" by any stretch; in my *Chasing Adonis* poll only 4 percent of the men who responded described themselves as members of the brawny, heavily muscled tribe of men with bodies that could grace the cover of a Joe Weider–type magazine. Many more, about half of the total number of men I surveyed, said they spent "a lot" or "some" time in the gym, and we'll talk about them in just a few paragraphs. But let's start with the guys like Chad, who seems typical of the thousands of gay men out there who are pounding weights, shoveling in massive amounts of protein, and doing anything they can to achieve a massive look. Make no mistake, the ultra-beefcaked gay bod may be relatively rare, but it's still out there; just the other night I was nearly shoved off my bar stool by a couple of passing NFL lineman-like studs who gave new meaning to the phrase "size queen."

So I ask Chad how it is he first came to realize he was gay, and what it was like coming to such a realization, ensconced as he was in the macho world of team athletics and the gym. "I guess I always knew, since I was like 8 or 9 years old, that I was different . . . then once puberty hit I figured out what the difference was. But I was already 'different,' being so much bigger than most guys my age, so I don't remember losing much sleep over it. Looking like I did I didn't have a lot of problems worrying about my masculinity, or that someone would try to bash me for being gay. I'm the nicest guy in the world, but I look pretty scary if you don't know me, so no problems about that." Chad says he was maybe 17 or so before he started sharing his secret with a few close friends. "Nobody's business unless I wanted them to know," is how he puts it now. "I'm pretty outgoing, but also kind of private."

And what about losing his virginity? "It may surprise some people to hear it, but there's more gay stuff and experimentation going on than a lot of people think when it comes to some team sports, it's just something that no one is ever going to talk about openly. My first time was with this other kid on the high school football team . . . it was the classic 'everybody gets drunk after the game' kind of deal, and we just ended up in his room when everybody was passed out and his parents weren't home. I sort of suspected he had a crush on me, and I let him blow me, which I really enjoyed a lot. I lost touch with him after school, but I'd love to run into him again, see if he's still a hottie like he was back then. Who knows, maybe one day he'll walk into my bar."

Since he brings up his social life, I ask him what kind of man he's drawn to, and what it's been like to be such an obvious object of attention; men with his kind of build draw all sorts of looks and stares, and not just from gay men. "I'll tell you the truth, I can't stand anyone who's too skinny—they look ill to me. And I really don't care for guys who are soft, flabby, or fat—that tells me they don't give a shit about what they look like. All I need to see is that someone takes care of their body. I really dig older guys who stay in shape, because I know that takes a real commitment when your metabolism slows down."

So does he get into other bodybuilder types like himself? "Nah, dude . . . not at all. Too much competition. I just started dating this older guy, a doctor . . . he's a little taller than I am, but maybe 50 pounds lighter. He's a runner, and a rock climber, so he's really tight. I think he's pretty sexy, gray hairs and all."

And what about the guys who find him sexy? "People tend to gawk at me all the time," he admits, and confides that most of the time, he "really digs" it when they do. "But it can get confusing sometimes, because straight guys in the gym will watch me to see what exercises I do, how hard I lift and how much. I have to remember all the time that they're not necessarily looking at me 'that way.' When I'm single—and I usually am, this dating thing is kind of new for me—it's fun to get hit on. But I always wonder how much people are liking me for me, or just my body and the way it looks. I know a gay bodybuilder is a real fantasy for a lot of gay guys—you should see the way some dudes hang out or take their time when I'm in the locker room, like they're hoping to see me naked—and most times it's okay by me, if you like my body, great, look all you want, I kind of get off on it. But there is a lot more to me than just my chest and biceps. I like to travel, sing and dance, I read a lot and I'm into movies, all sorts of things. I wonder how many guys even bother to think I might cry sometimes, or worry about the future like everybody else."

"Jerry" is a 38-year-old Chicago resident who works freelance for a security agency as a bodyguard; he's 6'5," and goes a good 250 pounds when he's "tight," as he puts it, and closer to 275 if he's "been slacking off" on his training. "I can put on a little around the middle really fast if I don't watch myself, it's one thing that really sucks about getting older."

Jerry tells me he also played football in college, and he didn't want to say good-bye to his beefy build when he hung up his cleats. "I saw too many of my old teammates just get fat and sloppy, so that's when I hit the gym hard. I actually slimmed down a bit, got real lean (for me, anyway) and really started enjoying the way I looked and felt." Like Chad, Jerry says his size was always a magnet for attention when he hit the clubs. "People won't believe this when I tell you, but I'm really not all that egotistical, I don't train hard so people will notice me, at 6'5" they're going to notice me anyway. Do I like the stares when I walk into a gay club? Sure, sometimes . . . sometimes my size can get in the way of ever having a real conversation with somebody. You get tired of people asking 'So how much can you lift? Could you lift me up with one hand?' Shit like that. Part of my job is looking big and intimidating so you scare away the bad guys before they get any stupid ideas in their heads . . . it can get in the way of a relationship, though, it's hard for people to see past the outside."

I ask Jerry what his idea of Adonis might be, the kind of guy that really gets to him or turns him on. "I haven't had too many boyfriends, or any long term things . . . it's funny how most people assume that a big, muscular guy is only into other big, muscular guys. Maybe that's the case with most big guys, but I actually like younger, slimmer guys, and pretty much always have. A lot of guys like that seem to be fascinated by me, which is great at the start . . . I don't mind someone being drawn to me by my size, at least at first, but the ones who stick around the longest are the guys that kind of get past all that, and just see me as 'Jerry,' not 'The Incredible Hulk.' Been single for awhile now, and when I meet people these days it's usually from the Internet or something. That way they get to know my mind a little first, not just my body. Of course when they see my stats they always want to see a picture—I wait awhile to see if we click first—then I send them the pic and we see where it goes after that."

A CHANGE IS GONNA COME

Though my polls and surveys show me that men like Chad and Jerry are much more the exception than the rule, they're really just an extreme manifestation of a fairly common phenomenon: gay men who make visits to the gym as regular a part of their daily lives as sleeping or eating, and are careful to watch what they eat, as well. My polls show that just about half of all those surveyed are pumping iron to some degree, and many of them started out the same way as our two muscle studs, similarly blessed by their genetics with bodies simply waiting to be developed by iron and sweat; although they may not achieve a Herculean physique like Jeremy or Chad, they find that their gains of muscle and lean body mass come relatively easy. "I'm not a body builder by long shot, but I'm still fairly muscular," says Steve, a 47-year-old animal care worker in San Diego. "I was in my 20's before I picked up my first weight, but within a few years I had what my friends call a 'hunky' body, and I've kept it that way . . . I won't say it changed my life drastically like it does for other guys, it's more like having a little money in the bank than winning a lottery. It's just nice to feel confident when you take your shirt off that someone might see you and go 'damn, he's hot.'"

Ben is a 28-year-old "military man," stationed in North Carolina. "I was never going to be a big massive dude, I just didn't have the genes for that," he tells me. "But I do have the kind of genes that give me the ability to stay really lean, and put on some good muscle mass in my chest and biceps by working out with weights . . . I don't want to sound like I am bragging or anything, but it turns out I have exactly the kind of body that most gay men seem to like the most, narrow waist, wide shoulders, you know what I mean?" So does that mean getting laid isn't a challenge for him? "You really want me to sound totally conceited, don't you? Ok, I'll be totally honest then . . . between the fact that I'm in the military, tall, reasonably good-looking, and well-built, I have more opportunities to have sex than most, sure . . . that doesn't mean I always act on them, but they're there."

I ask Ben if there is anything on his body that isn't "perfect," and he laughs. "Well, my ass is flatter than I'd like it to be, and I'm working on it. Maybe one day I'll make myself a bubble butt and complete the package."

A lot of other men tell me that they just got tired of what they were looking at in the mirror every day, and started hitting the weights to bulk up what muscle they could, or trim down some extra flab, all with varying degrees of success. Take Tommy, a 30-year-old delivery driver from Charleston, South Carolina: He explains that he was a "really skinny" kid in high school; at 19 he decided he'd had enough of that and got himself a gym membership. "There was a brochure at the gym with a guy's torso on it, a perfectly proportioned body with a great chest and abs. I stared at that body a lot . . . that was the body I wanted to have for myself."

Over the next few years Tommy spent countless hours on his quest, until working out became second nature. "I wouldn't even think about letting a day go by now without some kind of physical activity, mainly because I love to eat!" And he tells me that a few years ago he found a copy of that old gym brochure tucked away in a drawer when he was moving. "You know what? I had a better body by then than that guy in the picture . . . and I'm in even better shape now." As Tommy sees it, the confidence he gained by working out was an immeasurable plus when it came to his self-esteem, and his social life. "I have to say I am pretty proud of how I look, and while I'm not going to say that having a good body gets me every man I want, it sure makes the game a lot easier to play."

Tommy's story is typical of about a third of the men I surveyed, who say they started out as "thin" or "skinny," and at some point decided it was time for a change. Mark is a 38-year-old Houston resident who tells me he was "always skinny growing up, and I started working out serious about six years ago. Now I am thin and toned, with enough muscle that some people make comments like 'muscle boy' when they meet me."

Mark says his favorite part of a man is his torso, probably because that was the part of his own body he wanted to work on himself. "I do get compliments on my body when I am out at a club. There is nothing better than hearing someone tell you how good your body is after years of being skinny and out of shape. Some people may think it is shallow to put so much attention on the body, but for me it feels good."

It's not just the formerly skinny boys who take advantage of the magical transformation that simple exercise can create. Dozens of men I've talked with say they came at weight training from the other side of the fence, as soft and chubby guys looking for a way to firm up; a full 21 percent tell me they began life in a "large" way, then slimmed down, often with the help of weight training and cardiovascular exercise. "I was always rather fat as a child, and stayed fat into my mid-20's," says Casey, a 40-year-old middle school teacher in Lincoln, Nebraska. "I don't remember if there was a specific reason I started to work out, but I seem to recall looking at myself in the mirror as my 30th birthday approached, and said 'you can be better than this.' So I started with a little running—I could barely make it around the block, and I only ran at night because I was embarrassed that someone would see me—but little by little I found myself going farther. After I slimmed down enough not to be mortified to actually be seen by others, I joined a local gym, and learned—painfully at first—how to lift weights. I remember quite clearly—it was just after my 32nd birthday—the first time anyone said anything to me about it . . . it was a colleague of mine pulling me aside in the teacher's lounge, asking me 'how I did it.' I had no clue what he was talking about . . . I later learned that my obvious physical transformation had been a hot topic of conversation for quite awhile."

Bob, the 51-year-old personal trainer we heard from in Chapter 2, says it was a "heart incident" in his forties that "scared" him into weight training. Before that, he says he'd evolved from having a thin body in his twenties and thirties to a "pear-shaped" physique that threatened his overall health. Now he's 6' and 210 pounds, with what he calls a muscular "non-competitive" build. "My remaking of my physique has been and continues to be one of the most remarkable undertakings of my life. It has brought me a more optimistic view of live, a loving partner, and a new career."

You don't necessarily need to lift weights or even belong to a gym to get fit, of course; a little more than a quarter of those who took the *Chasing Adonis* poll say they exercise all the time but prefer to stay away from anything that smacks of a fitness club. In fact, many of the men I talked with say they wouldn't be caught dead inside of one. "You can have all those preening gym bunnies and muscle boys," is how Andrew puts it. He's a 33-year-old computer software specialist in Boston. "I don't like that whole 'body Nazi' culture we've come to embrace. Give me my yoga, and my stationary bike, and that's all I need to stay slim and trim."

"The whole gym thing is a crock of shit," avers Sal, a 44-year-old health care worker and part-time student in Philadelphia. "A lot of people are making tons-o-money off gym memberships. There are a lot of other ways to exercise and increase one's level of physical activities to help be fit and healthy." Sal tells me he started off life as a thin child and then became heavier, especially as he moved into his teens. "In my late 30's I put on a lot of weight, and then two years ago I was diagnosed with diabetes . . . since then I have kept the weight down and exercise daily by fast walking. I am much more health conscious and participate in activities that are health promoting . . . I just do what I have to do to be healthy. I have noticed, too, that more people look at me because I am in better shape, people who would never have glanced at me before. I'd be lying if I said that didn't feel good. It does."

"MOTHER'S LITTLE HELPER"

As it happens, I am writing this chapter just as the national headlines are filled with some not exactly surprising revelations, that dozens of well-known sports figures may have taken performance-enhancing steroids and hormones in order to hit a baseball farther, jump higher, or run faster. Very few of the men I surveyed would admit to anything of the sort; one exception is "Chad" (now you know why he wants his identity disguised) who tells me he's entered a few bodybuilding contests locally and done "okay so far, no big prizes," but he's still pounding away, hoping to get noticed. "I don't know yet if I can really compete at the professional level, I'm starting to get a little old for the game."

As Chad tells me, that "game" includes using what he refers to as "mother's little helper," a carefully calibrated combination of the latest steroids and human growth hormones available. "Officially I have to deny it, but since you're not using my real name, of course I have. You can get a certain amount of size and definition naturally, but if you're talking the kind of body I have right now, only a true freak gets it without some chemical help."

Just how do steroids provide that "help"? Simply put, they behave in the body the same way that your natural testosterone does—the male sex hormone that makes muscles develop and grow strong—except steroids kick that development and strength up several notches.

According to the Office of National Drug Control Policy (2006), there are currently more than a hundred different types of steroids out there that can make one bigger, stronger, or faster; they can be taken orally, injected, or rubbed on the skin in gel or cream form. Many users will often take them for a period, stop, then start again in a pattern called "cycling"; sometimes they take several varieties at one time—a process that's called "stacking"—or users will gradually escalate their doses, increasing the amount of one steroid or adding others to the mix before tapering off; that's called "pyramiding."

Though illegal without a prescription—and make no mistake, there are a number of medical conditions that steroids can treat effectively—millions of Americans are taking them without a doctor's proper supervision. How many millions, there's just no way to tell, but the ONDCP says a 2003 survey showed that 3.5 percent of twelfth graders had already reported trying steroids at least once, and even 2.5 percent of eighth graders had also tried them. About one-fifth of those eighth graders said getting their hands on the drug was "fairly easy" or "very easy"; more than 40 percent of the seniors said the same thing.

So if some high school jock who's still bugging Dad for spending money and the keys to the car can get his hands on 'roids without too much trouble, what's going to stop a motivated gay man who already has a passion for size? (Not much, as we shall soon see.) But taking steroids can often be like asking the Devil to the big dance; in other words, there can be hell to pay. In this case, according to the U.S. Drug Enforcement Administration, hell can come in the form of "baldness, development of breasts, painful erections, shrinkage/loss of function of testicles." Ye, gads . . . but that's not all, boys and girls. The DEA also lists the following side effects: "Acne, jaundice, swelling, fluid retention, stunted growth, increase in bad cholesterol levels, decrease in good cholesterol levels, mood swings, increase in feelings of hostility, increase in aggressive behavior." (If you still have the stomach for it, you can check out "Anabolic Steroids—Hidden Dangers" on the Drug Enforcement Administration Web site.)

A lot of men will just tell you that that all that is just the government bogeyman, hard at work as always trying to dissuade anyone anywhere from having a good time. Chad, who tells me he's been "using the latest, greatest stuff that has little or no side effects" that he can detect, says he hasn't experienced anything of the sort. At least, not yet. "I haven't pulled a gun on the pizza delivery guy [referring to a famous steroid-induced episode involving a college football player back in the 1980s] or tried to run anyone off the road in a rage. My skin is just fine and my balls are just where they're supposed to be, which is how my boyfriend likes them. Did I tell you I'm dating a doctor?" he asks me, laughing. "Sure makes getting the best stuff a lot easier."

And some will tell you the best stuff out there isn't steroids, or steroids alone, but rather the other half of Chad's "helper": human growth hormone, or HGH. A natural substance that's manufactured by your pituitary gland, HGH controls many growth factors in your body, hence its less than imaginative name. Doctors tell me its major legitimate clinical use is predominantly aimed at children with an HGH deficiency, kids whose bone structures aren't developing at a normal rate, in effect stunting their growth. In adults HGH is usually used for folks who find themselves with some kind of hormone deficiency that, in some cases, starts to accelerate the aging process. Older people who take HGH won't find their bones starting to grow again—at least not usually, and not unless the adult in question is subjecting himself to major doses—but it will make muscles develop, cut body fat percentages, and improve overall skin tone, leading some to liken it to a virtual "fountain of youth."

Originally, "human" growth hormone wasn't very human at all; scientists harvested it from cattle pituitary glands at slaughter. But about 15 or so years ago scientists managed to find a way to synthesize it by cloning the active protein into yeast cells, thereby making it possible to create HGH in a lab. Back then the only way to way to get the hormone into your system was by injection, and doctors tell me that's still the most effective way to administer it; of course that hasn't stopped a lot of companies—many perhaps not so reputable—from selling HGH in oral or nasal form. If you're looking to try it, it looks like a case of "you pays your money, you takes your chance," as the carnies used to say.

But be ready to spend a lot of money, more than one would for steroids, as much as a couple of hundred bucks a week. And although researchers say the effects on the body can be very dramatic when it comes to building more muscle and less fat, they're not as dramatic as those of steroids are; still, there appear to be far fewer side effects and long-term harm to the body with HGH than there are with steroids, which is not to say there are none. Doctors say HGH can cause otherwise healthy people to become diabetic, and some of those rare folks who do experience bone growth can develop some pretty painful joint disorders; but those side effects, I'm told, are more likely if someone takes more of the stuff than he needs to give his muscles an extra pump.

Where HGH does come in handy for those taking it—and trust me I'm not advocating anything of the sort—is that it's much less detectable in the bloodstream or urine than most steroids, and that's why some athletes use it to give them a stealthy edge over their opponents. But steroids, at least the latest variety that our bodybuilder Chad espouses, are becoming less and less detectable all the time; when you factor in the growth potential when the two are taken together, you can see why so many who want to get bigger, stronger, and faster are drawn to it.

But as for the other big man who talked to me at length, "Jerry" tells me he doesn't use any kind of "size-enhancing" drugs, not anymore, at any rate. (His choice to remain anonymous has to do more with his profession, not his workout ethic.) "I played around with that shit for awhile in school, but I started worrying what the long term effects would be. I've seen a lot of guys get addicted to what it could do for them, and then when they stopped, all their gains just disappeared. I didn't want that, so besides the occasional legitimate supplements I stay clean. But ask me again in ten years, I might have a different answer."

One product that used to be available for folks who wanted to steer clear of steroids or HGH was androstenedione, a "steroid precursor" that isn't a steroid in and of itself, just the next best thing. (In effect it tells your body to make more testosterone, which then goes about all that bigger, stronger, faster business on its own.) Despite its nominally nonsteroid status, "andro" has still been a subject of controversy; sales took off after baseball slugger Mark McGwire freely admitted to taking the stuff en route to his homerun record in 1998, but that higher visibility also put sports leagues around the world on notice that there was a new player at the table. Over the past few years it's been banned by one sport after another, and as of January 2005 andro sales were officially banned altogether in the United States.

Why ban andro if it's not a steroid? Researchers admit that the product—which first appeared on the market in the late 1990s—really hasn't been around long enough to study comprehensively—certainly not as long as steroids have—but many are convinced its side effects and long-term impact are the same. There was also grave medical concern about what effect andro might have on young weightlifters and athletes using it to get an edge; whatever one might think about its effects on adults, just about any expert will tell you that teens and young 20-somethings can severely damage their bodies with too much testosterone. (It's not like they need it, anyway, their young 'nads are pumping out plenty, the little bastards.)

Yet right up until the moment it was pulled off the shelves, many gay men tell me they were happy to have a little andro stored in their medicine cabinets next to their multivitamins. "I'd been stuck at 150 pounds for years, no matter what I did to try and get bigger," says Sam, a 36-year-old cable television installer in Richmond, Virginia. "I heard about andro, read the pros and cons, and decided 'what the fuck, can't hurt to try it.' Two years later I was 175, and it was just about all muscle. When I heard they were going to ban it I started stocking up, now I have about a year's worth supply. I've never had any kind of side effect or problem, in fact I haven't even had a cold since I started using it. Typical government overreaction, it's all bullshit . . . I just hope I don't start losing what I've gotten." I ask him if he'll look for andro on the black market, or maybe even go whole hog and try actual steroids. "Hell no, I keep it all legal. And forget steroids, that shit scares me."

Most of the men I surveyed and interviewed have pretty much the same view and tell me they rarely take any kind of supplements beyond the few you can get in any health food store, stuff such as creatine—a common supplement that purports to help your body maintain moisture and assist in muscle recovery—and protein powders. But while that's most men, it's not all; though I found a few mega-men like Chad who use 'roids for the classical reason associated with building a behemoth physique, I also found a small but ardent segment who use steroids, HGH, and andro to keep their "gym-toned" bodies looking, as one man put it, "top notch and tasty."

"I'm part of a pretty hardcore party group," says Jason, a 28-year-old designer in Los Angeles. "We all work out, tan, go out clubbing, you name it . . . we're the kind of guys that most people want to look like, and want to be friends with. And that's because we all look really hot. One reason we look the way we do is that we're all cycling on something. I know people will read that and think how shallow it is, how superficial, but we don't care, or at least I don't . . . this is the time in my life when I want to look fabulous and be fabulous. You'd understand if you saw me naked. I don't want to be anything less than perfect."

Other men who admit to using illicit substances say they've taken them for only a very short period, or for a specific purpose. "When I have a 'party' coming up I'll get my hands on a little something-something and really train hard," says Mark, a 32-year-old self-described "circuit boy" who lives just outside of Atlanta. "All I need is about a month and a half and I can really get pumped and ripped. The pecs get nice and round, the biceps pop, the abs are smokin' . . . if you're gonna hang with the crowd I go with, you have to do that or you won't get noticed."

"CIRCUIT" COURT

If you've been in a hole for the past 20 years or so, so-called circuit parties began in the late 1980s as a response to the general morbidity in the gay community brought about by the AIDS epidemic. They were originally touted as AIDS fund-raisers and morale boosters for a community that really did need a serious night or two out on the town, having been to a lot more funerals than weddings. Many social observers will tell you that two decades later that original noble purpose is a distant memory, and that these days such events—staged in just about any large city with a large enough gay club scene—are little more than an excuse for men with far too much time or money on their hands to zip off to South Beach or Fire Island or Montreal for a three-day binge of dance, drugs, and dick. It's an atmosphere, those critics contend, that almost encourages gay men to indulge in unsafe sex practices with virtual strangers, which is a rather curious contradiction, one might say, considering what created such events in the first place.

But just in case you've already got your hackles up—for one reason or another—rest assured this is not the introduction to yet another tired attack on, or defense of, the circuit party scene. I have to confess that I myself have never been to such an event—I burned out my party light a long time ago, and could never swing all that airfare, anyway—but I do have lots of friends and acquaintances who've been to a good dozen or so; they always return rather wide-eyed and stunned, like Moses come down from the mountain, having trod on Holy Ground in the presence of God Himself. "It was amazing, just being lost in this huge crowd on the dance floor," my 30-year-old friend Eric tells me; like a lot of circuit devotees, he likens it to a "religious" experience, and if that's where he finds his bliss, more power to him.

I delve into the circuit experience only at the prompting of party animal Mark's comments, those regarding the "crowd" he hangs with: that throng of sweaty shirtless men with near-identical builds and physiques, if all the stories I hear can be believed. "I never saw so many incredibly hot men in one place at one time," is how my 22-year-old friend Mikey put it after he schlepped home from the White Party, looking like he'd been "rode hard and put away wet," as the old saying goes. Two days after he got back he was still incredulous. "It was like everybody there looked about 25, even the guys who had to be 35 or more . . . and everybody just had the most amazing smooth pecs and six-packs. I felt like a freak, to be honest, I was almost ashamed to take my shirt off. And I used to think I had a pretty nice body."

Mikey's not a freak, of course, it's just that he refuses to use anything more than what nature gave him to get in shape at the gym, unlike LA's Jason and Mark the circuit boy, who freely admit to using steroids and anything they can get their hands on. But how many of their buddies out there on the floor with him, the "amazing smooth pec" crowd, are also juicing it up? And on the topic of the unreal bodies they're carrying around, far too often men with bodies like Mark & Jason et al. do tend to look down on those whose builds are "less than perfect." In so doing they help create what some have come to call a sense of "body fascism" run rampant. What are the implications of that example to gay men who see those bodies—and perhaps those attitudes—as an ideal to emulate?

"The gay men's party scene represents a very small subset of the overall gay population," says "Moody" Mustafa, a 47-year-old internal medicine and HIV specialist who practices in Washington, DC; he's also an avid photographer who regularly documents the party circuit. (You can check out his work at www.moodypics.com.) "I don't think the overall numbers [of steroid use] are all that high, but I would guess as many as 40-50,000 men use these drugs annually, and that the vast majority are in the major metropolitan areas with large gay populations, such as New York, Los Angeles, San Francisco, etc."

I've spoken with Moody before, chiefly while writing *Reeling in the Years;* that's when he told me that "terminal vanity" was the number one diagnosis in his practice, and that many of his patients were "very obsessed" with going to the gym, getting very "cut up," using far too many nutritional supplements, and using illegal steroids. "There is a lot of pressure in the male gay community to be physically 'perfect,'" he told me then, while those same folks tended to overlook other important aspects of humanity such as kindness, compassion, and humility.

Three years later, he tells me that, regrettably, not much has changed, either in those antisocial attitudes or in the propensity of gay men to ignore the prodigious side effects that steroids can present. "It is important to understand some of the thought processes that go on that lead one to make a decision to use these substances," he tells me now. "This group of men continues to give increasingly greater importance to body image. As time goes by, lots of guys are getting bigger and leaner; the 'bar is raised' constantly. But this is a group of men that essentially lives in a bubble; their frame of reference is other guys who go to the gym regularly or go to parties. Their 'norms' are moving further and further away from that of the general population with regard to body make-up, and the psychological pressure to keep up can be very damaging."

What might be most intriguing to me is how this nexus of gay men, steroids, the circuit, and perfect gym bodies has evolved, perhaps influencing millions of gay men unaware of its existence. Psychotherapist Michael Shernoff tries to help me make sense of it all. "There are numerous complexities involved with the focus many gay men have on bodybuilding," he tells me. "In the 70's, most gay men were slim . . . there were a few very well-built and muscled men, but they were a distinct minority. As AIDS ravaged the gay community in the 80's, people with HIV wasted away and all too frequently looked gravely ill. It is no coincidence that the interest in pumping up by gay men began during the early days of this health crisis."

It should also be noted that it wasn't much later that the party circuit launched itself in a few key gay cities such as New York and Miami, but a funny thing was happening on the way to that spinning disco ball. "In an effort to stem AIDS-related weight loss and wasting, physicians began to prescribe steroids, testosterone and human growth hormones," recalls Shernoff. "The onset of combination antiviral drugs brought countless people with AIDS back from the brink of death. Weight training in combination with the above-mentioned drugs changed the way many people with AIDS looked. People who had once been very gaunt developed into imposing hunks . . . in addition to the medical reasons for keeping fit, a pumped up body also became a symbol of health for some people."

Shernoff acknowledges that the vast majority of gay men aren't HIV infected of course, but that for some of those who work out, keeping fit and pumped up remains one very dynamic way that they announce to the world that they're not ill. And somewhere along the way from the 1980s into the 1990s and beyond—helped along by the media barrage we talked about in Chapter 3—this brave new world of a gym-pumped body has developed into our current gold standard of physical attractiveness and sexual desirability. "One way of coping with the internal attacks of the virus and the external oppression of unsympathetic and overtly hostile politicians was—and is—to work out and get 'pumped,'" Shernoff suggests. "This is one tangible way gay men can regain control of their bodies and feel powerful . . . many gay men remember being skinny and awkward kids who were never strong or athletic, and cite the important emotional as well as physical benefits from regular exercise and lifting weights."

We've already heard stories from several men who attest to that last point. But things get dicey, Shernoff says, when gay men begin to believe that the gym's front door is some kind of gateway to nirvana. "Some men who equate being pumped, having a chiseled body, or less than a certain percentage of body fat with being sexually desirable, often can find themselves never achieving the bodily perfection they seek," he points out. These men have come to believe, consciously or otherwise, that a ripped gym body will cure all their ills, the same way some folks become convinced that winning a lottery will solve all their problems. (A recent study of past lottery winners suggests their general level of happiness after five years roughly equates to that of a crime or accident victim; think about that the next time you play the Megamillions or Powerball.) Although most men who weight train undergo at least a modest improvement in their self-esteem and self-confidence—and find that a fit body does in fact improve their quality of life—this is a group for whom no loss of fat or gain in muscle mass will ever be enough to meet their unrealistic expectations. Some will eventually come back down to earth and deal with their situation; they'll get tired of the gym rat race and find some fulfillment elsewhere. For a smaller but still substantial number, they'll be stuck on that treadmill for a lot longer, for reasons it might take a professional to fathom.

IMAGE PROBLEMS

"I can't remember when it started, when I stopped worrying about what I looked like, and started obsessing about it," Ryan is telling me. He's a 24-year-old college student in Alabama. "I used to be a fat kid, which was bad enough . . . I got tired of being fat, exercised, lost the extra pounds, started weight lifting, and people tell me I look great . . . but I don't feel great, not at all."

I ask Ryan what he thinks the problem is. "I still feel fat, and I still look fat when I see myself in the mirror, even though there's a part of me that can see I have abs now, that I have a decent chest . . . I've gotten sick from starving myself sometimes and working out too much, like I'm convinced that any amount of food will make me start gaining weight again, so I have to try and burn it off."

Ryan says his obsession is starting to affect the way he acts and behaves with other guys as well. "Once in a great while my friends will drag me out to a club, and some guy will come up to me and flirt, and I'll be happy . . . for a second or two . . . then I start worrying if he hugs me or touches me he'll feel how fat I am, even though my best friend has convinced me—intellectually—that I'm really not."

And just how did he do that? "It's actually a funny story . . . or it would be, if the whole thing wasn't so pathetic. I don't know how he did it, but he snapped a digital picture of me when I was just getting out of the shower, I was drying off my hair with the towel and I didn't see him, I would never ever let someone see me naked . . . later that night he sent me the picture online, told me it was this really hot guy he knew . . . he'd played around with it on his computer, took my bathroom out of the background and everything, shaded the thing kind of red, but you could still see the body . . . then he took my head off of it, so I was just seeing the torso down to the legs . . . I said 'wow, he's got a great body' . . . my friend said 'do you really think so?' and I said 'yeah, I do, I would love to get with a guy like that,' and he says 'Ry, you're that guy' . . . and he sent me the original."

At first Ryan says he was really mad, but then little by little he came to see what a favor his buddy had done for him. "He made it possible for me to see myself the way a stranger would . . . and I do have a nice body, all that fat is gone, and there's more muscle than I thought." But even after seeing the evidence before his eyes, Ryan says it wasn't long before those old feelings started creeping back. "I was at the gym, riding the exercise bike, I looked up in the mirror, and I saw that fat boy again. It was me."

What Ryan is describing is a condition called body dysmorphia, a psychological disconnect between a guy's actual body and the body he sees when he's looking in the mirror. It's an equal opportunity malady, affecting both men who yearn for ever-more muscle and those who feel "fat" even as they approach shapely, or even spindly, status. Not every gay man who's unhappy about the way he looks has BD, just as not everybody who's regularly convinced he's left his front door unlocked—and has to go back home to make sure—has obsessive-compulsive disorder. We all have a little touch of madness in our souls, and some men simply take their attention to their bodies to an extreme, walking up to but not necessarily crossing the line into pathology. Some bodybuilders even make fun of their obsessive yearning to be bigger, and bigger still: they call it "biggerexia," a gallows humor term to be sure, but one that shows a certain self-awareness that, when it comes to lifting, they know they're a little "out there."

True body dysmorphia is a much tougher nut to crack, and the best evidence suggests it's linked to chemical imbalances in the brain and may even have a genetic component. Men and women seem to be affected equally, though women are more likely to seek help, and gay men more likely than straight men. Why look for help just because you're a little disconnected from reality when it comes to your body? The psychologists I talk to say folks with BD are much more prone to depression, have major anxiety attacks, even contemplate suicide; though most people affected achieve a certain level of functionality, some lose concentration when it comes to work or school, and like

Ryan, they may try to avoid certain social situations or any kind of dating at all.

"I've had clients who come into my office, telling me how unhappy they are with the way they look, and all I can do is sit in wonder," says Bill, a clinical psychologist in Chicago who asks me not to use his last name. "I am fully aware of the insidious power that a body image disorder can have on the mind, but I'm still taken aback on occasion, because often the individual is rather objectively good looking, with an obviously fit physique." Bill tells me that to such people reality is meaningless. "They're stuck in a world that's rather hellish, really, and rather unimaginable if you don't have that particular condition."

So what's the difference between someone who's simply a little obsessive about his appearance and someone with true BD? "We all find ourselves checking out our 'look' on any given day in a mirror, or wearing a hat if the hair just isn't working for us," Bill explains. "Now imagine looking in the mirror, or any available shiny surface, about every five minutes, or shaving your head because you're utterly convinced your hair makes you unattractive. Imagine wearing layers of clothing or bulky outfits, even in warm weather, because the idea that anyone will discern your true body shape is too nerve-wracking . . . I had one client who measured his chest and biceps daily, because he was sure they were just way too small. And he was huge!"

Simply telling someone with BD that he's totally okay, that his body is just fine, Bill says, is rather pointless, akin to telling someone with clinical depression to cheer up, or telling someone with panic disorder to just calm down, already. "It's not like these folks want to feel this way, they just do, and it can take some serious therapy—and often anti-depression or anti-anxiety medications—to get them back on an even keel."

I tell Bill about Ryan's sneaky friend, and his stealthy camera. "That's actually rather clever, though I wouldn't recommend it as a matter of ethics. But it's not far off from the kind of cognitive and behavioral therapy we use, to help give clients a more 'realistic' sense of their actual physical appearance. Ryan's little buddy showed him an 'objective' view, let him see himself as if through a third party's eyes. But as you can see by the way he started feeling bad about himself soon thereafter, the condition will constantly try to reassert itself. It can take a long time to get it under control, and some people never will."

"When I heard about 'body image disorders,' the first thing I always thought about was people who were anorexic," says Kenny, a 31-year-old officer worker in Watertown, New York. "I had this image of people who were eating a ton, then puking it out, because they thought any amount of food would make them look like a lard ass . . . I felt bad about them, but it didn't have anything to do with me . . . I was the guy who was eating all the time, lifting weights, running, taking the right kind of vitamins, all that stuff. The last time I had a fight with my ex-boyfriend about all the time I was spending at the gym instead of being home, I went to a relationship counselor, and that's when he had me sit down and think about how and why I was working out so much. We started going over why I wanted to be so buff, everything I was giving up just to try and look more muscular . . . I'm still not sure if I have a real case of [body dysmorphia] but I can definitely see some of the traits. I still workout a lot, but I try not to go overboard with it."

Admittedly it can be a very fine line; anyone who's worked out and made good gains will tell you how "addictive" the gym can be. For the uninitiated, the strategies that some men take can look pretty extreme, and even obsessive. But that doesn't necessarily mean they're ready for the couch. "I'd been going to the gym for several years, but there was no significant change in my body," says Rutledge, the 24-year-old teacher from LA we heard from in Chapter 3. "A year ago I decided to drastically change my body and I stopped doing cardio, did strength training four times a week, began taking creatine and ate over 4,000 calories a day. On that 'diet,' I gained 50 pounds of muscle and fat in about five months. When I reached 225, I cut all carbs out of my life, consumed about 1,500 to 2,000 calories a day, and began doing cardio, four times a week for 45 minutes. In six months, I lost 40 pounds of the weight I had put on, and I looked GOOD."

Rutledge tells me that over the course of an 11-month period he had a net gain of ten pounds of muscle, which is pretty remarkable. But he admits that the constant fretting over his physique strikes some of his less-buff friends as somewhat odd. "While I wouldn't say I have a body image disorder, no matter how 'in-shape' I am I will always pinch my stomach fat in the mirror and wish for bigger arms. People around me think I'm crazy."

WHAT'S THE SKINNY?

Diego is laughing as we stand there together near the doorway of one of DC's more popular weeknight hangouts, a strip club called Wet. He's come to enter the Wednesday Night Amateur Contest, and he's not reacting to some small witticism on my part; seeing him scooting about for the better part of the night without his shirt on, I've simply asked him where he's been working out to get that tall, thin, lanky build that any would-be underwear model would run over his grandmother for.

"Me? In a gym? That's just too fucking funny," he says, then explains that he's looked pretty much the same way for all of his 23 years. Well, not exactly the same . . . he didn't top six feet until he was 17 or so, about the same time people started complimenting him on his ripped abs. "I never really did anything for them, and I eat like a fucking pig . . . the only thing I can figure out is I like to dance, a lot . . . and I still get together with my friends on the weekends and play soccer." At that last I discreetly glance back, and I see that, yes, he may own a thin and toned upper body, but south of the border it's all bubble butt and thighs. I make note of that to him, and he smiles. "Sometimes I feel a little weird, because a lot of gay guys are just the opposite, all chest and biceps, and no legs at all." [My doctor, Doug, has a great term for that: he refers to such men as "UBQs," or Upper Body Queens.] "I hope these guys"—he motions to the crowd around us—"don't think I look weird, too," he says off-handedly, then heads back into the crush, to lobby for some votes come contest time. I don't see again him for an hour or so, and by then he's up on the platform, about to take it all off. By the hoots and hollers he's getting when he slips off his boxers, it seems clear he had nothing to worry about. He's a great-looking boy, and in the overhead lighting his stomach looks like it could cut a diamond. He spots me and smiles, and does a satirical little flexing move for me with his upper arm, barely making a muscle. But with the applause he's already getting, it's pretty obvious no one is put off by his lack of mass—that tall lanky body is very much appreciated. For one night at least, thin is very much "in."

We'll get back to Diego and Wet a bit later on—you want to know how he did in the contest, right?—but for now I bring him up to represent what seems to me to be a growing subset of gay men, especially young gay men; they're thin guys, who either can't or don't particularly want to pack on muscle.

I may be totally off base—trends are awfully hard to spot at the cusp—but it does seem that fewer young gay men are joining gyms these days, forsaking any attempt to build up their bodies with weights and machines. My polls show that 22 percent of the total number of respondents list themselves as thin or skinny, and the vast majority of those gay men under the age of 25 who took my survey place themselves in the same category. That's not to say that many older gay men aren't also keeping themselves fit while trim, or have simply been blessed—some of them might say cursed—with thin bodies from birth to adulthood. "I am the very proud owner of a 28-inch waist, and my age is twice that now," says Benjamin, a 55-year-old account executive in San Francisco. "I was always thin growing up, and after college I started taking yoga classes and light martial arts training . . . I think I can honestly say that my body hasn't changed in any significant way since I was about 22 or 23." Simone, a 43-year-old travel agent from Fort Lauderdale, says he always "wanted" to have the big beefy build, but it wasn't in the cards, genetics-wise. "It made me rather unhappy for awhile, to spend all those hours in a gym and get little out of it, but now looking back I realize I was at least keeping myself in good shape from a health perspective . . . people who meet me think I am much younger, and my partner is always marveling at my 'twink' physique. At least I don't have to worry about my muscles sagging, since I have absolutely none there at all to sag."

But most of the self-described "skinny boys" I talk with are much younger than men like Benjamin and Simone; they're usually members of the under-30 crowd. Most of those guys tell me they "almost never" work out, and relatively few of them even belong to a gym. Several cite the price involved; memberships at a gym, at least the good ones, don't come cheap, and it's hard for some youngsters to foot the bill. A lot of college students I talk with tell me they have access to fitness equipment at school; they just don't have time between classes and their part-time jobs to actually make it there. And blessed by youth with bodies that haven't yet started that long slide toward middle age, they just don't feel the need that many of their older counterparts do.

"I've been a skinny kid all my life, and at 22 I'm still skinny," says Zach, a college student in Tennessee. "My older friends give me a hard time about it, but I think they're just jealous that I can eat McDonald's three times a day, every day, and nothing bad happens." [Might want to get your cholesterol checked there, Zachary my boy.] Junk food jones aside, Zach tells me he's got a "healthy" lifestyle overall, doesn't drink or smoke, and likes to take his mountain bike out on the hilly trails near his college with a guy from town he's been dating. "We do the club thing once in awhile, but mainly we just chill together, two skinny boys just hanging out." I ask him if he's ever wanted to hit the gym, and maybe put on some muscle mass. "Nah, that's okay," he says. "Sounds like too much work for me. I'm not about muscles much... I like skinny guys just like me, always have."

Jonathan is a 23-year-old accounting student and bartender in Pembroke Pines, Florida. Unlike Zach, he tells me that he happens to like older, muscular men quite a bit, but that he himself has always been thin, and doesn't mind it in the least. "Besides, as caught up in my self-image as I am, I'd be too nervous to stick my head in there and see someone younger than me doing more weights than I could ever possibly do." Justin, a 19-year-old "skater boi" from Littleton, Colorado, says he doesn't think he could "put on any real weight" if he tried, and right now he's not at all interested. "I think that really shredded skinny thing is hot, and older guys hit on me all the time telling me they think so, too. I hope I always look this way."

Stories like those—and I hear more and more of them all the time, from young men who no longer use the phrase "swimmer's" build, and instead say "skater's" build like Justin to demote their slimness—seem to confirm the growing dichotomy I've noted myself on occasional forays into the dance club scene; skinny young boys congregating over here, beefed up and bulky men gathering over there. Certainly a muscular build can take years to create, so it's not terribly surprising that youth and relative slimness might go hand in hand; what is a bit surprising is the frequent utter lack of interest in doing so, even among some gay youngsters who love the idea of being with a man bigger and stronger than they are.

"Maybe I'm just too lazy, but the idea of actually going to a gym three or four times a week, eating all the right food, the whole drama of the experience isn't for me," says Adam, a 24-year-old waiter in Baltimore. "Don't get me wrong, I think muscles are hot! I'd love to get with a guy like that, feel his arms around me and his body on top of mine, the whole deal. I just can't see myself ever being that guy."

I'll be the first to admit that my small survey and poll samples may not be comprehensive enough to provide the truest picture, yet rest assured I'm not the only one who believes a small shift might be under way. In the October 2004 issue of *Out* magazine, editor Brendan Lemon observed that "among the many 18-to-25-year olds I know, I detect much less desire to bulk up like the queens of yesteryear and much more yearning to have the kind of 12-pack abs that seem to snap into relief with hunger-strike skinniness" (p. 31). Braden, a 26-year-old graphic designer in Tampa, says he's noted the same desires among his cadre of companions. "My buddies and I like to hit the gym, play racquetball, swim, all that kind of stuff . . . when we lift weights we're not really going after bulk . . . I don't have anything against a huge muscular body, but we're not really built like that anyway . . . it's easier to get a 'cut' that shows off your abs than it is to throw on 15 pounds and have a huge chest. Abs are hotter anyway."

Some men who talk to me tell me they have spent some time in the gym, pounding away to put on those pounds, but in the end, "thin" won out. "I used to want to look like your typical Abercrombie boy, like the guys that have a young college jock body," says Christopher, a 27-year-old accountant in Philadelphia. "I swear I worked out like hell, and once I got to that point, I wanted to look even bigger, like the guys you see on those exercise magazines that closet cases buy, because they're too chicken shit to actually buy gay porn." Christopher tells me he was "very much inspired" to work out and pump iron when he saw all those "biceps and pecs and abs and whatnot," but he says that in the end that "look" was just too hard to maintain. "I just have a real fast metabolism, and keeping any kind of meat on my body is really hard. So I stopped what I was doing, went the other way, and just got ripped. I'm smaller than I used to be, but tighter, and it's all good now. I don't even have an A&F body anymore, but I happen to think I would look right at home on a 2xist box."

Craig, a 36-year-old personal trainer in Phoenix who works for a gym with a predominantly gay clientele, says he gets the occasional "young gay guy who is a bit overweight or out of shape" and wants some professional advice and training. "I also see a lot of guys, maybe a little older, who say they're 'thin' or 'skinny' when we talk on the phone to set up the appointment, and they're really not all that thin or skinny when they show up . . . they're undeveloped, sure, but they also have a lot of body fat that's starting to accumulate around their waists. I give them high marks for showing up and starting to address it before it gets out of hand."

Craig tells me he takes the most issue with the young gay guys he sees out on the town, the "thin raver/skater kids who wouldn't know a bench press if it bit them in the ass, and they don't want to," as he puts it. "They're happy just as they are, but that's only because they don't know what's going to happen to their bodies if they don't stop abusing them, or if they don't get in some kind of habit of regular exercise."

As a former Marine staring at 50 in a few years, I don't have to ask Craig what he means by regular exercise; the habit to run and lift weights is so deeply ingrained in me that my brain and body seem to go into withdrawal if work keeps me off the gym floor or running track for more than a few days. But long before those Marine Corps days, I too was a pretty damn skinny boy; at 18 I was 5'11" and weighed about 125 pounds. At 19 I got inspired to start lifting weights and take better care of myself, so that by the time I hit 20, I was weighing in at a much more substantial 160. And now I've been around long enough to have seen former skinny boys like myself grow quite unbelievably fat and unhealthy—over a surprisingly short interval—because they never developed the life habit tools to stave off those extra pounds once that "fast metabolism" they're so proud of inevitably ticks down a few notches.

But I do want to know what Craig means when he talks about "abuse"; is he implying that most of the thin gay boys and young men are delving into areas best not explored? "I'm not going to say that they're all using drugs, but I'm sure lots of them are," he says. "What steroids are for big and beefy guys, keeping them huge, well . . . there's crystal meth, there's lots of other club drugs around, hell even smoking all the cigarettes these kids smoke, and never eating anything of substance . . . it will give you a really thin body, that's for sure. So no, I wouldn't say all the club kids or all the skinny kids I see are using, just like I wouldn't say every guy with a big body is juicing it up . . . but too many guys are doing both, God help them, they're turning their bodies into chemistry sets, all because they want to have fun, or just look 'hot.' It's really a damn shame."

A lot of what Craig tells me may sound a bit extreme, but there are some statistics that back up his claims, numerous studies that show recreational drug use on the rise among young people, and among young gay men in particular; one study conducted in the late 1990s by the Seattle and King County Department of Public Health surveyed about 3,500 "men who have sex with men," all between 15 and 22 years old. The survey found that West Coast methamphetamine use in that age group, of at least an experimental nature, approached 45 percent in some areas; East Coast stats were much lower but still hovered around 20 percent. The authors of the study, which appeared in the November 2003 issue of the *American Journal of Public Health* and was widely publicized by a number of national gay newspapers and magazines, admitted their research by the time of publication might seem dated, but they also suggested that current arrest trends and treatment data indicate that if anything, usage these days might be even higher (Crea, 2004, p. 1).

As for smoking, well that's even harder to disagree with; recent studies show gay men and lesbians are 70 percent—yes, 70 percent—more likely to smoke than their heterosexual counterparts . . . and that as many as 59 percent of gay teens and 20-somethings are lighting up, as compared with 35 percent of the straight kids. Experts point out that many if not most young gay people suffer from some degree of self-esteem issues, so taking care of their bodies often isn't exactly priority number one; the same experts also say that, since so much of gay life takes place in smoke-filled bars and clubs, there's a lot of implicit permission to have a smoke and a smile. If either study is right, or even on the right track, you can see why so many youngsters are in fact skating that skinny line.

And Bill, the psychoanalyst from Chicago, tells me that several current studies show that between 10 and 20 percent of gay men—especially young gay men—are experiencing some kind of eating disorder, a figure many times that of straight men. "It's self-esteem issues, it's the pressure a lot of gay men feel to look young forever, to have that thin, waif-like body they've come to believe is all the rage, there are lots of factors coming into play," he tells me. "For some young people it's an ingrained disorder along the lines of those with body dysmorphia, a condition that may require professional help and therapy . . . others literally talk themselves into starvation, or become part of the binge-and-purge set because they feel every bit of pressure to be 'pretty' that the stereotypical supermodel feels."

But as you might imagine, those facts, formed as accusations by some such as Craig, are often met with a lot of criticism, if not outright anger. "I find it pretty insulting that people would just assume I'm anorexic, a meth head, or that I do any kind of drugs, just because I'm skinny and like to go out to clubs," says Jeff, a 24-year-old business major in Columbus, Ohio. "That's a really arrogant assumption, if you ask me. I may not have the best eating habits in the world, it's hard when you're in college sometimes, but the only thing I do when I go out is drink, and I'm so thin it only takes a few drinks to put me out. [Jeff explains he's 6'1," and 160 pounds, and most of it is in his legs.] I don't smoke, and none of my friends smoke. We're not that stupid."

"I won't deny that I know some people who use drugs occasionally and probably party too much," says Travis, a 22-year-old college student in Austin, Texas. "I don't, and I don't think I ever will, but it's out there. I just don't think it's as bad as some people say it is . . . and by the way I know some so-called adults who are a lot more cracked out on club drugs than any kid I know." And Clay, a 23-year-old veterinarian's assistant in Indianapolis, also strikes a somewhat defensive stance. "Some guys are fat, some guys are muscular, and some guys are skinny, because that's just the way they are. I really can't believe how judgmental gay people can be sometimes . . . I mean, damn . . . it's hard enough just being gay . . . now I have to get somebody's approval just for the way I look? Do straight guys have to go through this, too?"

LARGE AND IN CHARGE

"I started life fat," says David, a 40-year-old library worker in suburban Atlanta. "At birth I weighed about 11 pounds, you should see the pictures, I was just immense . . . but that was actually pretty normal in my family . . . Mom was big, Dad was bigger, and all my brothers and sisters were large as well. By ten years old I was already well over 100 pounds . . . at 18 I was 220 . . . now I weigh about 275 pounds, and I am just under six-feet tall."

Growing up both fat and gay, David says, was a pretty difficult proposition. "You're an outsider twice," he explains. "At school you're such an object of ridicule and teasing. I used to hear 'hey fat boy, did you get enough to eat today?' and 'look out, it's the Pillsbury Doughboy!' The other kids were really horrible, and they would make fun of the fact that I didn't have a lot of clothes, and that the seams of my pants had been sown and re-sewn because I used to split them a lot. At home I didn't get teased about being fat—we all were—but my brothers picked on me a lot and called me a 'sissy' because of the way I talked. To be honest it's pretty painful to bring it up now, I don't know how I made it through without going crazy."

Still, David says in some paradoxical ways dealing with both issues helped him get a stronger sense of himself. "When you get picked on long enough you learn to find a refuge somewhere, and for me it was in books. I used to read constantly, and that set the stage for me to do well in school, which helped me get accepted to college far away from the places I grew up . . . I left as soon as I could."

I ask him if things got better for him once he got away from all that childish cruelty. His response is a sad sigh. "You'd think so, right? You're still kind of an outsider in college, everywhere there are gorgeous boys and their gorgeous bodies, though I found it much easier to make friends, at least straight ones . . . I think I've gotten more 'childish cruelty' from gay men than I ever got from kids in grade school.

"In the gay world it's completely acceptable to laugh at fat men, because we give gay men who've always felt picked on someone they can pick on, and feel better about themselves. You can't read a gay newspaper or go online without coming across the 'no femmes, no fatties' thing, and I score high in both areas. Now that I've crossed the threshold of 40, the gay world also considers me 'too old.'"

But lest you begin to believe that David has let himself grow bitter and jaded, think again. "Oh, I'm not bitter at all. I suppose I might be, if I didn't have an active social life and satisfying job, but I'm actually doing pretty well. I have dozens of good friends I see often, and I've just started dating a wonderful man . . . he's a big guy, like me, just a year older, and we have tons of stuff in common, if you'll pardon the pun. I'm as happy as I've ever been."

It's no secret that Americans in general are fat, and getting fatter; by most estimates, as much as 60 percent of our population as a whole is overweight, with a smaller percentage considered outright obese. Although some people have always been born with some sort of genetic predisposition to a certain amount of "largeness," the U.S. Department of Health and Human Services says obesity in adults has doubled since 1980, and in adolescents it's tripled over the same time period. All sorts of factors have helped contribute to that condition; experts point to improvements in technology that provide for less physical labor in daily life, and on the job, and that same technology is creating more and more jobs of a relatively sedentary nature. Meanwhile, the amount of food available to Joe Citizen at the grocery store has also expanded, much of it prepackaged, and laden with calories . . . not to mention the concurrent expansion of fast-food outlets from coast to coast.

As for the kids, well . . . when is the last time you saw a teenager actually exerting some kind of physical effort when someone wasn't making him do it? Your average 15-year-old these days is more likely to be playing football or basketball on his Game Boy or X-Box than he is to be outside, playing those games for real, burning up those super-sized fries he's been gobbling and the Cokes he's been guzzling.

And although we've seen already that gay men are notoriously body conscious—often to a mind-numbing degree—we are not immune from the same genetic, nutritional, and occupational situations that can lead to lots of packed on extra poundage; of the men who took my *Chasing Adonis* poll, 20 percent list themselves as overweight, and 2 percent say they're obese. When I read the more detailed surveys, however, where gay men describe themselves to a greater and more personal degree, it seems likely those figures are probably a bit low.

"I know the popular stereotype says all gay men are thin and fabulous, but honey, that just ain't the case, and I'm here to tell you," says Harry, a 37-year-old painter from Pittsburgh. "I'm about 5'9" and I weight 183 pounds . . . do the math and that'll tell you I am pretty chubby. All those skinny boys or muscle men you see in the press may represent what many of us might want to be, or think we want to be, but that's not who we are, at least not where I live, and not back home in the Midwest where I grew up." Harry says the gay men where he hails from in Missouri are largely a "large" lot, and don't have "a lot in common with those folks who live 'out there on the edges.'" [By that I assume he's referring to those of us living on or not far from the East or West Coasts.] "You want to see how real gay life is in America, what real gay men look like, you guys need to stop flying over us and land once in awhile."

Peter is a 43-year-old Kansas native, currently working for a consultant firm in my "edgy" hometown, Washington, DC. "I have always been over my height/weight ratio standard," he tells me, "and I am commonly called 'a chub.' Since college, I have gained about 75 pounds . . . I am healthy, great blood pressure, and have no disease associated with being overweight." Just how much does he weigh? Peter says right now he tips the scales at 306 pounds, but would "prefer to weigh about 225 to 250, because it would be easier to buy clothes and fit into airline seats, booths at restaurants, and amusement park rides." Peter tells me he was never much for muscle men, or the young skinny boys that Harry also dismisses. "The thin or muscled body doesn't do much for me. I want a man under whom I can feel their weight and have something to hold with confidence." He also asserts that such desires are becoming more and more common. "It's always difficult to be one who likes things that are 'out of the norm,' but little by little, big men like me who like other big men are slowly coming out of their closet."

James, a 37-year-old office worker in Northern California, wasn't born out there in the breadbasket of America; he's a Golden Stater by birth who started out life "thin as a rail, but then the rail started to get a little thick" by the time he was in his mid-twenties. "I was never one to exercise or work out much, but I did always like to eat . . . right now I would classify myself as somewhere between chubby and downright fat." I ask James what that's meant in terms of his love life, or his overall quality of life. "It's been harder to meet guys, more and more as I've gotten bigger. Well, I meet them, but they're not usually going to be 'into me' sexually, the men I like look more like I used to when I was younger, they're the thinner or in shape guys. I do have some health issues, I can't walk as far as I used to, my knees hurt a lot, and my doctor tells me I need to start trying to lose some of this weight."

In that last, James's experience runs in consonance with what most experts will tell you about obesity, and about gay or straight men who are significantly overweight. With all apologies to Peter above, who says his 300+ pounds hasn't affected his health, the vast majority of men who carry a significant amount of extra fat on their bodies are risking a lot, to be sure; HHS calls obesity the nation's number one health issue, more dangerous in degree and epidemic in scope than any drug or alcohol abuse. Such weight conditions can lead to heart attacks, stroke, diabetes, the list gets pretty long. But for our purposes here, I was more curious to find out how such large gay men—who may or may not be dealing with those health issues already—are also coping with life inside a gay community that, as David suggests in the paragraphs that started this section, often tends to bear them little good will.

"I have no fat friends, but I know some fat people," says Chuck, the 39-year-old HR recruiter from Miami. "I just won't hang out with them. I watch them eat or sweat, and it drives me nuts . . . then they bitch about their weight. It's called discipline, people. If you want it bad enough, you can lose weight." Timmy, a 22-year-old college student in New Jersey, says putting on weight is just about "the most unattractive thing" a guy can do to himself. "It tells me he doesn't give a shit about what he looks like, it tells me he can't control his appetites, it says he's too lazy to get up out a chair and do some kind of exercise. I see a fat guy walking up to me in a club I am going to go the other way fast."

I'm sorry to report those kinds of comments were pretty common among the folks I surveyed and interviewed. But you don't need me to tell you that; to find out for yourself, all you have to do is take a look at any gay newspaper that has a personal ads section, or any gay-themed Web site with a members' area that has profiles, just as I did while researching my previous books that dealt with effeminacy and ageist attitudes. Sometimes it seems just about every ad or profile is from a "lean, in-shape GM seeking same," or "slim and smooth hottie, ISO muscleman"; only a very few will single out fat or chubby gay men as an object worthy of pursuit or desire. And you'll frequently discover a good representation of that group David speaks of, the gay men who go out of their way to be hostile to other gay men they've judged by the size or appearance to be beyond the range of desire; not five minutes ago I was surfing through a popular site, and I encountered no fewer than a dozen members online in my local area alone, with profiles that specifically asked anyone who was "fat," "obese," "chubby," "overweight," or "out of shape" to please not contact them, else they face being rejected or simply ignored.

"If I'm chatting with someone and he asks to see my 'stats,' I really hesitate before telling him what a big guy I am," says Frank, a 32-year-old writer from Massachusetts who explains that he weighs on the "high side" of 250 pounds. "I know when guys are online cruising, that they're looking for the guys who are going to turn them on, and I should probably understand their motivation and their lack of interest in talking with me if I am not their type. I just wish they wouldn't be so damn rude about it."

Frank's situation reminds me of the same thing I started going through about a decade ago, when people online—and sometimes in person—started ignoring or rejecting me solely because of my age; those experiences in fact helped inspire *Reeling in the Years*. They also call to mind certain threads of discussion in *Sissyphobia*, where my interview subjects suggested they shouldn't have to apologize for not being attracted to effeminate men; in both works I referred to older men, effeminate men, and overweight men as members of that "unholy trinity" that many gay men do their best to avoid, something our bud David says he's been dealing with as well.

Certainly it is a touchy subject, that rejection any of us confront when certain facets of our being don't meet the muster of folks we'd like to make a connection with. And in all brutal honesty, I think we have to grant other people the freedom not to accept us on that level, just as we would like to feel free to reject them if they had certain traits we didn't like. As Frank suggests, a little less rudeness would be nice, and the whole topic of rejection is such a potent one from all sides that I've dedicated a whole chapter to it later in this book; but how odd is it that many of the large men I speak with tell me they're not attracted to other large men—just as many of the effeminate men I have interviewed don't like effeminacy, and several older men I've talked with are interested solely in those younger than they are?

"You can certainly call me a hypocrite in that respect," says Matt, a 26-year-old retail shop employee in Frederick, Maryland. "Where I live about an hour outside of DC most of the gay men are pretty fat and sloppy, and I find them to be grotesque and disgusting. But when I go to Nation [a now defunct DC dance club which held a weekly gay dance "event" called "Velvet Nation"] on Saturdays no one wants to talk to me, because I too am out of shape." I ask Matt by how much he exceeds his desired poundage. "I could easily lose 50 pounds, which would put me at close to 160 or so, that would be normal for my height. I still go out and manage to have fun most of the time, I love watching all those hot boys dancing with their shirts off, even though I know lots of them are looking back at me and thinking 'why are you so damn fat?'"

So I ask him the obvious question: Why doesn't he just go ahead and make the effort and lose those extra pounds? "It's not like I haven't tried, but you said it right there, it's the effort . . . I just can't manage to stay on a good diet, or find the time to exercise. I hope one day I can find the motivation, I can't imagine life wouldn't be at least a little better if I was thinner."

"I'd like nothing better than to look like the guys I find the hottest, to be lean and well-toned like they are," says Kevin, a 30-year-old computer technician in Cincinnati. "I like to think that a lot of the unhappiness, and sometimes bitterness, that I feel about gay life would vanish if I could manage to shave off some fat. [Kevin says he's not obese, but still far beyond what he thinks would be his optimum weight.] I keep trying to find the right diet that works for me. So far, nothing seems to work."

"It is one of the hardest things to do, losing weight that took years to put on," says Mike, a 38-year-old fitness trainer who lives and works in South Beach. "Especially down here, where there are so many hot men around . . . you'd think that might serve as motivation, but I have clients tell me it actually works the other way . . . they set such an impossible standard that a lot of men don't even bother, and give up before they even really try." Mike says he tries to put the end to those notions immediately the second someone voices them. "I tell them to compare it to money, or investments, that it doesn't matter what you did ten years ago, or yesterday, if you want to start saving or investing, it's today, tomorrow, and next year that matter more. It's the same way with proper diet, and fitness training . . . you work on today, make sure you do the right things now . . . you have to work on undoing a life of bad food, and lack of exercise, and that takes time. But in the end, if you really stick with it and make some lifestyle changes, it will pay off, sometimes just a little, sometimes a lot, depending on how much dedication you can apply to it."

Mike makes all the standard comments any fitness professional or nutrition counselor makes. "You really have to check with your doctor first, find out if your overall health is solid enough to start the kind of regimen you need. Just about any doctor will tell you that absent any condition that negates physical activity, there is virtually NO ONE who won't benefit from a better diet and getting more physical in his or her day to day life."

I can surely echo and confirm everything Mike says, based on my past experiences as a fitness trainer myself. And I would encourage men like Matt and Kevin, convinced that a thinner build will right a lot of the wrongs they experience, to go ahead and make the plunge, the health benefits are simply too important not to. But I would temper their expectations of a complete life change, as would Mike the fitness man. "People turn to food sometimes as a kind of comfort or security blanket, to the point where a lot of people simply have no idea just how many calories they're consuming in a day. Sometimes they're overweight or obese for a host of psychological reasons, and that can include gay men who have a lot of self-esteem issues. If you've just been a bit lazy and you know it, and you want to turn it around, that's honestly not all that hard to do, you just have to make the commitment and stick to it . . . but if you're really, really fat, and you've been that way for a long time, it's probably a good idea to look at some counseling along the way while you're starting that diet and fitness routine. You may have some issues that need to be addressed, just like the weight you want to lose. You'll be a lot more likely to be successful in the end."

Make no mistake, losing weight and creating—or re-creating—a slimmer body, or even a hunky body, is no guarantee of happiness. Let me share with you an exchange I stumbled on in "Bitch Session," a compendium of caustic commentaries published by Window Media in its chain of gay newspapers from New York to Houston. Sometimes wry, often rude, the single-paragraph missives are anonymously submitted by a toll-free number or by going online, and cover topics both broad and narrow; the one that caught my eye appeared in the October 31, 2003, edition of the *Washington Blade*.

> To all the men who never used to speak to me when I weighed 45 pounds more than I do now but who all flock to me since dropping my weight to tell me how good I look: I'm the same person I've always been, and you are self-centered bastards. (p. E-3)

I'll admit I uttered a little "touché!" when I read that; it seemed to me that the Former Fat Guy was rightfully indignant that so many folks, used to overlooking him because of his size and never bothering to get to know him because he was overweight, were now pleased as punch to bask in his company. But several weeks later, in the December 5 edition of the same paper, came this trio of responses.

> To the formerly fat, yet still bitter guy who lost 45 pounds but is pissed that guys only now notice him when he's "the same person" he's always been: Why did you lose the 45 pounds? Because you're obviously unattractive on the inside and no one cared for your bitter, resentful persona.

Followed by this one:

> To the man who couldn't get anyone to talk to him when he was 45-pounds heavier: It's great that you found ways to control yourself, and your weight. Are you still looking to date fat guys? I doubt it. No one wants someone who obviously can't control even the simplest parts of their life.

And then one more, somewhat curt, but also cutting: "You may have lost 45-pounds, but you have not lost the bitter fat boy attitude" (p. E-3).

Ouch. I followed the next several issues, hoping to find that our Former Fat Guy would come back with his own witty rejoinder, but it seems he never answered back. Pity, because that trio certainly needed to be dressed down in devastating, Dorothy Parker fashion. Their words only bear out the negative assumptions that so many gay men have about larger men, that just because they happen to be fat, they're also bitter and cynical, and "obviously unattractive on the inside." That's not to say while researching this book I haven't found plenty who are bitter, men who could stand to lose several pounds and can't stop carping about their extra 25 to 50 as if it's a burden that they're forced to carry, something they absolutely have no control over; hell, I used to live with a fellow who would complain to no end about his weight, while I watched him stuff mounds of food into his mouth just before he hit the hay every night. I remember getting a headache from the self-control it took not to shout out, "Then put the fucking fork down and do something about it!"

But our FFG did do something about it: he dropped his excess weight, and though he may still carry some emotional baggage from the experience, one can't blame him now for calling out those "bastards" he speaks of—even as we realize how common their attitudes are and how much we might quietly share their viewpoints. But at least some men are a lot more upfront about it than most. Back to the "Bitch Session" we go, this one from the *Blade*'s April 16, 2004, edition:

> Either I find you attractive or I don't. No amount of politically correct hogwash about how beautiful you are on the inside is going to change the fact that I find you physically repulsive on the outside. Meanwhile, we can still treat each other with dignity and respect: I respect the fact that you're a cow and you respect the fact that I'm shallow. (p. E-3)

Of course there are thousands, maybe hundreds of thousands, of large gay men who don't give a rat's ass what thinner, muscular, or just "in shape" gay men think of them. They look at those massive tummies and ample asses on their fellow big men with a leering, lusty eye, the same way your average club kid might go all aflutter when he spots an Aberzombie in the house. Leroy is a 42-year-old club bouncer in Southern California; you make trouble in his place, you have to deal with all six-foot-three and 300 pounds of him. "I guess I can see why so many dudes go for the muscle boys, the circuit boys, what have you, just like I can tell you that this woman here is hot, this one over here not so much. But none of that does anything for me . . . maybe it's because I see how flighty and flaky they all are, I don't exactly see them at their best. My man waiting for me at home is bigger than I am . . . he's my rock and my anchor, beautiful in so many ways inside and out."

"You give me a mountain of a man, and my thing just goes schwinggg!" says Lee, a 30-year-old physical therapist who hails from a small town in eastern Tennessee. Lee tells me that as a man who weighs "well over 250, I stopped stepping on the scale a long time ago," he simply isn't satisfied by anyone who can't match him, pound for pound. "All those little sweet twinky boys, they're like rug rats to me, barely legal, barely there. When they're around I feel like I do when someone brings their tots into a restaurant. I need a real man, and that means some serious girth!"

And speaking of "girth" . . . that just happens to be the key word for large gay men seeking others like themselves; a very large friend of mine turned my attentions to groups that call themselves "Girth & Mirth" clubs, loosely affiliated chapters of big guys and their admirers—big and small—that can be found in cities across the nation, even around the world. Through their many Web sites I've met a number of their members, and there's nary a "bitter fat guy" among them. John is a 41-year-old writer who belongs to the Chicago chapter; as he explains it, G&M clubs aren't just for hooking up—though a fair amount of that happens—they're mainly about giving big men some room to roam around in the company of others, away from all that nastiness and backbiting they often encounter on the slimmer side of the street.

"I hate to call it a 'safe space,' as if we're great big sissies who need to be protected," John tells me. "But some of us have been brutalized or marginalized by the mainstream gay world, in a lot of subtle and not-so-subtle ways. You don't see much of us in advertising, or in the main gay magazines unless we make the news in some freakish way . . . there's a lot of catty chatter whispered behind our backs, sometimes to our faces . . . our clubs make for a welcoming environment where no one of ANY size is ever made to feel like he's an outsider. We arrange all sorts of activities and events, parties and trips, it's just wonderful. The worst thing that's going to happen is you're going to make a boatload of new friends; the best is what happened to me, I met my partner of the last five years there."

The DC G&M Chapter got its start almost a quarter century ago, back in 1983; it's one of several other big-men's groups—including the Gentle Giants of Oregon, the Houston Big Men's Club, and other G&M clubs from Philadelphia, Central Florida, and New York City—that get together every year for a convention called Convergence. It's been going on since 1988, and it often attracts heavyset men and their fans from overseas as well; the 2003 Convergence in DC welcomed members from nations as far-flung as Europe and Australia.

Mark is 34-year-old member of the G&M Big Men's Club in Long Beach, California, a group that bills itself as among the best of its kind anywhere. He points me toward the group's Web site gallery, page after page of photos showing pool parties, barbecues, trips, and nights on the town. Mark tells me he's not a "big guy" himself, that he's actually kind of tiny compared with he men he likes to rub elbows with. "I always found big guys sexy, long as I can remember, but I didn't see many of them out and about in the clubs I used to go or the places I used to hang out . . . then I heard about GMLB, and joined up . . . can't tell you what a great environment it is, it's hard to believe I used to worry I might not be accepted. But they took me under their wing. Only wish the rest of the gay community could be half as nice as supportive as these guys have been."

I ask Mark if he ever gets any ribbing—good-natured or otherwise—about being such an admirer of large gay men. "I guess someone might say something from time to time, if you're not into big guys it probably looks awful strange, like some kind of weird fetish . . . but why is it any stranger to be attracted to a man with some meat on his bones than it is to like some skinny chicken? That's exactly the kind of attitude I haven't found much of here . . . these guys know what it means to live and let live."

And some big guys are living quite well, and aren't ashamed to brag about it a little, as this final (for now) glance through "Bitch Session" shows, this one from February 6, 2004:

> Yes, I overheard your "stage whisper" at the bar the other night. And yes, I agree that I am about 25 pounds overweight. But I ran (and finished) a marathon last year, I'm on Atkins, and I'm not a queeny "blond" waify little bitch like you. Besides, when you got a tool like mine, it's okay to build a shed over it. (*Washington Blade,* p. E-3)

BEAR HUNT

It's a cold, snowy, and somewhat dreary day in Washington, DC, but you wouldn't know it from the stifling heat inside this Dupont Circle hotel, or the loud and rather raucous crowd that crushes into the lobby, and spills over into the adjoining bar and conference rooms. This is the great Mid-Atlantic Leather Weekend, and except for the handful of men walking around in little more than thongs or chaps—and the occasional assless pants—it's a group so bedecked in thick animal hide that one can safely say they're well equipped to face whatever fearsome elements Mother Nature might care to dish out.

To my eyes as I stand in the lobby, lots of these guys might not even need the leather for the weather; their own natural fur would probably suffice, growing as it does on virtually every square inch of their exposed skin, and quite likely that which is not exposed as well. Though these so-called Bears—a term that means different things to different people, but is generally used to describe large, hirsute gay men—aren't specifically here to meet as such, the MAL tends to draw more from their subset of the gay community than it does from any other. Outside in the hotel's courtyard, blowing in the snowy wind alongside the American and DC flags—and the large rainbow flag, of course—you can find their paw-spangled banner with its stripes of black and brown, tan, white, and gold; it's a sight, one man tells me, that almost brought tears to his eyes when he arrived to check in for the weekend. "It makes me feel welcome, and it shows that we've really arrived."

As I learn this weekend in a nation's-capital-turned-Bear-den, despite commonly held beliefs, the whole Bear thing isn't so much about the hair, or even the size of the man sporting it; it's more about a worldview, a bit of a swaggering attitude that refuses to be a slave to whatever the mainstream gay community says is hot or not. "This is an Abercrombie nightmare," one fellow says to me as he shops for some, um, accessories inside the makeshift MAL Mall, a series of booths and kiosks set up in several of those hotel conference rooms and banquet halls. "Being a Bear is all about being natural and comfortable with who you are and what you look like, it's not about spending days in the gym and waxing off every stray hair on your body." He pats his round tummy, which protrudes prodigiously from under the shiny black leather vest he's wearing with matching pants and a jaunty little cap. "They can have their six-packs, I am happy with my keg right here."

I will also learn that among the Bears, you have your Cubs (usually a younger man who aspires to be one of the crowd) and other species lurking about as well; "Otters" are normally younger, and mainly slimmer men who'd like to count themselves in, as well as "Wolves," who are thinner, older, and generally more aggressive types than Otters. I confess I was starting to picture the whole experience as something off The Discovery Channel; what a documentary that would make!

As it turns out there's already a fair amount of documentation going on. "It was through the happy convergence of several factors that gay men began bandying about the term 'bear' to apply to themselves or other masculine men they were interested in, in the early years following the arrival of AIDS," says writer Les Wright on The Bear History Project Web site (www.bearhistory.com). "While similar things were happening all across the U.S., the geographical compactness and density of the San Francisco gay community produced several 'bear' manifestations simultaneously in the mid-1980's." Wright says by the early 1990s Bear clubs were popping up all over the country, along with regional "Bear fests" from Denver to Chicago to Orlando. The phenomenon has even spread around the globe; in fact, Wright suggests, Bears are likely to be at least as popular—if not more—in the Land Down Under than they are in the United States. (And you thought they only had koala bears in Australia.)

What led to such a rapid expansion of this "community within a community"? Wright says that "early bears proudly proclaimed being 'average,' masculine gay men, neither effeminate queens nor hyper-masculine leather men. In fact, many of them were former 'clones,' now heavier and graying at the temples. A bear subculture rapidly developed along three trajectories, all emanating from San Francisco—the underground press, private sex parties, and the newly emergent medium of electronic communications . . . word-of-mouth broadcast of 'bears' via computer bulletin boards, and then the Internet, spread the concept even more rapidly. Bear spaces, particularly bars and private sex parties, occurred where various subcultures within gay male communities, including 'chubbies,' radical faeries, bikers, blue-collar men, rural men, computer geeks, and fetishists, came together."

Jeff, our assistant professor from Virginia Tech, echoes that scholarly discourse with his own real-world experience. "I grew up in Appalachia, where there are still lots of beefy, hairy, bearded sorts," he tells me. "I had crushes on some of them before I knew what I was feeling. No wonder I'm a bear, and am into bears . . . thence come so many of my fetishes—body hair, facial hair, muscles, a little bit of beer belly, boots, pickup trucks, wife-beaters. . . . well, you get the picture."

And the proof in that pudding is right in front of me, as I make my way around the convention floor; many of the large men we talked about in Chapter 3 also think of themselves as members of the Bear community, and certainly many of them are. Here at the Leather Convention I speak with two very large and burly men—37-year-old Bob and 42-year-old Steve—who've traveled all the way here from Minnesota. "The last time I came to DC some friends of mine took me out to The Eagle [that's a DC leather bar] and we had a pretty good time," Bob tells me. "But this just blows me away, I've never seen so many hot men in one room in my life." He looks around at the crowd and smiles at two other large men walking by on their way to a backroom that displays yet another assortment of accessories, the purpose of which even I might blush to explain. (Let's just say the item getting the most attention back there is suspended from the ceiling. It looks very much like a swing. It is not.) The men smile back at Bob, now clearly itching to get away from my nosy questions and get back to business. Steve is obviously amused by his friend's eagerness to mingle. "Don't mind him, he just doesn't get out that much." Steve tells me he does, however, from his G&M club back home, to membership in some leather clubs, and various other gatherings tailor-made for the larger gay bon vivant. "I've been out for years, but Bobby here is a bit of a newbie, he still has that kid in the candy store thing going on."

I confide that at 37 I'm not sure how much I'd call "Bobby" a "kid," but once again there are lessons to be learned among the burly men. "You'll find that G&M'ers, bears, and leatherfolk all have several things in common, and one of them is a respect for age," Steve tells me. "We're probably the only part of the gay community that doesn't think getting older is a bad thing . . . my friends and I call it 'seasoning.' You're just not as interesting until you have some years under your belt, and some gray in your beard."

"I consider myself lucky to be a part of the leather and Bear communities, because men over thirty are still regarded as desirable in those communities," asserts Virginia Tech's Jeff in agreement. "I suspect, were I a part of mainstream gay culture, I would have been 'put out to pasture' long ago. As it is, being a bald, goateed man in my mid-forties, I get more attention from men now than I ever did in my twenties!"

Sure enough, this crowd around me now is not one you'd likely find hanging out at your average metropolitan mega-disco on a Saturday night . . . if I had to guess, I'd say the average age in this room is definitely on the high side of 45, maybe even higher. Younger men can be found, but they're sporting a sort of updated clone look—twenty-first-century clothes with classic Tom of Finland bodies—and I notice that I don't see many of them who aren't in the company of one or two older men. "We're throwbacks to that time when we all had older gay friends who helped us come out," Steve explains. "You just don't see the twinks doing that these days, not to the degree we do."

Just as Steve mentions "twinks," lo and behold I actually spot a few them standing together off to the side, dressed in jeans and khakis and pullover shirts, watching the scene passing by in front of them. (They don't want to give me their names, so I'll just call them by monikers appropriate to their twink status: Chad, Ryan, and Josh.) In any gathering they'd probably be on the smaller side—I doubt they're any more than 21, and weigh barely more than 140 pounds—but here they are as Lilliputians in a room filled with Gullivers. "We just wanted to see what was going on, we heard this was in town," says Ryan, the largest of the three. "I can't believe these guys are gay, they look like football players or truck drivers." Josh—the most petite of the trio—is wrinkling his nose. "I can't believe these guys have bathed," he says, somewhat disapprovingly. I suggest that might be mostly leather he's smelling; it's a singularly distinctive aroma that hangs rather thickly in the air. "If you say so, sweetie . . . I think some of these guys have hygiene issues."

The other member of their little group isn't saying much; Chad is just watching the Bears and leatherfolk in action, and something in his eyes tells me he's somewhat fascinated by a spectacle totally beyond his experience. A few minutes later bitchy little Josh has had enough and wants to leave, and he pulls Ryan out the door with him into the snow. But Chad heads off in the other direction, vanishing into the leather-clad crowd. I wander around a bit more, just talking with folks, telling them about this book, and asking what they'd like to say to people who don't know much what Bears are really all about. "Tell them we're more normal than people think we are," says Jimmy, a 44-year-old construction worker who's traveled here from Virginia Beach. "I know some of these guys look really out there with all this leather stuff, but most of us are pretty regular, and down-to-earth . . . you have some really queeny Bears, but mostly you have really butch Bears, with a little of everything else in between." Another furry gentleman, down from New Jersey with his partner of 15 years, wants to explain that "Bears are a lot of fun, and we hardly even bite. Nibble some, but we don't bite."

I continue my wanderings and run into Bob and Steve again; they invite me to join them later at The Green Lantern, a refurbished bar a few blocks away that's historically known for its masculine patronage. I tell them I just might, but I'm not sure where I'll end up later, having gotten a number of similar invitations from other people I've been talking to. This is easily the friendliest gay crowd I've ever been in, even if to be honest most of the men here are not my type. But I could see getting drunk with them and laughing the night away; that would be a blast.

I'm making to leave when I hear some hootin' and hollerin' erupt behind me, and I turn back to look. That's when I see Chad again, but his former outfit of khaki pants and preppie shirt has undergone something of a transformation. Well, actually more of a removal; all he's wearing now is what can best be described as a leather bikini, and a studded collar . . . and he seems to have made a lot of friends, including one older man twice his size that he's now walking around with, arm in arm. He gives me a wave as he walks by, and his older buddy gives him a good-natured pat on the ass to move him along.

I could be wrong, but I think Chad is going to have a really interesting evening.

Chapter 5

Rejected!

> You're my obsession, who do you want me to be
> to make you sleep with me?
>
> "Obsession"
> Animotion

"I had been talking with this really cute guy for most of the night," says Vince. He's a 32-year-old marketing specialist at a Boston firm, telling me about a recent evening at a Bean Town bar. "I was getting pretty good vibes from him . . . seemed to be making him laugh, he didn't seem like he wanted to get away from me, and he came back and sat back down beside me after he got up to use the can, when a lot of guys would have used that as an excuse to move on and talk with other people. We probably talked for an hour and a half or so . . . and I decided to try and move things to the next level."

By that I ask Vince if he means he invited the "cute guy" home. "We don't do that in Boston," he explains to me. "In fact it doesn't seem like many people talk to each other at all here unless they're friends already, which is one reason why I thought he might be into me." Vince says for him the next level was giving the fellow his phone number. "I figured we'd had such a nice time . . . and it would be great to carry it over to a dinner or coffee sometime." But "cute guy" had other ideas. "He looked at that piece of paper like I'd dipped it in poison, then looked at me like I'd just spit in his face. Forget about getting his number . . . he said he had to go, got up, and went. I can't tell you how stupid and useless it made me feel, looking at that piece of paper lying on the table after he left."

Since Vince and I are talking real time on the Net on this particular evening, and not via delayed e-mail or a survey filled out and left in my database, I am able to give him my instant assessment of his would-be date. We have some of his type in the DC area, I tell him; they're called "crazy," and I suggest to Vince that he should thank his lucky stars to have found out so early, before wasting any more time—or God forbid, money—on such a loser with serious people issues. "I know you're right about that," he says in agreement. "He really did me a favor, showing me that really odd side of him before I made any real investment in him . . . but then I think wow, I was rejected by a loser. And I'm not sure how to process that."

But as bad as getting rejected might be, I could tell Vince that being the guy doing the rejecting isn't exactly a walk in the park; a short time after our conversation ends, I'm talking webcam to webcam with Jake in Austin, Texas. He's a very attractive postgrad student, 25 years old, telling me about the time not long ago when he had to turn away the unexpected affections of a longtime friend.

"I must have been clueless not to spot it, all my friends kept telling me that it was obvious this guy had a thing for me," he says. "But we'd known each other for years, and I just didn't think of him like that. A few weeks ago I was driving him home from a party, and he started getting really touchy-feely with me. I thought he was joking around, then I realized he was serious . . . and that's when he started telling me that he was in love with me."

Jake goes silent for a little while, then continues. "I didn't want to hurt his feelings, because I really liked him a lot, we always had a great time together. But I had to tell him I didn't return his interests, not physically, and not to the depth of the emotions he had. He called me up the next day to apologize, but it puts a real strain on a friendship when one guy feels something that the other doesn't. I haven't had any contact with him since, and I'm not sure if I should. I don't want to feel like I am leading him on."

Getting rejected—or finding yourself in a situation where you have to reject someone—is just one of those unfortunate facts of life, like Republicans, or having to take a dump once or twice a day. It happens. For our purposes here, I was interested in finding out what happens when our chase for Adonis runs into a major stumbling block, and what happens when we have to cut someone else's pursuit off at the pass. What's going on inside a guy's mind when he has his heart set on some kind of relationship with Mr. Right—or that good ol' Mr.

Right Now—and he suddenly gets the message that, nope, it ain't happening. What does that really do to you, and how do other people's reactions vary? What's it like on the other side of the fence, when you're the one who has to play the bad guy? Since rejection of all sorts is something we all go through, I talked with some experts who deal with such issues professionally, to find out what they recommend when it comes to effective coping strategies, and how those strategies might differ according to who has to do the coping. We'll hear from them in just a bit.

Some other men tell me stories about guys for whom mere rejection isn't enough for them to get the message; some I've talked with actually were those guys. Their tales are, by turns, amusing, sad, and sometimes chilling; also often sad and chilling in many ways are the stories of those men who've played both roles in the rejection scenario, at the very same instant: they've rejected themselves. Despite all outward appearances and their basic intrinsic sweetness, they've become convinced—or allowed themselves to become convinced—that they are just not worthy somehow. Rather heartbreaking, that.

There are other men, of course, who seem to believe that not only are they totally worthy, but they are also all that, and the proverbial bag of chips. Consider this snippet from the October 2004 issue of *Instinct,* a letter written to advice columnist Joel Perry:

> I'm what a lot of people consider good-looking. I get hit on a lot, especially by guys that should realize that, basically, I am out of their league. But if I'm curt with them, they tell me that I should stop acting stuck up. I'm just being honest, but they see my rejecting their advances as pretentious. Is there a way to way to tell them I'm not interested without them projecting their insecurities on me? It just makes going out so uncomfortable. (Perry, 2004b, p. 94)

Before I give you Joel's answer, reread that few times. Savor it. Admire the utter chutzpa it took to commit such words to paper. Ready? Okay, here's Joel's reply:

> You poor, uncomfortable, good-looking man. There is indeed a way to go about keeping such presumptuous peons from pawing your perfect person. Get a smart, stylish sweatshirt. Then have the word 'ASSHOLE' emblazoned on it in large, red letters . . .

do not remove said sweatshirt until you realize you are not acting stuck up, you are stuck up.

Joel goes on to refer to our letter writer as a "shallow snob," who's missing out on a potential "gold mine" of a mate, because he is "unable to see beyond slightly imperfect packaging" (p. 94).

I heard from several such "gold mines" as I researched this chapter, men of good hearts and great minds with slightly "imperfect packaging," and yes, they often ran afoul of such "shallow snobs" as Joel talks about. Sadly, very few of the latter were wearing the sort of sweatshirt he recommends, and therefore, far too few of the former managed to escape unscathed.

IT'S NOT ME . . . IT'S YOU

"The one that sticks out in my mind was way back in college," says Eric, now a 47-year-old medical researcher in Sacramento, California. "He was a classmate named David, devastatingly beautiful, with an intelligence that a lot of people found to be intimidating. But his brain was actually what probably drew me to him most, the part of him I found most compelling . . . all that unearthly beauty of his was just the icing on the cake."

As Eric recalls, he and David worked together as lab partners often, and forged what seemed to be a rather easygoing and stable friendship. "He never came right out and said he was gay, but he seemed to be sending me the signals so he never really had to spell it out . . . whenever we were grabbing some dinner or working on a project, I could feel this closeness with him that I had never experienced before, and haven't many times since. I'd really fallen for him, and thought of him constantly."

Eric tells me the friendship took a bad turn one night, after the two had been slamming back some beers for a few hours to celebrate a well-received paper. "I told him how I felt about him, and he just sat there, looking at the floor. Then he looked up and told me he considered me a dear friend, but wasn't at all attracted to me 'that way.' He was probably as nice to me as anyone could have been under the circumstances, but even telling you the story now 20 years later I can still feel a little pain inside. Our relationship soured after that, it was just too hard for me to be around him."

Other men tell me about rejections where "nice" never figured into the equation. "I met this guy at a club, gave him my number, got his, and I called him up to ask him out to dinner, which he accepted," says Sean, a 31-year-old photographer in New York City. "We met at the restaurant, ordered drinks, and were looking at the dinner menu when he just looked at me, said 'sorry, I don't think this is going to work,' got up and left. We'd hardly made any small talk at all, I can't imagine what I might have said to set him off like that." Richie, a 27-year-old store manager in Salisbury, Maryland, says he was similarly dumbfounded by his dinner date. "We'd been eating, drinking, laughing, you name it, for hours at this place in Baltimore—that's where he was from—and this guy was just perfect for me, or so I thought. You know those nights where it's like everything seems to be going your way? That's how it was . . . then just as soon as I paid the bill and we were talking about what to do next, he's telling me that hey, he had a great time, but he's going to make an early night of it. I tell him ok . . . that I would love to see him again . . . he smiles this really plastic smile and says sure. When I get home there's an email waiting for me, and he's saying I'm not his type, please don't bother him anymore."

But at least Richie and Sean got to the dinner stage. Lots of other men tell me such tales of woe when it comes to approaching guys they're attracted to that you'd think they were describing a veritable nest of venomous vipers. A fellow who simply calls himself "Student"—he lists no age or hometown—admits he has a bit of a "pale and gothy" look about him, but also explains he has a nice, defined build brought about by several hours each week in the gym; he also tends to be attracted to older muscular men. One night at a club he approached just such a man: "He looked me in the eye and told me I was too pale and feminine . . . he said I and should go find a straight guy and be his bitch. I went home and cried." Kevin, an 18-year-old anthropology student at the University of Illinois, tells me about the time he was approached by a man fascinated by his smooth, well-toned body. "He said 'God, you've got such a great tan!' and I replied with 'It's not a tan, I'm part Native American,' and all of sudden he wasn't interested in me anymore. Really odd how what was apparently so physically attractive to him, turned into such a turn off so quickly."

Bill, a 35-year-old banking executive in Tacoma, Washington, says he spent a good half hour screwing up his courage not long ago to go talk to a very attractive guy he'd been eyeing for most of the night. "He was standing there not really talking to anyone, just ordering drinks. So I walked over and said hello. First he looked surprised, then annoyed, then he just walked away. I'll admit I'm not Brad Pitt when it comes to the face department . . . but no one deserves to be treated that way."

And yet . . . so many are. Greg, a 30-year-old municipal worker in Louisville, Kentucky, tells me that his rejections had piled up so high on the social scene that he finally gave up and started letting his friends fix him up on blind dates. Soon he started noticing a curious trend. "Whenever or wherever we arrange to meet, within a half hour or so the guy's cell phone or pager goes off, and he has to go home because of an 'emergency,' or he's getting 'called into work.' It's insulting, not just because it's an obvious 'bail out' call they've arranged with someone so they can get out of the date if they want to, but because they don't think I'm smart enough to figure it out." [Reading Greg's tale prompts me to make the confession that I used to use that "bailout call" strategy myself, back in the day when I was first getting back in the dating scene. But I had no idea people still did that. It's so 1994.]

Not every gay man I talked with came ready with a nightmare rejection story; many say that although they can remember things "not working out" with this guy, or that guy telling them "sorry you're not my type," it was simply something they took in stride, like having a bad day at work or getting caught in the rain. "Hey, shit happens," says Adam, a 32-year-old firefighter in Oklahoma. "Someone doesn't like me, that's cool. Just means it wasn't meant to be."

Michael is a 55-year-old communications worker in Boca Raton, Florida. He's also a self-described "big burly Bear type" who weighs about 350 pounds. He says he "liberated" himself from what mainstream gay culture considers "hot" a long time ago, and that upbeat attitude comes in handy. "I'm not bothered by people's rejection anymore," he tells me. "I figure it's their loss and move on. Believe me, in my experience people can be turned on by all kinds of things if they allow themselves . . . but most won't let themselves stray outside that tiny little box they've gotten so comfortable in."

Bradley is a 25-year-old actor/singer in New York City: "Being an actor means being constantly told by strangers that you do not look the way they need you to look. You get over it. As for being rejected for sexual or romantic encounters by someone... that's them, not me, and it doesn't affect me in the slightest." Or, as Charlie, a 34-year-old bartender in Fort Lauderdale, puts it, gay men "love to fall in love with their pain and drama. You get rejected, so the fuck what? Just move on, already."

Easy for you, maybe, Charlie. For others it's just not that simple. Doug, a 29-year-old receptionist in Philadelphia, says he knows what a "great catch" he'd be, if someone would just take the time to get to know his mischievous sense of humor, perhaps become acquainted with his skills "in the kitchen, and in the bedroom." Instead, Doug tells me, they all seem to focus on his thinning hair, or the fact that he's not exactly tall, dark, and handsome. "I'm not dumpy or anything, but I'm pretty short, which makes it easy to spot the fact I'm going bald. I guess it must make me look older, which in the gay community might just as well be a death sentence when it comes to a lot of guys in the bars and clubs." Doug says it's a routine he's almost getting used to: "I say hello, they might say hello back, we exchange a few words, then they find an excuse to go talk to someone younger (or younger-looking) or just someone better-looking."

That sort of face-to-face rejection has driven many men right out of those bars and clubs, and straight to their nearest computer; so many gay-themed communities have sprung up in the past decade that it's possible there are just as many if not more men meeting online now than off. But the rejection many men experience is just as common. "I've had a profile up on [a popular gay male Web site] for a few years and just about every time I get on there it's the same story: I message someone interesting, and they don't reply," says Danny, a 27-year-old hospital employee in New Mexico. "You'd think with all the horny guys out there I'd get a nibble, but it rarely happens. The few times it does, the conversation only lasts up to the point where I really get my hopes up, then he disappears."

"There's a site I go to where you can 'hook up' with someone any hour of the day or night," says Jason, a 24-year-old college student in Columbus, Ohio. "But that's only if you have no standards. If I find someone incredibly hot there, or even someone reasonably hot with an interesting profile, odds are he won't even respond because my picture and profile aren't anything particularly special. I don't really like going to bars because I'm very shy and afraid of being rejected to my face. The funny thing is, though, getting rejected anonymously ain't a whole hell of a lot better." I ask Jason if he isn't also rejecting a similar number of folks, by use of those "standards" he mentions. "Oh, sure, all the time," he admits freely. "I'm as guilty of it as anybody else."

Whether it's online, out at a club, or just somewhere out in the world, getting shot down in flames by someone they were attracted to is a pretty common phenomenon for most gay men; my *Chasing Adonis* poll shows that just over half of respondents admitted that they had experienced such rejection, based "solely on their physical appearance." And rejection isn't just a matter of the social scenes one travels in; 31 percent of the men I've polled say they've "been treated badly" because of the way they look in other environments as well, such as the workplace. And if not treated badly exactly, they're at least certain someone better-looking got a leg up on them, purely because of his looks. "Working in retail men's clothing you'd think I'd be used to the really shallow nature of things," says Jimmy, a 25-year-old in Charlotte, North Carolina. "But it never fails to piss me off when one of the good-looking new guys gets promoted over me. And my manager actually told me to my face that maybe I should think about toning up . . . she says I'd go farther in this field if I kept myself in better shape. The sad thing is, I know she's right."

"I'd given up going out to gay clubs because I was putting on weight, and I was never all that much to look at in the first place," says Larry, a 26-year-old department store clerk in Pittsburgh. "Now my co-workers have started cracking jokes about my weight, and the fact that I work a lot of overtime because I don't have a social life. Last month my doctor told me I'm starting to show signs of clinical depression. Not exactly a surprise."

Sean LeSane knows a little bit about depression and lots of other problems gay men face: he's a Washington, DC-area-based clinical social worker and psychotherapist who's worked with such men for more than eleven years. As such, he's heard the whole cavalcade of gay men's woes, whether it's dealing with coming out in a hostile straight world, or all that internalized homophobia so many of us carry around. The religious conflicts many gay men experience, along with anxiety, and various relationship issues? He's heard it all. And rejection, he tells me, is a constant theme he encounters, though just how his clients have reacted to it is as varied as those clients themselves. "For some men, rejection has no impact on their desire to find a relationship, whatever kind it may be," he explains. "They remain optimistic that they'll find the right guy . . . if they didn't meet him this time, it wasn't the right guy after all. But I've heard other guys say that there are no good men, and they become frustrated and somewhat jaded. Sometimes there is the belief that men only want sex and are not serious about building a long term intimate relationship, or that there must be something wrong with them, that they can't manage to meet the right guy, and always end up getting rejected. Men in those 'Mr. Right Now' situations may also experience anger and sadness if they are rejected in a sexual situation, especially if the initial contact was hot and intense."

Ronald La Fleur is also a DC-based clinical social worker, who's been working as a psychotherapist for 23 years; he's seen the same gamut of gay male issues as his colleague LeSane, many of them dealing with rejection. But he's also watched some gay men go through a different sort of experience, first getting rejected as a lover or boyfriend, but sort of kept on as a "friend with benefits." Although many gay men have no problem at all accepting that kind of status—in fact I can tell you from these surveys that it's the most sought-after arrangement I hear about, with most of the advantages of having a partner and fewer of the disadvantages—a smaller number seem to find that sort of relationship debasing and lacking in worth. Still, as La Fleur explains, they stick around, despite the effect on their psyches. "[They] remain in a sexual relationship with the rejecter and on the surface appear to accept that the rejecter has sex with other men," he tells me. "This arrangement often leads to feelings of resentment toward the rejecter, feelings of powerlessness by the rejected, low self-esteem and perhaps depression."

And it can get worse than that. "A small number of men—who may be bi-sexual but strongly attracted to same-sex relationships—react by dating women, rejecting that [other] part of their sexuality," says La Fleur. "These men often begin to internalize this hatred of their sexual attraction to other men, contributing to their low self-esteem, compulsive sexual acting out, followed by extreme guilt, and possible anxiety disorders and depression."

To hear La Fleur explain it, many men who experience a number of rejections over time get pretty gun-shy about putting themselves out there; he tells me they "become extremely apprehensive about pursuing relationships for a very long period of time if ever again, out of fear of repeated rejections. This [kind of] person may simply turn off this feeling of emotional love by compartmentalizing his feelings . . . others remain in an extreme state of ambivalence."

"Of course, what they'll tell you is that they don't like the bar/club scene, or the gay scene as a whole," echoes Sean LeSane. "While this may be genuine, sometimes it's a mask for not wanting to deal with having someone else say 'no, it's not going to work out.'"

For many of those social "rejects," getting turned down, rebuffed, or ignored is such an assault on their self-esteem that they virtually isolate themselves; LeSane doesn't use the term "bitter old queen," but Martin, a 60-year-old retiree in Florida, certainly comes close. "Maybe if I had come out earlier, if I had been bold enough to get out and meet men when I was younger and a little hardier when it comes to affairs of the heart, I would have learned how to navigate those shark-filled waters a little better. I might have met someone less caught up in physical appearance and more willing to see inside my soul. But it never happened, and now I would in fact say I've become very bitter. Except for the people I chat with online, I rarely cross paths with anyone gay in a social situation."

Other men who've encountered constant rejection might find themselves coping by trying to "correct" their perceived deficiencies. "Guys may engage in working out at the expense of socializing, unless it's to show off the great arms and abs . . . or they throw themselves into other activities to compensate," says LeSane. As he puts it, such men aren't really "chasing Adonis" at all, but rather "running from the pain and the fear and not knowing where to start in confronting the misconceptions they have about themselves, and the assumptions they make about whether people will accept them as they are."

"I think that describes me rather aptly," says Louis, a 45-year-old activist from Oregon who works for a number of political and environmental organizations when he's not working at his "day job" as a lawyer. "I don't want to be a 'bitter old queen' cut off from all human contact, even though I'll admit to a certain amount of bitterness that I've never been able to find a suitable partner. (I've been told I am 'too intense' or 'too driven,' which has the tendency to drive people away when they first meet me.) Now I just keep myself as busy as possible, while holding out the dwindling hope that one day, in the midst of all the chaos, I'll stumble on the right man, or he'll stumble on me."

I ask Louis if he's ever thought about getting some kind of counseling, perhaps seeking out some professional help to work through his "rejection issues." He admits that it's crossed his mind from time to time, but in the end he never makes the call. "I suppose I simply feel that whatever problems I have, I have to solve them on my own."

But LeSane tells me nothing could be further from the truth; he's encountered dozens of clients over the years who've dealt with anxiety and depression brought about by rejection, men who've come to doubt themselves in intimate situations, or men who don't feel that they are deserving of a caring and nurturing relationship. Getting them to open and talk about their experiences can be challenging, but it's often the first step toward getting them back on an even keel. "They may be able to find better ways to minimize the pain of rejection or to see how their thinking has impacted the situation," he tells me. "I do a lot of work with men on affirmations and identifying positive qualities about themselves. I do this as a way of building their ego strength so it is less hurtful when they experience someone saying no. With more ego strength—a stronger, healthy sense of self without being dismissive of others—they're better able to recover from disappointment and rejection with less damage. I also encourage guys to talk to their close friends or even someone outside of their social circle to get a different perspective that may challenge some of the beliefs they have about themselves. It can be huge ego boost to hear someone validate an aspect of yourself that you have doubted or negated."

Ron La Fleur agrees that in some extreme cases of rejection reaction, some kind of psychotherapy can help. But he seems to also believe that folks like Louis are on the right track, at least when it comes to keeping busy while waiting for that slow-footed Mr. Right to rear his pretty head. "Personal challenges tend to build esteem," he says, things such as daring one's self to run a marathon, pursuing a degree, or starting a new company. There's also volunteer work—a great place to meet people of similar interests, outside the "meet market" atmosphere found in bars or online. Most important for a fellow resolved not to give up and give in to despair, says La Fleur, is the matter of creating some "balance" in your life. "That includes a balanced diet, exercise, meditation, the practice of good sleep hygiene—going to bed and waking up at the same time every day of the week—along with abstinence (or minimal use) of potentially harmful substances . . . and establishing relationships with people that are affirming."

Everyone is going to go through a rough patch from time to time, but not all of life's experiences are bad, he says, especially if you learn from them. And navigating some of those "shark-filled waters" can be pretty rewarding, as long as you make it safely to shore.

SORRY SEEMS TO BE THE HARDEST WORD

"On the rare occasion that I go out to a bar, it's never the good looking guy that will approach me," says Rory, the 43-year-old South Carolina furniture maker we heard from earlier. "It's inevitable that the least attractive guy in the place will make a beeline right for me . . . I try to be polite and either make an excuse to extricate myself, or through body language indicate that I'm not interested. I think, 'if I actually try to enjoy this person's company, just being polite, he'll get the wrong idea and I'll actually have to hurt his feelings by rejecting him more directly.'"

Xavier, the 22-year-old college student who also hails from the Palmetto State, took a slightly different tack when he was approached by a fellow he found less than desirable. "This one time an overweight and completely unattractive older guy hit on me at a club and I just danced with him out of . . . well, sympathy, I guess. I excused myself after a couple songs and he thanked me profusely for not being a jerk."

Then there's Jonathan, 23-year-old student in Pembroke Pines, Florida. "I had a younger, chubbier guy trying to get with me at a club once . . . I managed to get away quickly by turning to an ex and giving him a huge kiss, just so the chubbier guy would think I'm taken and he'd have to go somewhere else. His image just wasn't one that I would consider associating myself with."

If gay men deal with rejection in a myriad of ways, so too do they have multiple strategies for letting the other guy know they're just not interested, letting him down easy, or simply avoiding the situation altogether. Some strive to be polite, to maintain the highest standards of decorum even if they find themselves less than interested in the guy making the advance. "I have a tremendous sense of social protocol and I always like to practice 'good manners,'" says Peter, the 43-year-old Kansan working in DC that we heard from in Chapter 4. "Therefore, I bend over backwards to 'reject' someone in a respectful fashion. There is never a reason to be rude or mean to someone who is attracted to me. I also believe in being direct; I do what I have to do to allow the guy to leave with his dignity, and me with mine. I could have been a diplomat." Darren—he doesn't give me his age—is an e-commerce worker in Lindenhurst, New Jersey, who tells me he lets the other guy know he's not interested in a "very gentle or subtle" way. "For the more forceful guys, I usually tell them that they are 'not my type.' I rarely have to be mean to get my point across. I don't like to hurt anyone's feelings."

"If someone flirts with me, I flirt back and enjoy it," says Greg, a 26-year-old actor in New Carrollton, Maryland. "I'm really just a whore at heart . . . if someone kisses me or grabs me, I'm thrilled. I've been at clubs and some guy has come up to me and wanted to kiss me, and I always do it. Why not share the joy? That's what it's all about." Greg tells me that "joy" usually stays in the club, however, as he rarely "hooks up" with anyone from a "safety" standpoint. But the other guy's feelings are always a principal concern. "When I have rejected someone, I say something like 'I really like talking to you, or I'd like to be friends, but I don't want to take it any further.' I never say, 'You're not my type.' I don't know . . . I just feel shitty doing that. Gay men have enough neurotic bullshit going on without me adding to it."

Other men aren't so kind or thoughtful. "I believe I have a certain reputation to live up to, based on all the time and effort I've put into working hard, and working out, and trying to have the best of everything," says Keenan, a 31-year-old broker in Chicago. "That means I'm looking for a guy with a great body, and a great face. People should know when they approach me that I'm not going to settle for anything less . . . yeah, I've been rude to people when they don't measure up, but it's usually just the fat guys or old guys who really should know better than to open their mouths and try to talk to me."

"I get pretty pissed off when some ugly dude gives me 'the look' in a bar or the gym, or if he sends me his picture online after he's seen me," says Brett, a 30-year-old machine shop worker in Detroit. "I'd describe myself as a pretty rugged, pretty handsome guy, very physical, great body, etc . . . when some fat disgusting pig, or some old hairy monster, tries to hit on me, it's like he's saying we're on the same level, and we are so totally not. I'm not afraid to let him know it." [Author's observation: We need to get these last two fitted for Joel Perry's T-shirts, and pronto.]

If getting the old heave-ho is a relatively common experience for gay men, even more common is the experience of doing the heavy lifting yourself and merrily—or not so merrily—chucking that other guy over the side. My polling shows that about two-thirds of gay men—65 percent in fact—have rejected someone else's advances, based on his physical appearance alone. As we've seen from just the handful of stories above, gay men take very different approaches to the effort; it also has vastly differing effects on gay men's psyches.

"Some people have very little difficulty rejecting others," says Ronald La Fleur. "These individuals have a very clear idea of the kind of man they are looking for, and may even feel offended if approached by a lesser attractive man. Whom they are able to attract—or pull—attributes to their status in the gay community, their level of 'fierceness.' Others anguish over having to reject someone; they procrastinate by sending the 'soon to be rejected' very mixed messages. These individuals may offer numerous excuses for not engaging and may manipulate the other man into ending the relationship by being emotionally unavailable and uncommitted. Then there is the one that we so affectionately refer to as 'Houdini.' He simply disappears from the radar screen without any dialogue."

"I had a guy pull the 'disappearing act' on me not long ago," recalls Lee, a 29-year-old computer software specialist in Seattle. "His name was Mike, and we seemed to be hitting it off after the first time we met at a club and our first date a few days later. I was pretty hot for him, and he said he found me attractive as well, but we didn't 'hook up' because both of us agreed that dating shouldn't necessarily involve sex right away. We made plans to get together again, but he never called to confirm, and he didn't return my calls or emails. I feel dumb now that we didn't hook up, at least I might have gotten a good lay for all my troubles."

"Having been on both sides of the fence, I can say that it's not easy to do the rejecting," offers Sean LeSane. "The thing that is hard to convey sometimes is that it's not a matter of saying 'you're a bad person,' it's more that there just isn't a connection. Now, having played Mr. Nice Guy, some guys are very upfront and believe that being honest about what is/is not going to happen is the best approach. At the very least, there is the potential to build a friendship. The bottom line is, I think that most guys will respect the honesty and directness, even if they want to throw their drink on you before you leave. It saves time and minimizes the guessing and anxiety on both sides."

SWAN STORIES

"Being fat made me appreciate life in a different way," says Mike, the 20 year old theatre student from New Jersey we heard from back in Chapter 2. (He loves the "couch potato" boys with "amazing asses.") He tells me he was born a "little large," which became "extremely obese" by the time he was ten and lasted through high school. Dealing with his weight has been an epic battle, but right now it's one he's winning; he's lost 90 pounds in the past year, putting him back in medium-size clothes for the first time in more than a decade. "Numerous times I've had guys tell me I'm 'too ugly' to be their friend, and when I lost weight I was suddenly eligible for friendship," he tells me. "I mean, when you go around and you know other guys just won't talk to you because you're over a size 36, but you lose weight and suddenly they're all over you . . . you realize what kind of people are pathetic, shallow, lonely little jokes, and what kind of guys are worthwhile."

Mike's story calls to mind those of several men, who explained how they encountered rejection for years, and convinced that their physical appearance was the cause, took whatever steps necessary to "correct their deficiencies"; some, like Mike, who were fat lost weight, while others who thought themselves too thin and spindly bulked up and gave themselves new physiques. Some younger men with bad acne or other skin conditions took medical steps to clear up their problems; other men who were balding had hair restoration, and still others had full-fledged plastic surgery to reshape their noses, or their entire faces. Yet instead of feeling joy that they weren't rejected at face value any longer, they've come to doubt the value of the attention they had sought in the first place.

Al—he doesn't give his age—is an interior designer living in Calgary, Alberta. He started life out tall and thin, put on some weight in college, and got even heavier while he was married to a woman. Growing ever more uncomfortable with his looks, he turned things around at 30, joined a gym, and started shaping up—he's also had some electrolysis and laser hair removal—and he's at the point now where he tells me he feels "pretty good" about himself. "Having been on the heavy side, I know that since I take better care of myself, I get more looks," he explains. "And I get more people approaching me.... so now I often find myself wondering, 'Would you talk to me if I was 40 pounds heavier?'"

Of course, plenty of men who gave themselves a makeover of sorts are happy about their newfound self-image, and the new attention they garner. "Maybe I should be a lot more wary about men now, than I was before I made the big change," says Mark, a 43-year-old doctor in Manhattan who tells me how he embarked on a strict diet and fitness regimen, after having 20 pounds of fat whisked away courtesy of liposuction. "It's utterly remarkable how people who ignored me for years out on Fire Island or Provincetown are doing double-takes. There's a part of me that says 'how shallow,' or 'fuck off, you didn't want me then, why should I want you now?' but the reality is I love the attention I get. It's one reason I made the change, so it doesn't make a hell of a lot of sense to get all pissed off that it actually worked, now does it?"

But other men, though equally happy, are wary. "I'm not sorry that I look better, not at all," says Jonathan, a 45-year-old computer tech in Ontario who bought himself a nose job as a present on his fortieth birthday. "I had a really ugly nose, misshapen and malformed, and frankly it made me look hideous. Once I had the surgery I was shocked... to be honest, I looked rather handsome for the first time in my life, and I wouldn't trade that feeling I have when I look in the mirror every morning for anything. But I seriously doubt the intentions of people who used to know me, and didn't have the time of day for me, and now they want to ask me out for dinner."

I know exactly how those guys feel, having experienced a bit of all that myself. My trouble growing up wasn't a huge schnoz like Jon, or any extra weight like Mike or Al. Far from it, in fact; at 18 I was skinny as a rail—I used to say I was built like a "pencil with ribs"—and I had that awful, bushy, unkempt 1970s hair, like Beethoven after a real bad night. I was also very, very nearsighted, and from the age of ten I had to wear these thick eyeglasses just to make my way around.

But worst of all, I had acne. Face, neck, chest, back, even the occasional zit on my dick—how wrong is that?—where there was skin, there were pimples. I was called all the usual names—"pizza face" is the one I remember best—and for the life of me I don't know how it never came to affect my inner self-esteem. Actually, I do know. I was already such a nerd and a basic outsider that having the zits, glasses, and skinny body just seemed to be part of the package; as a bookworm and would-be writer—want to see my handwritten, 300-page science fiction novels some time?—most social interactions, where I might face rejection from the popular kids, just weren't part of my reality.

Then came Billy. I've spoken of him briefly before, both in *Sissyphobia* and *Reeling in the Years;* if you've read those books—and God bless you if you have—you'll hopefully forgive the repetition: he was my next-door neighbor, and my straight best friend, two years my junior. And yet when I saw him for the first time in the apartment building corridor I thought he was much older, so tall and well built he was a literal genetic freak, not yet even 16, whose muscles were preternaturally formed so that they seemed ready to burst out from under his smooth, taut skin.

Unlike many of the men I've talked with who tell me how the images of their first or most devastating crushes live only in their memories, I actually do have a picture of young Billy from that initial summer of our friendship; he's frozen forever in time, standing in his low-riding Speedo boxer trunks beside the apartment pool where he worked as—of course—the lifeguard. I still take it out and look at it from time to time, marveling at that fantastic body, the V-shaped torso, the ripped abs. And his face . . . simply breathtaking. If you've ever seen the *Smallville* series on the WB, and noted the beauty of the young actor Tom Welling who plays the teenage Clark Kent, you've seen Billy's virtual twin, 30 years later; the resemblance is remarkable. I became absolutely and completely smitten.

And again, unlike so many gay men interviewed for this book, I had the chance to fully enjoy that smitten-ness; for reasons I still cannot fathom, Billy took a real liking to the skinny, pimply faced nerd I was at the time. He was among the most popular kids in his class and a star on the football and wrestling teams besides; we moved in very different worlds away from the apartments. But on nights and weekends we'd take long walks together—people actually did that back then—and do battle in chess game after chess game; we'd watch TV, play music together—me on piano, him on sax—and have ridiculously long talks deep into the night.

How our friendship proceeded from that point is something you're going to have to stick around for later on—you may just find it worth the wait—the point I'm getting at here is the effect that the constant exposure to his perfect physique had on me. Little by little, almost beyond my notice, I started not wanting to look like I did anymore. And just as gradually, I started taking steps to make it happen; first it was long runs around the hilly neighborhood where we lived, then it was buying a book on basic weight training, followed by a month or so of begging Pop to buy me some weights by which I could apply my newfound knowledge.

My first weight bench? It was a real bench, stolen from the patio picnic table outside. (Functional, but murder on the back.) The first dumbbells and barbells? Those primitive concrete-covered-with-plastic kind, laughably light by my current standards, but sufficient for my needs way back then. I spent a year with those things, sweating and grunting and stuffing myself with food, and gained ten solid pounds. (That may not sound like too much, but on my spindly body it was quite dramatic.) About the same time I started going out to my first gay bars, and although I got the attention that almost any young guy is going to command by virtue of his age—the chicken hawks just loved me—I wasn't getting quite the amount of desired attention from the boys that I happened to find hot.

Then a number of rather fortunate events started to fall into place, all in the space of several months. First the acne disappeared; a doctor finally prescribed an antibiotic—tetracycline—and the pimples were gone within a few months, leaving no scars behind at all. Then I started working at my first real job—and bringing home some decent money—and as soon as I could make it happen those Elton John-sized specs I had to wear were history, replaced by soft contact lenses. And I joined a real gym for the first time in my life, relegating those old plastic weights of mine to new careers as doorstops and paper weights. Within a year I weighed better than 160 pounds; people who had known me in high school would literally walk right by me, without any idea who I was; but more important to me at the time, suddenly the hot boys at the bar who wouldn't talk to me before were now virtually clamoring for my company. It was like coming out all over again, but this time with a new face and body.

Had I been a little older I might have had the same reaction as Mike or Al or Jonathan; instead, like our surgeon Mark, I mostly reveled in the attention I was getting. Like the night I found myself driving back to my apartment with a beautiful young man I'd recognized as an old classmate from high school when I spotted him in the bar earlier that evening. He wasn't one of those guys that had ever picked on the skinny, younger me, that would have been too perfect; no, he'd simply never acknowledged my existence sitting two rows behind him in class. And I didn't exactly have a crush on him—my emotions were far too tied up in Billy at the time—but he was still a wicked hottie then, and even hotter looking three years later. I had never for one moment suspected he might be gay; now after a 20-minute chat in the bar he just couldn't wait to get back to my place.

Later when we were lying there in bed he looked at me a little strangely, like I suddenly looked familiar to him. I toyed with him for a bit, then finally clued him in; at first he couldn't believe I could possibly be the same guy—apparently he had at least noticed me—then, rather touchingly, he looked like he felt real pangs of guilt for having never even said hello. I told him not to worry about it in the slightest; in all honesty, considering what I had looked like then—the zits, the glasses, the bad hair and skinny body—I couldn't say that I would have behaved any differently in his shoes.

It's too bad that kids like me—and I talked to so many of them for this book—didn't have someone like Chad for a high school classmate; these days he's a 23-year-old fashion designer and artist in New York City, who describes himself as someone who's always been an absolute "people person" who could "hold a conversation with a brick wall" if he had to. He tells me he's never "rejected anyone for any reason," and has always been cordial and polite to anyone who wanted to approach him and say hello. He tells me a pretty compelling story by way of explanation.

"In high school, I was the counselor aide in charge of new students," he explains. Part of that job was to give all the students the typical tour and introduce them to teachers. "One of the girls in my first tour was by no means anyone's idea of beautiful. She was pale, had bad teeth, and her hair was knotted and tangled and the like. When she didn't show up to her Friday morning classes, it was my duty to call home and check if things were okay. There was no answer so I called her parents at work, and they said they would go home and check things out. That evening I got a call from her parents . . . she'd committed suicide. They told me she'd left behind a note that said 'To Mom and Dad: Your ugly duckling can now be a swan, I only wish you could have seen me this way.'"

But that wasn't all, Chad says. The note went on. "'To Chad: You will never know what your simple smile and friendly hellos meant to this ugly duckling swimming in a pond of swans. I give you my life Chad, to pass onto the next ugly duckling in line that needs someone, just one person to make them feel like a swan, the way you did for me.' Now you can see why I don't base my life by physical appearance; all it takes sometimes is just that little acknowledgement to make a difference to someone."

Other men don't need anything as dramatic as a troubled girl's suicide, or something as random as a hook up with someone they used to know back in high school, to make them aware of how they might once have treated someone badly. Bill, a 39-year-old administrator at a DC-based nonprofit agency, shares this story: "In college there was a really nice guy with a terrible over-bite," he recalls now. "I avoided getting involved physically because I was really turned off by how he looked. He went and had his jaw broken and wired shut." You can guess what happened next: "When he healed, he was rather attractive and I felt so bad about avoiding him when he was ugly, that I couldn't bring myself to flirt with him once he was beautiful. My loss, but I wonder how he felt, or if he even had an inkling about my avoidance."

Rich, a 34-year-old investment banker in DC, has a lot more than an inkling; his weight has been up and down for years, and it's only in the past several months that he's gotten a handle on, well, his handles. "I belong to a local nudist group and yes, sometimes I've felt rejection because of how heavy I was at the time." Getting back to the gym and doing his cardio training has once again improved his all-over muscle tone, especially in areas below his waist, and he's resolving to stay in shape. And as far as men who suddenly find him attractive again? "Now I just say 'fuck you and the horse you rode in on.' I've always been happy being me and that's all that matters . . . but now guys are rolling down their car windows and whistling at me when I'm in my running shorts. (My legs are truly one of my best assets and I take pride in how they look!) I've discovered that some people who weren't as overtly friendly in the past are now making a point of saying hello to me. Eat your hearts out, girls!"

DON'T LET ME GET ME

I saw him for the first time when I walked down 17th Street on the eastern edges of DC's Dupont Circle neighborhood, about eight years ago as I write this; he was standing just inside the doorway of a Universal Gear store—or Universal Queer, if you like—and for a moment I thought he was just an incredibly lifelike and beautiful mannequin. Then he smiled at someone inside the store, and I did a double take, nearly walking directly into the telephone that sits on the corner of Q. That's a real boy, I said to myself, and spun around and headed back for the Gear.

Since he still lives in the area I'm not going to give you his real name; much of what you're about to learn about him are most likely facts he might not wish to share with the world, at least not with his name attached. But since his story still resonates in my head all these years later, and fits perfectly within the framework of the topic we're going to delve into, I'm going to go ahead and spill that story anyway. We'll call him Matt—he was all of 22 on that day we met—and it turned out he'd been hired to do precisely what he'd just accomplished with yours truly, i.e., snag the occasional passerby with that pretty mug of his and induce them to come into the shop, perhaps to drop some cash or credit on hideously overpriced and often dubious clothing and stylish accoutrements.

Funny thing about Matt, though . . . he didn't seem to think he was very pretty at all, at least not to the degree that I found him attractive. (For the record, he was about six feet tall, with close-cropped dark brown hair with bright blue eyes, and possessed of an extremely sexy, muscular build; he was also terribly sweet and charming.) Over several dinner and movie dates—including one very memorable evening where we sat out along the street and talked until dawn broke over Massachusetts Avenue—I slowly but surely found out why.

He'd grown up in a small rural town about six hours south of DC—he was only beginning to lose his country accent when we met—and like so many young guys out there in the sticks he had had no way to express the same-sex longings we all feel as young teens . . . that is, until a certain fellow came into his life. (We're going to call this guy Jim Bob, because, well, why not?) Jim Bob was a few years older, and the way Matt told the tale in retrospect, not particularly attractive. But he what he lacked in looks he more than made up for in craftiness and a well-honed ability to manipulate; thus, he immediately spotted Matt for the extremely beautiful, but terribly naive and vulnerable youngster he was at the time. So Jim Bob took Matt under his evil wing, and for a time Matt was happy just to have the companionship, and a mentor. But only for a time.

Most likely sensing Matt would soon sprout wings of his own and fly that mighty small coop of a town, Jim Bob started to convince him that, far from being the beautiful young man he was growing into, Matt was in fact actually quite unattractive, not very smart, and totally unlikely to make it on his own, without Jim Bob's constant help and guidance, of course. There was still a lot of sadness on his face as Matt explained how he'd bought into Jim Bob's bullshit, then endured a few years of emotional—and occasionally physical—abuse at his hands.

But fortunately for Matt, Jim Bob's eyes finally wandered elsewhere. One day he abruptly told Matt that he was moving out of the small apartment they shared. And just how did he tell him? Seems good ol' Jim Bob left a note tacked to a closet door, which Matt found waiting for him when he came home one Friday night; besides informing Matt that he was gone, Jim Bob also let slip that Matt would have to be out of the place himself in a few days, since the rent was due, and Jim Bob wasn't about to pay it.

That started a chain of events that landed Matt in DC, where, despite Jim Bob's assertions to the contrary, he did learn to make it on his own. But those scars the bastard left took a long time to heal; in fact, the wounds were still so fresh when we met that Matt's self-esteem was far too battered for us to have a real chance at any kind of relationship. (He didn't have a lot of self-confidence yet, and he had too many residual issues to work through that I just didn't know how to help him with.) We parted on friendly enough terms, and the last I heard of him, he had a partner of some years standing. It looks like things finally landed right for him, and I'm happy.

As for Jim Bob, I don't know what happened to him, but if there's a hell I hope there's a reservation waiting in his name: Major Asshole, party of one.

What's all this have to do with rejection, you ask? It's actually not a side trip or a tangent at all. I found more than a few stories like Matt's among the men I surveyed and interviewed—and a few among men I happen to know personally, like Matt—stories that illustrate what might be the cruelest kind of rejection any of us can face: those times when we come to reject ourselves, either through the influence of someone else or through other circumstances which convince us that we're just not very worthy of human contact. And while it's tragic that anyone ever comes to such a point in his life, it just seems—to me at least—even more sad when the guy involved does have a lot to offer and, like Matt, cannot see the true face that's looking back at him in the mirror.

That old science fiction show *The Twilight Zone* played around with the concept; in the episode "Eye of the Beholder" we meet a young woman whose face is wrapped in bandages; she's been told how hideous-looking she is for all her life, and now she's had surgery to correct her "defects." When the nurses and doctors remove those bandages, we viewers see a radiant beauty, but she only looks in the mirror and screams her miserable disappointment; that's when the camera pulls back to show her doctors and nurses to be strange beings with piglike faces. On her world, such a "beauty" is anything but.

I can easily see Matt in the role of the "beauty," here—and even more easily I can see Jim Bob as a pig-faced freak—and you don't have to travel to a distant planet, or even out to a rural area, to find the same sort of stuff going on. Doug is a 28-year-old health care worker in St. Petersburg, Florida. He tells me now his friends, co-workers, and even random people he meets often remark about what a good-looking guy he is. Half-Latino and half-Irish, he tells me he got "the best combination of both," and that "tall dark and handsome" are the words that other people have used to describe him to someone else.

Yet Doug is only now coming to see that in himself; throughout his entire upbringing he was made to feel ugly and worthless. "It was my family," he explains. "I was your stereotypical 'sissy boy' when I was younger, wanted to play with dolls and not toy soldiers, definitely wasn't the average rough-and-tumble kid like my bothers and cousins. They made me feel like I was a freak, and to a smaller extent, so did my parents. My dad was always saying 'why can't you just be normal?' and I knew what he meant . . . he was already sensing I might be gay when I was barely into my teens, probably before I did."

Doug tells me that being gay in his "rabidly Catholic" family was just about the worst thing possible; he was made to feel so miserable that he ran away from home at 16, stayed away for a year "basically living on the streets," before returning to an uneasy peace with his folks that lasted until he moved out for good at 19.

Doug says that when he looks back now at pictures of himself from that time period he can't believe he felt so horrible and useless. "I see a sweet-faced little boy, smiling for the camera," he says, adding that he eventually started seeing a therapist who helped him begin to resolve a lot of his anger and self-esteem problems. "It was really hard for me to ever have a decent relationship with someone, because I could still hear my brothers and dad talking in my head about what a 'sissy fag' I was," he says. "I'm a lot better than I was, but I still have a ways to go."

Psychotherapist Sean LeSane says that, unfortunately, stories like Doug's and that of my friend Matt are quite common among gay men. "Many guys grew up experiencing rejection from family and peers, and sometimes it had very little to do with being gay," he explains. "For some men, home was abusive and they found ways to cope; some rebel and fight against it while others internalize it and struggle later in life. For gay men specifically, there may be rejection because of their sexuality, whether it was known or just perceived. Couple that with being told that you are worthless, or that you are not good enough, and even the most gorgeous man may have difficulty . . . growing up hearing that being gay is wrong and that you're not equal to your straight counterparts makes it difficult to believe that you're worthy as an adult."

"My parents never abused me as such, but I'd have to say they were pretty distant," says Steven, a 29-year-old computer software store manager in Youngstown, Ohio. "I was their only kid—I came late when they were both in their 40's—I just don't think they ever knew what to do with me." Steven says that although he was a "pretty popular" kid at school, his popularity level sank to zero once he got home. "The older I got the more it seemed like they didn't want me to be around . . . I saw how the other kids' parents went places and did things together, but mine were too busy and didn't want to be bothered. Without sinking into 'psychobabble,' they didn't give me the 'validation' I wanted and needed, and it made me feel like I wasn't good enough." Steven says it was only after getting out and going to college out of state, where he made "dozens" of new friends—and had a few boyfriends—that he realized the problem wasn't him at all, but his absent parents. "I'm happy I turned out okay, because I realize talking to other people that it could easily have been much worse. But I hate going home. The second I get there I find myself feeling kind of ugly and gross again. Isn't that odd?"

Of course, it doesn't necessarily require any kind of outright abuse or absent parenting to fuck up your self-esteem; some guys are just drawn that way, even if the rest of the picture is pretty stunning. Take my friend Cody, for example, a 20-year-old marketing student at Kutztown University in Pennsylvania. When I met him at a club in DC a year and a half ago I was stunned he'd bother to speak with me; tall, slim, and blessed with the most angelic face you can imagine, it seemed a slam dunk he could just about have his pick of anyone in that crowd. (Not that there's anything wrong with me, you understand, I'm just old enough to be his . . . err . . . older brother.)

Anyway, getting to know him over all the time between then and now it's become pretty clear there's always something just a little amiss in Codyville. It's not that he doesn't realize on some level how attractive he is; the boy has as many pictures of himself as you can imagine, if not more. It's just that he never seems to believe it, or believe in himself, for very long. "I never realized when it happened, it came as such a surprise," he says about realizing he'd grown out of his "weird and awkward" stage to become the total babe he is now. "As I got older more and more people started talking about my looks. I remember this girl that I graduated with said 'Oh my God, you got so hot since high school,' then it was just random people at clubs and in person that would just say things like 'You're really attractive, have you ever thought about modeling?' My favorite times were when guys would tell me I was 'beautiful' because that meant more than any of the other compliments in the world. I guess it just started sinking in that I wasn't just 'average.'"

But, as Cody tells me, he's never really grown very "comfortable" with himself. "I figure if I was so damn attractive then I would have somebody. Don't get me wrong, I know I am 'above average,' but I seriously don't think I am anything special. I am just like everyone else except my face just might be a little bit more attractive, not any 'better' than anyone else, maybe just 'better-looking.' When it all comes down to it I am pretty insecure, I never think I am good enough for the person I am dating."

That doesn't mean he hasn't been a beneficiary of whatever magical combination of genes it was that gave him such a pretty face. "I have never once been turned down for any job interviews, and most of the time I can always get what I want," he tells me, which has its positive and negative aspects. "Take for instance my first internship . . . when I was interviewed I was going against a bunch of people that were incredibly smart. Not that I am not intelligent, but I didn't compare to these people in the 'smarts' department at all. When they made the decision I was one of three that got hired. Later on while working there, I asked one of the ladies who interviewed me why I got the position. She said 'Honey you can thank your mother that you had the looks, because your looks are just what we wanted at our front desk.' It really hurt my feelings in a way. I was taken aback, and felt like I didn't belong there, because the other people were so qualified. I don't know it just bothered me for a little while, but I'm over it now."

Cody's story could almost be substituted word for word for a tale told to me by Dante, who's now a 31-year-old officer manager in Atlanta. "I was young, I was pretty, and I used it to my advantage whenever and wherever possible," he tells me. "The jobs I got, the men I dated, even getting out of traffic tickets when I'd play 'cute but stupid' with the cops. It seemed like all I had to do was smile, or sometimes look crushed like I was about to cry, and people would just melt for me, and give me whatever I wanted."

But Dante tells me he came to realize what tenuous footing he was on. "After awhile it starts to eat at you. You begin to feel like you don't deserve what you have—that job, or that guy—because you 'only' got them because you were 'beautiful.' Other people start to resent you, whisper things behind your back, you really start to doubt yourself." Dante says it was only with the passage of years—along with the passage of his lean tight body and a good percentage of his hair—that he started to believe more in himself. "I would never tell you I was ever sorry that I was a good-looking kid. I'm not. But now I'm balding, a bit heavier, and no one seems to think I got where I am today on looks alone. It might be easier to find a partner if I was still 'pretty,' but you can't have everything."

Lots of the men interviewed for this book think that "everything" is exactly what Cody and the younger Dante have—or had—and wish they would stop all their whining. "I've heard all those stories about hot guys who end up going home all alone because other guys were too 'intimidated' by their looks, and wouldn't walk over and start a conversation," says Martin, a 40-year-old banker in Milwaukee. "Let me tell you about those guys. They're usually snobby and spoiled. We may not walk over and say hello, but it's not because we're afraid to, we just don't want to get your attitude thrown in our faces." Josh, a 19-year-old student in Texas, says he never sees any "pretty" guy out at a club or bar who isn't surrounded by a half dozen other pretty boys. "They travel in packs like dogs, and that's just how they treat the not-so-pretty guys like me," he tells me. "When I hear them talking about 'woe is me, it hurts to be this hot,' I just wanna smack them. They should be more thankful, and they should try walking in my shoes, I don't get everything handed to me like they do."

When he hears that statement, Cody fairly bristles with anger. "My looks make it so much harder in the gay world," he tells me. "First of all, people do say really nice things, and do treat me with a lot of initial respect, but then it usually goes downhill. Let me tell you a little something about the 'attractive guy equals slut' misconception. I cannot tell you how many times I have been called a slut for no apparent reason. Usually it happens when I decline someone's offer to dance, hook up, or join them for a party after the club or something . . . that's when call me a slut and say things like 'you're not that attractive anyways,' which sends my insecurities sky high and I have to start all over with the whole 'I am not a bad-looking person' complex. I just think it's really hard to be nice and attractive at the same time . . . I know I don't have the best personality in the world, but I try to be the best person I can be. People need to realize that life is too short to worry about looks all the time. Some days I just want to wake up and go to class in sweatpants and have fuzzy morning hair, but I know I can't just stop trying to dress well, doing my hair, and doing all the junk that makes me think I'm attractive. I wonder how people would treat me, or if it would be any different at all."

NEVER GONNA GIVE YOU UP

"I dated this one guy (his name was Ed) for a week, maybe ten days, and it wasn't going anywhere," says Grant, a 22-year-old who just graduated from a small college in Indiana. "Maybe it's because he was a little older, and seemed like he was inflexible about some things . . . or maybe it's because we just didn't click, or that I didn't find him all that attractive in the end, it's hard to say. Anyway, I told him in the nicest possible way that I didn't see us going anywhere."

Grant says Ed's reaction took him totally by surprise. "It wasn't that he got angry, I was kind of expecting that. It was this . . . rage . . . that's all I can call it. You know how some people out driving will just go ballistic, go from calm to crazy in 10 seconds? That's how Ed was. Luckily we were in public, and I had a friend to come pick me up right in front of the restaurant. There was something about the way he stormed off and left me there that scared me."

If this was a Lifetime movie, here's where the creepy music would start; it turns out Grant had every reason to be scared. "First there were phone calls, even though I asked him to please stop calling me. (I ended up getting my number changed.) Then there were flowers, with notes telling me he was sorry and why couldn't we give it 'another chance.' That really pissed me off he wasn't getting a clue. Then it was other notes, like the one he left in my locker at the gym while I was at swim practice, or on my car on campus, and later when I was out at a mall or seeing a movie."

What kind of notes were they? "He was never threatening, or telling me shit like he couldn't live without me, but damn . . . we only had a few dates, and now he wouldn't leave me alone! It got so I couldn't go anywhere by myself, I was getting so scared, because he was obviously watching me."

Grant tells me that besides whatever obsessive tendencies the notes betrayed—which was bad enough all by itself—they also made his life very complicated. "I wasn't out then to all that many people, and it was really hard to explain why a guy might be following me around." But finally Grant had had enough, and he called the cops. "They were surprisingly helpful and understanding . . . they told me they'd take care of it, and I suppose they did, because I never heard from him again, and now I'm living in another state. But I still find myself getting a little creeped out sometimes at night when I'm walking to my car, like I half-expect to find another note . . . or worse, I'll find him waiting for me."

When you chase your heart's desire, sometimes it's not all that easy to give up just because you got shot down the first time. Literature is filled with stories of men who pursued women—and occasionally, other men—even after being told to get lost, wooing them with romantic songs or letters until their fair intended finally gave in and everyone lived happily ever after. Indeed, lots of men shared such stories with me about their own lives.

Paul, a 25-year-old officer worker in the Cleveland area, says he met another guy at a party and ended up spending the night with him after festivities wound down. "He was everything I had always wanted in a guy, and we had almost everything in common down to the year and months we were born. Even that first night we joked about being twins separated at birth." But Paul says that right after that first night together his newfound friend didn't appear interested any longer. "He'd given me his phone number and email, but he didn't return my calls or messages, and I was ready to pack it in.

"But the more I thought about it, the more I figured he was too special to just let go . . . besides, I was curious why suddenly he wasn't interested in me after we'd had so much fun." Paul says he got in touch with the host of the party where they'd met, convinced him he wasn't a psycho, and found out where his "twin" liked to hang out. "I didn't stalk him. I just wanted to make sure he knew I was still around, and I also made sure I went with a buddy or two so it didn't look like I was only there to see him. After a few weeks of that he finally walked over one night and said hello, and we started talking again. He told me that he never hooks up with anyone like we had, and that basically, he was ashamed and feeling like a slut. So we made a 'real' date, and waited almost two months before we had sex again. He's been my boyfriend now for about year."

Some guys tell me they wrote long e-mails or letters to their "rejecters" after getting the boot; others went the classic candy/flowers/diamond jewelry route, and with a little time and persistence, wore the other guy down and managed to get back together, for at least a little while. Jon, a 43-year-old investment manager from Connecticut, tells me he persuaded a local deejay to play all his ex's favorite songs one night at the place he loves to hang out at, then to pass him the mic so he could make a rather public plea for a little more time. "Good thing for me his friends found it romantic and sweet, and they told him he should at least go talk to me. We didn't date for very long, maybe a few months more, but at least I had a chance to see him again and see if he was the right guy for me. When we parted company the second time it was much more mutual."

"I'd gone out on a few dates with a guy who was very attractive in a lot of ways, but I thought he was too much of a workaholic," says Kyle, a 29-year-old stylist in Houston. "And I explained that to him when I told him I thought we should stop seeing each other. A few weeks later it was my birthday, and some friends invited me out to dinner . . . I walked in and it was this huge surprise party they could not have afforded in a million years . . . then in walks Robert, he'd paid for it all, and wanted to know if I might allow him the chance to show me that he could always make time for me. My God, it was so romantic, like something out of a storybook."

But all too often the real-life tales of men who chased after other men who had told them to get lost—or just weren't interested—are a different kind of fairy tale altogether; frequently they sound a lot less like Cinderella and more like Grant's tale of Obsessive Ed. Barry, a 19-year-old college student in New Hampshire, says he was literally stalked by a local guy he'd met first on the Internet, then consented to meet in person at a coffee shop. "I was still 17, with a few months to go before my 18th birthday . . . he was in his mid-20's. I wasn't sure if I'd want to have sex with him before we met, but I was awful damn sure after that I didn't want to . . . we were in public and he kept pawing at me, it was disgusting. So I told him I had to go home, and when he called me later I didn't answer. He called again, I didn't answer. Then he started sending text messages, and he threatened to out me to my parents if I wouldn't go out with him again."

Though Barry was already out to his folks, he didn't want them to know he was arranging dates with random people he was meeting on the Net. "That would've grounded me for months, and they would have taken my computer away. As we all know a gay boy without his computer is a very unhappy gay boy, so I begged him not to do it . . . but I also asked him to please respect my decision not to see him again."

No dice, there. The threats in the form of e-mails and text messages kept coming, but Barry was saving them all to his computer and printing them out. "I sound like a drama queen, but if he ever did anything bad to me I wanted there to be a way they could catch him." And Barry may not have been too far off. "They found him loitering on school property, and a security guard called the cops. They showed his picture around, and I decided 'fuck it, I've had enough of this shit,' I gave them everything he sent me. They took his ass to court, and he had to agree to stay away from me and not contact me again, or else he'll go to jail for a long time."

Jeff is a 28-year-old bartender in San Francisco who tells me about the time a regular patron of his started to get the wrong idea about Jeff's affections for him. "Well basically those affections were nonexistent, but he misread what I do for everyone who's a regular, like slip them an extra drink or a shot here and there, 'forget' to charge them once in awhile, exchange a few extra words . . . he thought that was all aimed just at him. I feel sorry for guys who are lonely, that's why a lot of them are in the bar in the first place, but this guy was really out there, man. He was always asking me out, and I told him I had a boyfriend, but he kept asking anyway. Then he started giving me shit if I spent too much time, or what he thought was too much time, with another customer. I hated to do it, but one night I just asked him to leave if he was going to keep making a scene . . . you would have thought I slapped him, he was almost in tears when he left."

Cue up that creepy music again. "So I close up, lock up, and start walking home, and there he is, sitting on my front steps, crying. To think he'd followed me before and knew where I lived was bad enough . . . now he was in this bizarre emotional state, and blocking my way in." Jeff says he speed dialed his boyfriend who was sleeping upstairs, then called 9-1-1. "Maybe that sounds harsh or something, calling the cops on him, but you just never know how mentally unstable some guys can be. They took him for a ride, and they must have talked some kind of sense into him, because it's been a year and we haven't seen him around since."

According to the Stalking Resource Center on the Web site of the National Center for Victims of Crime (www.nvcv.org), few formal studies of same-sex stalking have been conducted. Statistics show that one in a dozen women, and perhaps one out of about 50 men, will be stalked by someone of the opposite sex at some point in their lives; some experts suggest that gay men might be more prone to stalk or improperly pursue another gay man than their straight counterparts.

In any case, as we've already seen, the prospect of being stalked presents certain unique problems for gay men, especially those who aren't fully out and for those who've so far remained completely closeted. As the SRC Web site explains, such victims

> fear that they will be "outed," that their homosexual orientation will be disclosed. Victims have to tell the police about their relationship with the offender; for closeted victims, such disclosure may endanger their relationships with family members, friends, landlords, coworkers, or employers. Outed [gays and lesbians] sometimes lose their jobs and homes, as well as custody of their children simply because they are gay. Abusers can also use the threat of outing the victim as a tool of manipulation and control.

Other victims, even those who are fully out, are often loathe to come forward because they don't want to shine a spotlight on one bad relationship or situation, and thus risking painting all same-sex relationships in an unhealthy or abusive light. And many gays and lesbians simply don't want to open their door to law enforcement officials, because of their long-standing belief that police and prosecutors are biased against them.

But often that's not the case in most big cities with sizeable urban areas and large gay populations. Take my hometown of DC, for example. For the past several years the Metropolitan Police Department here has been noted for its Gay & Lesbian Liaison Unit, which provides 24-hour assistance to the gay community, combining street-level law enforcement with traditional outreach and community policing techniques. I've been the beneficiary of their services a number of times, from both the active and passive perspectives; I've been rescued from hordes of overzealous street bums demanding I give them money outside a few Capitol Hill clubs, while the GLLU patrol vehicles regularly dissuade similar types from trashing my car while I'm inside those same establishments.

Sergeant Brett Parson has served with the GLLU since 2001 and currently commands the unit; as he explains it, "stalking" is a well-defined concept on the DC law books, and includes everything from physical confrontations that smell of violent intent to harassing phone calls. It's been updated and beefed up several times in the last decade and a half, and now violators face hefty fines and possible jail terms. For those who think police can choose to look the other way,

Parson tells me, in the nation's capital at least, that's just not an option. "We've investigated or assisted in many cases of same-gender domestic violence and stalking," he says. "We are required to investigate and make an arrest if we have probable cause to believe a crime has been committed, and if we identify the person responsible for the crime." And for anyone who even suspects he might have a stalker on his tail, Parson has the archetypical law enforcement officer's plainspoken and direct advice: "Report it," he says. "Tell others and ask them to be extra eyes and ears. Be vigilant, and document everything. And don't be afraid to call 9-1-1."

But if a call to the police or a judge's gavel puts an end to a stalker situation—and many cases end precisely in that manner—where does the journey start? Just what creates a stalker, and just how far will a stalker go in pursuit of his apparent obsession? Frankly there's a wide range of opinion. Some studies seem to show very little commonality in those who take the chase for Adonis to such an extreme; there are otherwise ordinary chaps who've been rejected or rebuffed, and simply refuse to give up. We call them stalkers only if they fail, and fail again, but keep trying anyway, looking for that elusive happy ending. At the other end of the spectrum we find the real scary types lurking; they're often quite mentally deranged to some degree or another, and often have potential for real violence. Their idea of a happy ending might entail some poor Adonis laid out in a box, surrounded by flowers and weeping relatives lamenting his untimely passing.

It's in between those two extremes that we find the real gray area. As Ron La Fleur suggests, some stalkers have become addicted to the idea of a relationship with their intended, an addiction every bit as powerful as alcohol or narcotics. "They may develop denial around the possibility of a relationship with the 'rejecter'," he explains. "They will use 'self-talk,' such as 'if he would just get to know me he would change his mind.' In some extreme cases the rejected may develop a pathological reaction to the fellow who spurned him . . . the rejected might become obsessed with the rejecter and feel that he'll never experience pleasure ever again, unless he has a relationship with the one who rejected him. Such a person believes that the two of them were meant to be together, and that no one else will do." La Fleur says if the rejected suitor perceives further rejection, "then threats of coercion or violence may surface."

It was relatively easy to find men who had tales of being stalked, who could relate their fear and anger at being pursued in such a way. It was much harder to find men who'd done the actual stalking, or used coercive methods to try and win back the man they wanted. But after months of trying I managed to find two guys who would open up. "Tom" is a 40-year-old Detroit resident who doesn't want me to reveal his true name, or occupation, lest anyone recognize him in the slightest; he's deeply ashamed of an episode in his not-too-distant past. "It was like a lot of the shit that goes bad in your life, it started slow, and built up," he tells me. "I met this guy, we went out a few times, and I was head-over-heels crazy in love with him in no time." This despite the fact, he explains, that he'd just come out of a five-year relationship that had ended badly, and he'd promised himself he wouldn't get hooked on anyone until he'd gotten his head on straight. "But this guy was a lot like my ex, which should have been my first warning sign . . . I should have realized from the start that he reminded me of the guy who dumped me and moved to the other side of the country." Tom says the new fellow—we'll call him "Harry"—was like a younger and "much studlier" version of his former partner. "It was like I'd met my ex when he was barely out of college, they had so many things in common, and the two of us clicked in exactly the same way." For a few weeks, Tom says he was very much in heaven. But hell was waiting on the other side.

"As a younger guy he had a lot of friends in his social circle, and I didn't want to share him," Tom tells me. "I started throwing what I can only now call tantrums, really acting like a stupid jerk, eventually telling him that if we were going to be partners, he'd have to choose." So that's exactly what Harry did—and he chose his friends, and not Tom. "That should have ended it, I should have just kicked myself in the ass for losing a good thing, and moved on." Instead, Tom tells me he chewed on his mistakes, dwelt on them, counted all the things he'd done wrong, and decided he and Harry should make another go at it, now that Tom had seen the error of his ways.

Harry, however, wasn't interested. "Told me to get lost, get a life, get out of his face," he recalls. And again, Tom says he knew that should have been another exit ramp back to Sanity Land. "But I just couldn't take no for an answer."

Got the music ready? Good, here we go. First, Tom tells me he sent the obligatory flowers and I-am-so-sorry notes; they went unthanked and unresponded to. "That pissed me off, that he wouldn't even acknowledge me," he says, now fully understanding why. He tried telephoning next, only to find that Harry's home phone and cell phone numbers had been changed. "He was really cutting me off, and I didn't like it at all," he says. Even his e-mail address no longer worked, and Tom's messages bounced back to him, unread.

That was his final chance to make a U-turn away from a very bad road, but Tom says he drove right past the sign. "I just had this constant theme running through my head all day, from the time I was taking a shower in the morning to the moments I was lying in bed at night, trying to sleep, that if we could just spend some time together like we used to, I could make him see that we were really a good match," he says. But how was he going to make that happen, if Harry refused all contact?

Enter a third party, whom I will quite rightly call "Dick." He was, even by Tom's description, a rather "low life character" that he had met online in a chat room. "I'd told him all about [Harry] and he said I needed to do anything I could to get him back and make things right. We talked a lot about it, and though I don't excuse myself one bit, a lot of what happened when I was stalking [Harry] was inspired by this guy." One night, Dick suggested that maybe he had to find a way to "get [Harry] away" from his friends, the ones Dick convinced him were probably helping to keep them apart. "The more he said shit like that, the more it seemed reasonable." One night, Tom says, Dick suggested a rather extreme course of action, and Tom was certain he had to be joking. "He said I should follow [Harry] to a club some night, and when he wasn't looking, spike his drink with something, then get him alone and get him to come back with me to my place. I thought it was a really dumb idea, and probably dangerous . . . then he said he could get me the exactly the drug I needed to make it work."

Tom didn't take Dick up on his offer, at least not right away. "I thought I should try one last time to see him, that maybe after not having seen me or heard from me in so long maybe it would be different." So Tom waited a week, then started looking for Harry in some of his favorite haunts, finally spotting him out on the town with some of his buddies. "I just wanted to say hello, how have you been . . . he saw me and took off in the other direction, and his friends stood in my way, almost screaming at me to just leave him the fuck alone."

That public embarrassment sealed it. "I decided that maybe [Dick's] idea wasn't so bad, and might be worth a try. It had been more than six months since [Harry] dumped me, and he had obviously moved on . . . for me it was like it just happened yesterday. I was thinking that if I could just be alone with him again, just talk to him, I could turn back the clock." Tom says he arranged to meet Dick during his lunch hour at a nearby mall to pick up his "dating aid"; just how and when he'd use it he'd have to figure out later. "Meeting [Dick] should really have been a wake up call . . . he was this little rat-faced guy, a lot older and creepier than I thought he would be, and he said something about how 'it had never failed him before.' I should have just stopped and asked myself what kind of guy would use something like this, and for what, and did I want to be that guy. But I was just about psycho by then."

Tom says he started following Harry again, this time paying more attention to staying out of sight. "It's not easy to hide from other gay guys in bars, because they're always looking around to see who's coming in and going out . . . I had to wait for a night when [Harry] wasn't surrounded by so many people, it would've been too easy for them to spot me." Tom tells me it took weeks, but his patience finally paid off. "This is the part that's really painful to tell you, because the poor kid was on a date, it was just him and this other guy, sitting in a dark corner off by a pool table, and none of his other friends were around." Tom says he waited until they ordered some drinks, and waited a bit longer until they both got up to use the bathroom. "I never thought they'd make it so easy . . . I just walked over, and dropped a little in each of their drinks, then went back and stood in the shadows. I hate myself for this . . . it was so exciting waiting to see if they'd get back and start drinking again, I was half expecting them to just leave at that point or leave the drinks on the table and go order new ones from the bar."

But Harry and his friend did come back, and downed their cocktails as they got to talking in their quiet little corner. "The way they were making eyes at each other and laughing . . . I was getting so pissed, it was really hard not to go over and confront them." Then, like magic, the "dating aid" Dick had given him started taking effect. "[Harry] just stopped talking and started staring straight ahead . . . his friend kind of slumped over and put his head on the table. "If I had been in my right mind I would have panicked, and realized what I had done," Tom tells me. "But I hadn't been in my right mind for quite awhile."

Tom says he walked over and sat down, and Harry looked over at him, with a "bleary-eyed expression that looked half-dead" as Tom describes it now. "He didn't look mad or upset to see me, and it would have been very easy to get him to stand up, walk him to my car, take him back to my place, and I was planning on doing just that." But fate, or rather the regulations of the local ABC board, had other ideas. "Would you believe that during all that waiting and waiting, and hiding there in the shadows, that I never heard them say 'Last call for alcohol'?" Right when I was going to stand him up and get him out of there, all the lights in the place came up, and the music died. The place was shutting down, and there was just no way to do it... at least I was still sane enough to realize that." Tom says the only thing he could do was make a fast exit, and leave the catatonic pair to their own devices. Guilt kicked in on the way home, he tells me, and he was overcome with a near-screaming panic. "I started saying 'My God, what did I do?' What if they had some reaction to the drug—I don't even know what it was—what if they died, or went into a coma, or God-knows-what?" And of course, what if someone had seen him?

"I waited for the next few weeks, calling in sick to work every other day, certain that any minute now the cops would come banging at my door," he recalls. "I considered leaving town, at least taking some kind of extended leave, maybe go visit my folks, just to get away." In the end he stayed put, and somewhat to his surprise, nothing ever happened. "I saw [Harry] and his friend a few weeks later when I was having coffee one Sunday morning. They strolled in, [Harry] looked in my direction, looked away, and acted as if I wasn't there.... he didn't show any kind of reaction to my being there at all, didn't seem to be in a hurry to leave or anything like that, so that's when I knew I had completely gotten away with it."

But even though jail didn't appear to be lurking in his immediate future, Tom tells me he realized he still had a lot of issues. "Watching them together I felt the same burning rage start up inside me again, then I had my little epiphany... I didn't want to feel that way anymore." Bright and early Monday morning Tom called in sick, except this time he didn't stay home; he made an appointment with a shrink, and continued getting help for the next several months. "I'm not completely over him, but I've really worked hard to get a better grip on the way I handle myself . . . I also know I'm not ready to have any kind of relationship with anyone, until I get a lot healthier upstairs."

Rick feels equally guilty about an episode in his past, but at least he has the callowness of youth to chalk it up to, and the desperation brought on by being dumped by a boy he'd fallen deeply in love with. At 20 years old Rick was a college kid in the Northeast, trying to get over a closeted high school jock who just didn't want to be around him anymore. Now at 37 he can look back with something close to humor at the stupid stunts he pulled, getting stuck on "a kid," and trying to win him back. "If I did anything like that these days I'd be labeled a stalker for sure, and once in a great while if I'm in a relationship that's going sour on me, all I have to do is remember what I did to poor Jim, and it snaps my head right back to where it's supposed to be."

As Rick explains it, Jim was someone that he "had no business getting involved with in the first place." They met when Ricky was out using the local high school track, running laps one night before sundown. "It was late spring or early summer, and all I was wearing was my shorts because it was really humid that day. I had a few laps to go when I saw Jim on the other side of the track, just wearing his shorts, too. I slowed up a little so he'd catch me, and I couldn't believe anyone could be so hot." Rick—he points out he was called "Ricky" back then—started up a sort of grunting conversation, and Jim sort of grunted back . . . they continued that way until Jim waved good-bye and headed off toward the parking lot. "I always think I fell in love with him that night, us running side by side like that for a mile or so . . . I came back the next night hoping he'd show up . . . and the next night . . . it was almost a week before I saw him again."

This time they did a lot more talking, Rick recalls, as they lingered there after their run until long after dark. "You know how it is in warm weather at night when you're young, everything is so alive and your hormones are flowing . . . throw in a hot guy you're really attracted to, and he's liking you too, and that's just something really powerful. Nothing like that had ever happened to me before." Rick says neither he nor Jim ever said anything "outright sexual, it was just something you could feel in the air," and that somehow they "ended up under the bleachers just going at it." And they continued "going at it" for weeks, meeting at the track, in the woods nearby, in the backseat of Rick's car, you name it. "This is all pre-Internet, and the chances of us finding each other in that town were microscopic, so I felt like maybe it was something 'meant to be.' But he never said he loved me or anything, and I was afraid to tell him how I felt . . . he'd talk about his girlfriends, and how he had sex with them, I could see he didn't think of himself as gay, so I wasn't going to push him. I just didn't want to ruin anything."

As Rick tells me, it took Jim a long time to even tell him where he lived. "It was less than a mile away from my parents' place, and I was still living at home. Really amazing, the coincidence. But he didn't want me to visit him . . . he said he didn't want to have to explain a lot of shit to his parents about who I was or how we might have met." Since Jim was still a few months shy of his eighteenth birthday, Rick thought that was probably a good idea as well, though he says it hurt that they couldn't just go grab a bite to eat or see a movie sometime. "I loved having sex with him, but I wanted us to be more than that."

One night Rick says he got restless and went for a walk. "I took the dog with me on her leash, and what do you know we just happened to go by Jim's house." Rick says he didn't know yet which room was Jim's, or if he was even home, but was curious to check out his digs anyway. Jim wouldn't have to know about it.

"It was a small house, and the lights in the living room were on. I walked around back to the backyard—they didn't have a fence or anything, there was a small woods in the back, no neighbors nearby—and I saw one window almost at ground level that was lit up. I thought it was a laundry room or something, and I kind of crept over to peek inside just for the hell of it . . . what I saw was the blinds were tilted just so that someone could see in pretty clearly, and there was a bedroom in there." Rick says he was only standing there for a few seconds, when he saw Jim walk into the room with a towel around him.

"I fucking froze, I was afraid to move because I didn't want him to see me . . . then I figured out he probably couldn't, since he was in a well-lit room and I was standing in the dark." Rick says he was about to make his exit when all of a sudden Jim's towel came off, and he got down on the bed and started jerking off. "Wasn't anything I hadn't seen (or touched) before, but it was a lot of fun to watch," Rick recalls. It was only when his almost-forgotten dog started pulling at her leash that Rick got out of there, lest Jim hear any disturbance outside.

Rick says he played "peeping Tom" a few more times, but that it "wasn't really something I had to do since we were getting together a lot." Still, he says, he did notice that Jim was using "guy porn, magazines he had hidden under his bed, and I never saw him looking at any girlie mags . . . wasn't anything I could do with that information, but it was nice to know." Rick tells me his liaisons with Jim continued through the summer, once or twice a week, until Jim's family took him off for a two-week vacation that August. "I knew when he was supposed to be back home, and I couldn't wait . . . I got nervous though when I never heard from him. He was the one who always called me, from a payphone at the drugstore around the corner some from his house. I kept waiting, but he never called."

Finally Rick says he did something he'd promised never to do; he looked up Jim's number and called his house. "He picked up the phone (I was going to hang up if anyone else answered) and I thought that was really lucky. I said 'Hey man, it's Rick.' He didn't say anything, just hung up after a few seconds. I figured maybe his Mom was around, so I tried not to be too upset. About a half-hour later he called me from the payphone . . . I was all excited for about 5 seconds, then he started yelling at me to leave him alone, don't bother him again. Hate to sound pathetic, but I cried all night, mad at myself for fucking things up . . . but mostly mad at him for being such a dick."

As Rick recalls, the next few weeks were "really agonizing, I was already back taking classes, but I couldn't concentrate on anything else, I just had such an empty feeling inside, and every night I'd just lie there in bed, praying he was going to call me. My father even asked me if I was feeling all right, that I looked sick. I lied and said I was okay, but I wasn't. It was the first time anybody had broken my heart."

It would be October of that year before Rick gave in, and "took the dog for her walk" again, as he puts it. "I crept around back like I did before, and saw his light was on . . . at least that much was the same. I walked over to the spot outside his window, waited for about 10 minutes or so, and there he came, out of the shower with his towel on, lay down on his bed, and started going at it." This time seeing him was a lot more powerful, Rick says, since he no longer had his "daily access" to Jim's body. "It was titillating and heart-breaking at the same time . . . I loved watching him get himself off, but I was still so much in love with him. I don't know if a 20-year old has the capacity to handle that kind of complicated emotion, I know I didn't." Rick says he started taking that walk a lot, several times a week, in fact. "My parents started making these little comments about where I might be going and what I was doing, but they never had a clue. I don't know if I would have stopped if they did know, I was addicted to watching him by then."

But even that dark joy started to pale after a while, and Rick became obsessed with getting Jim back. "I know I still loved him, but there was this weird little resentment I started to get, like 'what right did he have to deny me?' that kind of thing." Rick decided to do something he would never have even considered a few months before. "I wrote a note that said 'CALL ME' and taped it so he'd see it if he looked out of the window. I watched him jerk off one more time, then put it there and left." Rick says a few days went by, then Jim called.

"I let him yell and scream for a few seconds, then I told him he better shut up and listen," Rick recalls. "I'd never talked like that to him before, and he stopped talking . . . that's when I told him I wanted us back like we were, and that if he didn't agree, I could really make trouble for him. Then I hung up on him." Rick says the memories are painful now, when he thinks of all that must have started going through Jim's head. "He must have been so scared, wondering if I'd really do it. He called back a few minutes later, kind of screaming at me again, and I hung up a second time. My God, that probably really freaked him out." A half hour later, Jim called one more time. "He sounded like he'd been crying, and wanted to know if I was really going to do it, and I said 'It's up to you. Will you see me again?' He told me to come pick him up, and that was it. I'd won."

But Rick says any joy he might have felt over their reunion dissipated rather quickly over the next week or so. "We mostly did it in my car, because by now it was getting pretty cold at night," he remembers, telling me how he'd pick Jim up and drive out to relatively remote areas not likely to have cops nosing around. "He was still just as hot, and we would still make out and do everything we did before . . . but all that . . . I guess you'd call it innocence . . . all that was gone. Part of me liked the fact that he was there because I'd made it happen, that he was sort of under my control . . . but most of me didn't. The guilt I felt took away a lot of the excitement.

"So one night I told him that I was sorry I had blackmailed him, that I really cared about him a lot, but that if he wanted to stop seeing me he could, and I swore I'd keep his secret forever." Rick says Jim actually called him a few times afterward—a horny teenager is a horny teenager after all—and they occasionally got together off and on for about a year, until Jim went off to college himself. "We fell out of touch pretty quickly, and I haven't seen him for years. I really regret doing what I did to him . . . he was the first guy I loved, and for all I know he might have cared a lot for me at one time. But I can't help but think that—if he ever thinks of me at all—it's a memory of the guy who had to use extortion to get him back. Wish there was some way to make that up to him."

Chapter 6

Dream Lovers

> I have scaled these city walls . . . only to be with you
> But I still haven't found what I'm looking for.
>
> "Still Haven't Found What I'm Looking For"
> U2

"I don't know if I'm the exception or not," writes Lester to me in an e-mail. He's a 39-year-old construction worker in Tuscaloosa, Alabama. "Most of the men I know are always talking about trying to find a boyfriend, husband, partner, whatever we're supposed to call it . . . the rest seem to be bitching all the time about how unhappy they are with the man they have. My guy and me have been together for almost eight years, and he still finds a way to make me happy just about every day. He's everything I always wanted, and he says the same about me. Since you're writing a book and talking to gay men about the kind of guys they find perfect, I was just curious to ask what you've found out about gay couples like us . . . are we all that unusual?"

That's a hard one to answer, Lester. Looking back over the hundreds of life stories I've collected, it does seem the vast majority of gay men are either between relationships, not looking for one, or resigned to the fact they may never be deeply involved with a partner, however much they desire it. That's not to say there aren't thousands and thousands of gay couples out there, for surely there are; whether you trust the numbers or not—and for the record most gay people don't—U.S. Census figures from 2000 showed more than 300,000 gay male couples living together. Even if those figures are lowballed—and most gay people think they are—that seems at first glance like a lot of His-and-His matching towel sets.

But hold the phone a second. If you figure a total American population of about 300 million, and use the classic 1-in-10 formula, you get something close to 30 million folks of the gay/lez persuasion, a little less than half of them male. Mind you, most gay rights groups do a little lowballing of their own, and use more conservative yardsticks, figuring the same-sex segment at 6 or 7 percent of the overall population. (But let's be honest, no one really knows how many 'mo's there are, so I'm sticking with my nice, round ten.) However you crunch the numbers, it turns out that here in the good ol' USA we probably have anywhere from 8 to 14 million gay dudes running about. Not every couple decides to cohabitate when their relationships go long term, but I think it's safe to say that most do . . . so can it really be true that less than a tenth have decided to hook up for the ever-after?

After all, it wasn't so long ago that we couldn't get away from all those happy couples, no matter how hard we tried; the TV news was filled with their smooching and smiling mugs, once those gay marriage floodgates opened up in Massachusetts—and, for a brief shining moment, in places such as California, Oregon, and upstate New York. Though you have to admit it seemed the greatest number of couples getting hitched were lesbian lovers, the menfolk were still pretty well represented at the altar or on the courthouse steps. (The last time I was in Provincetown—where the gates remain open, as of this writing—it felt like every other minute someone had to excuse himself from the beach or the cocktail party, and run off to a good buddy's wedding.)

That's not to say you have to have the ring and multitiered cake to signify a successful pairing. "We were thinking about that whole gay marriage business," says Johnny, a 44-year-old designer in Seattle who's been living with his partner for the past ten years. "But just when the conversation started getting serious the roof kind of fell in, and it was illegal again, at least out West." Now he and his partner say they've decided they don't need any outside authority "validating" what they already know in their hearts. "We've been married in everything but name since three months after we met; we use the day we moved in together as our anniversary. Allow me to be trite and say 'we complete each other' in every meaningful way there is. But we know for lots of other gay men finding a life-long partner is like 'Mission Impossible,' so we also know how truly lucky we are."

That takes us back to Lester's question: "Are we all that unusual?" I'm going to have to say yes, and congrats to him, Johnny, and all the rest of you guys out there that have found your own personal Adonis. Clearly it's not easy, judging from all I hear—and all I've seen, with my own eyes. Because even when you do find that elusive sucker, that hot boy or smoldering man who gets you going upstairs and downstairs, sometimes you can't make him stay for very long. "It seemed like forever that I was bummed after my ex broke up with me," says Drew, a 29-year-old communications worker in Boulder, Colorado. "After three years together, to break up like that . . . I was beginning to think I'd never find anyone to love again, someone like Bob who I thought was a perfect match. Then as time went by I started to realize that once you love someone, something in you changes . . . I grew up a lot because of the whole drama, and now I feel really optimistic that I'll find someone new. But I won't be looking for anyone like Bob, and not because he wasn't perfect for me. No one can be perfect. Learning that is part of the process."

Although they may or may not represent the majority of all gay men, the greatest number of guys I've surveyed tell me they've come to believe that a long-term relationship with the same man, forever after, isn't something they believe in very much anymore. And most seem to be fine with it. "I'm sort of a rebel against the whole monogamy wave," says Brett, a 35-year-old nurse in Orange County, California. "The idea of getting married is someone else's trip, not mine. Not that I don't think we shouldn't be able to get married, I hate those conservative assholes who say we can't . . . but I never would. I always thought the best part of being gay was getting away from all those heterosexual constructs and traditions, and making our own way. If I want to see one guy, or five, or five at one time, that's what I'm going to do."

"After three boyfriends in ten years it's clear I'm just not the monogamous type," says Adam, a 31-year-old customer service rep in Champaign, Illinois. "I'm not a slut or anything, I just get bored with the same guy. What looks to be 'perfection' when we first meet gets a little old a few years later. I never cheat or sleep around behind anyone's back . . . I've always been honest. Now I'm honest with myself, and I just make a few 'friends with benefits' here and there. That's 'perfection' for me."

Jake, a 33-year-old accountant in Torrance, California, says he and his partner of six years recently embarked on a bit of an adventure, relationship-wise; I'd heard of "trios" before, but Jake's "permanent threesome" was the only such situation I found among the men I sampled. "People don't think it can work, but Gus and Barry and me make it happen," Jake says. He and Gus met Barry in a bar in Mexico on vacation, and it turned out he lived just an hour away from their digs back home. "We played around down there, and it really lit a spark in us . . . later he came to visit a few times, and after we had a real long talk about it, we told Barry he should move in." Jake admits it can be complicated: "There's always drama with couples, and when you add a third guy to the mix it can be drama times ten. But we love him in our own individual ways, he loves us the same, and as long as there's never any ganging up in a 2-against-1 way, it works for us."

Much more common are couples who have "open" relationships, but their standard operating procedures are every bit as complicated as Jake's trio. Some are like Jeff and Miguel, a "40ish" couple in South Beach; they like to hit the clubs and find the occasional willing young man to take home. "We lavish all sorts of attention on them, treat them very well," says Miguel. "We just enjoy their boyishness and energy . . . then we drop them off or get them a cab. I know some people frown on it, but I have to tell you it's really injected some excitement and 'newness' that we felt we were losing after 15 years together. But we only 'hunt' as a couple, we never do it alone."

There's really nothing new about such unconventional relationships; gay men's partnerships, by definition, have always been somewhat unconventional. But with gay marriage so much in the headlines, I am hearing more and more criticism from those who believe that the "monogamy wave" is something gay men might try harder to take a ride on. Take author Christopher Rice, for example, who penned a commentary titled "Monogamy and Me" in the March 29, 2005, issue of *The Advocate*. Rice takes such couples and trios as mentioned above to task, asserting that in the long run, few of them manage to create an arrangement that achieves anything close to loving and functional.

> The fact is, the true open relationship—with its highly progressive blend of ménage à trois and solo expeditions under strict, mutually enforced ground rules—has so many dysfunctional imitators. For instance, if your new beau is super hot and half

your age and you have reluctantly agreed to let him sleep around because you want to keep showing him off at pool parties, think hard before you call this an open relationship. Turning a blind eye is not the same as linking hands and kicking open the barn doors to let in all the other livestock. (p. 72)

Rice suggests that those who man the barricades in the fight for legal gay marriage are losing more than a little patience with other men who insist their unconventionality is the true ideal. But most guys I've talked with tell me that such views as those of Mr. Rice are, to put it bluntly, a load of crap. "Gay men seem to be very susceptible to group think, like when one couple ties the knot, a lot of others feel pressure to do the same," explains Allen, a 39-year-old city employee in Manhattan who lives with his partner. "I can tell you first hand that an open relationship can be every bit as loving, and a lot less restrictive, than any supposed marriage. My man and I are open, and it works because we do have certain rules if you like, and we follow them: Nothing ever happens in the city, or with people we know as a couple . . . that works well since we both have jobs that involve lots of travel. The sex has to be safe always, there's no comparing or boasting, and our relationship always comes first. I have some straight friends, and even some gay friends, who say we're really not a couple if we allow each other to stray. I tell them that's the reason we're still together after almost ten years, because we took jealousy and possessiveness off the table a long time ago."

Those are just a handful of the stories and situations culled from my surveys and interviews; hell, one could write an entire book on the vast variety of gay male couplings alone, and maybe one day I will. But this book is about that "search" for a certain kind of flawlessness that many gay men have embarked upon, and as I pore over their tales I find that lots of them just can't seem to find the kind of "perfection" in the real world that they desire most, that "unusual" situation that Lester asked me about. Some are involved in long-term relationships such as those described above, settled in with a partner they find loving and comforting, but still they find themselves a little restless for a little spice; others have those more open relationships, based in part on that very sort of restlessness, and a yearning for "variety."

Still others are single, dating around in hopes that their Adonis might be waiting around the next bend in the road; lots of them have those "friends with benefits" that Adam spoke about to tide them over; one guy I know compares it to "settling for fast food, until the real meal comes along." A considerable number of men I've gotten with admit they're in the midst of a "long dry season," and haven't had company in their beds for quite a while. Many of them were like the guys we talked about in Chapter 5; they've grown a bit gun shy based on bad experiences with rejection. And some simply have such an idealized view of what a man can or should be that they don't believe they can ever be satisfied by an average Joe. Yet pretty much all of these men—partnered or single, looking around or just riding solo—tell me they still have healthy and strong libidos that require, shall we say, a certain amount of satisfaction from time to time, and they're perfectly prepared to indulge their fantasies with a dream lover until that "real meal" gets delivered.

So where do they find their fantasy man? It turns out he's just about all over the place: he might be a dancer performing up on a stage at some go-go bar, looking for a little something to get stuffed in his sock or G-string in exchange for an extra-erotic gyration or two—and in some clubs, more than just a gyration—or maybe he exists only in the frames of a video/DVD or the pixels on a computer monitor, an actor paid to play a role, or a less-well-compensated but slightly more "real" fellow, acting out some suggested fantasies on a webcam from his dorm room a thousand miles away.

Perhaps he's a guy encountered on the Internet, not a fantasy exactly, but someone so geographically remote that he might just as well be a product of the imagination, since he exists solely as a combination of digital photos, words on the screen, and, occasionally, a voice on the other end of the phone. But how much is real, how much illusion, and how much do we really care? Some men speak to me of deep, erotic fantasies involving men they work, work out, or go to classes with; unlike those long-distance or porn fellows this guy is flesh and blood, and right in front of them, with just one tiny problem standing in the way of any kind of consummation; to wit, his utter heterosexuality. But that doesn't kill the fantasy at all. Sometimes that makes it even hotter.

As I found out over the past several months, a gay man's "dream lover," his own personal vision of Adonis, is just about everywhere. The only caveat is, you often can't touch him. You have to be satisfied touching something else.

STRAIGHT FROM THE HEART

It's that last group of fantasy men we're going to start with first, if only because of the "utter" heterosexual's effect on every other group. When it comes down to it, we may not like the fact that so many of us are frequently drawn toward the occasional—and usually unattainable—straight guy, but let's be honest at least and admit it happens, okay?

Now remember, we're not talking about any closet-dwellers here, or any of that "straight acting/straight looking" crowd I had to contend with in *Sissyphobia*. I don't mean some hetero wannabe, the kind of guy who makes it his life's mission to run away from every outward association with homosexuality, even while he's bottoming six out of seven nights a week. We're talking genuine, 100 percent, ass-scratching, spit-on-the-sidewalk, why-the-fuck-should-I-shave-today straight. Got it? Good.

"Come we now to sing the praises of those straight boys we've known and loved, and been loved by—if only platonically—and lived to tell the tale afterward," wrote yours truly, in the premiere issue of the late, lamented *HERO Magazine* back in 1998.

> Just about any gay man has a straight story in his past or present; an Army buddy, a high school pal, or a friend from the gym. He's a co-worker, or that guy you see at the grocery store. Maybe he's tall and muscular, with an arrogant gait and carriage to him; maybe he's quiet and soulful, but possessed of a masculine air tinged with some vague suggestion of doability. We hear him speak of his wife or girlfriend, and that should be enough to send us elsewhere . . . but still we linger. We know him, and sometimes, we want him; we're just not sure how to get him, or what we'd do with him if we ever got close enough to try. (p. 18)

That was a fun article to write, and fun to read back through today, even if it does speak to a phenomenon that's anathema to many gay men these days. You probably know who I mean . . . they're the guys who tend to see such crushes or infatuations as a sort of backsliding, or as some kind of an expression of self-loathing. I remember talking to some gay friends about the "straight-boy crush" thing as I was compiling my *Chasing Adonis* interviews and surveys, and many of them were absolutely aghast that any gay man would confess openly that he might have a "thing" for a straight guy he knew or might once have known. They worried it would play into the hands of those who believe we're all out looking to "recruit" new members into the fold, in the process rejecting our arguably more attainable brothers in favor of a target with no opportunity, and embarking, so to speak, on a fruitless pursuit. What message does that send about us, they'd ask me, if it looks like even *we* don't like us?

But I have never been particularly concerned about political correctness, or that my digging toward whatever truths I can find will make people uncomfortable. In just about every survey I've received, my respondents mention at least one gay/straight alliance of this particular variety, even if the straight guy in question had no idea he was being lusted after. Sometimes, particularly among the younger men, it was someone they were acquainted with right now; for the older men, it was usually more of a misty memory.

Kevin is a 40-year-old lawyer in Chicago who fondly remembers his college buddy Phil to this day. "He was just the coolest, sweetest guy," he recalls. "One of those big, well-built and laid-back Midwestern lads that seem to come from another world, nothing at all like the ambitious and back-stabbing scrawny guys I'd known growing up in New York. I wasn't really out at school, and I didn't have that many friends, gay or straight. But Phil and I really hit it off, we spent hours together every day . . . in a lot of ways he was like a substitute for the boyfriend I didn't have at the time. I can safely say I loved him dearly, and yes, I did fantasize about what it would have been like to be 'with' him."

I ask Kevin if that ever came close to happening, or if there was ever a time when he wanted to tell Phil how he felt. "It may shock you to hear there's a lot of drinking in college," he tells me wryly. "And there was one night when we both got trashed and smashed, and stumbled back to the dorms. He lived down the hall from me, but somehow we both ended up collapsed on my bed . . . my roomie was away for the weekend, and we were just lying there, our bodies touching but neither of us making any effort to move away."

It's clear from his telling that Kevin has remembered that night many times since. "There is no way I can guess what was going on in his mind, but I can tell you that my heart was really racing. I didn't think he was gay or bi or curious or anything like that, but I had often fantasized about him letting me just 'enjoy' myself with him . . . and with the alcohol buzz at that moment if felt like anything might be possible." But as bad luck would have it, whatever moment might have happened never came to be. "The door flies open, my roomie comes back, I jump a mile from the shock, and Phil just kind of rolls off the bed laughing. For the next few days I kept thinking about how close we came, what my roomie might have seen if he'd come home five or ten minutes later . . . for some reason that kind of scared me off from ever even thinking about making a move on Phil again. I never even told him I was gay. I rather regret that."

Ryan, a 26-year-old postgrad student in Raleigh, North Carolina, has a much more recent tale of regret about his college crush, one he himself describes as "rather sordid" in its details. "His name was Jason, we were both 19. He was a little shorter than me (I'm kind of tall and skinny) and he was very muscular, always lifting weights and working out. I thought he was like the hottest boy I'd ever seen, and we'd been friends at school for about a year before I told him I was gay. The first thing he said was 'Well, I'm not,' which kind of hurt me a little. But he saw that, and said 'I don't care if you are, 'cause you're still my best friend.'" Ryan says he and Jason became even closer after that, but there was one secret he didn't share with him, at least not yet. "I was in love with him, even though I knew I wasn't ever going to get anywhere with it. I remember kicking myself for being so stupid to 'let' myself fall for him, as if that was something I could have controlled."

As Ryan explains it, his feelings for Jason remained pretty much under wraps for several more months. "I don't know how he couldn't have known, or that if he did know, why he didn't show it or ask me about it, but it never came up . . . we just hung out and went places together, just acting like regular guys. The only thing that was sexual between us was all in my head . . . I used to jerk off all the time thinking about him."

But everything changed when "Robin" arrived. (Ryan asks me not to use her real name, and suggests that one as a substitute.) "She was a transfer student who just blew in out of nowhere. We both got to be friends with her, but we had very different feelings . . . I was her 'gay pal' she had a crush on, while Jason clearly had a thing for her." Ryan says he won't blame you for thinking that all this sounds like the setup for a move. "As soon as she started hanging out with us, and found out I was gay and Jason was my straight best friend, she started joking about that movie *Threesome*. [That's a 1994 flick starring Lara Flynn Boyle, Josh Charles, and, God help me, Stephen Baldwin. Don't worry about the plot if you've never seen it; Ryan's about to explain.] Basically it was the girl-likes-the-gay-guy, gay-guy-wants-the-straight-guy, straight-guy-wants-the-girl scenario. Neither of us had seen it, but she had. One night we were all hanging out, and she suggested we rent it . . . then when it was over, she said she'd be into it."

Ryan says he pointed out how the threesome in the movie turned the three-way friendship into a train wreck, but that Robin said it didn't have to be that way for them. "The funny thing was how Jason was so excited by the idea. I didn't kid myself that he wanted me, I think he just wanted to get in her pants real bad, and if he had to go through me to get there, he didn't care. I was excited about being with him too, but I was more worried about losing him as my friend."

In the end Ryan says the two wore him down. "Robin really kind of harped on it, and Jason seemed like he was pissed I wouldn't give him a shot at her. I remember saying something like 'It's not really going to be a threesome, I'll just be watching you two do it,' and he said 'Maybe I'll surprise you.' So I caved, and we all went over to her apartment."

As it turns out, Ryan was very surprised. "She said she wasn't going to do anything until she watched us have sex together first and I thought that would end the whole thing, but then Jason said ok . . . I'm not going to lie and say I wasn't in Heaven for the first half hour or so, watching him get naked for the first time (he was really big down there) then rolling around in the bed with him. Feeling that body on top of me, then having him inside my mouth, then letting him top me . . . it was everything I had dreamed about. But once she got into the mix it did start to feel kind of dirty . . . women totally turn me off sexually, and seeing Jason and her together made me crazy jealous even though I was right there with them. I couldn't hide what I was feeling, and it ruined the whole thing. It was just like the movie, because nothing was ever the same after. They started dating, and he never spent much time with me again. It was all about her."

Not all the gay men I talked with had a bad or frustrated sexual experience with their straight buds; Dave, a 37-year-old former sailor in Bremerton, Washington, says he had several liaisons with a number of straight shipmates throughout his 15-year career. "It never failed that wherever I went I seemed to make one good friend I could confide in about my sexuality, and once in awhile stuff went beyond the just talking stage. I'm sure some of them weren't as 'straight' as they claimed to be. But I'm sure some were, and I just happened to catch them at a time they were curious or just plain old horny."

And most relationships I'm told about never had a sexual component at all, beyond whatever fantasies the gay man in question might have secretly harbored. "I used to jerk off thinking about some of my friends in high school," recalls Devon, now a "40ish" travel agent in West Texas. "Didn't tip my hand about it, always acted normal when we hung out. Don't think any of them ever suspected I was doing that. They'd be damn surprised to find out today I live with another man." Steve—a 28-year-old Army sergeant who is still on active duty at this writing—says that unlike the Navy's Dave, he'd never even consider approaching any of his comrades. "It's not worth the risks, to my career or my health. You never know what might happen to you. That doesn't mean I don't think about it. I never cared much for soft, 'faggy' or 'sissy' guys, and all the men I serve with are absolutely the cream of the crop when it comes to their bodies and the way they carry themselves. I'd defy any gay man to spend any time with them and not get some kind of 'crush.'"

Just what is it about a straight guy that many gay men find so fascinating, especially in a world where more and more gay men are coming out all the time? Like a lot of seemingly "straight"-forward questions, the answer can be pretty complex, depending on the situation and the guys involved. As some psychologists suggest, sometimes it really is a case of self rejection; for any number of cultural, religious, or simply situational reasons, there are many gay men who despise their own homosexuality and latch on to a straight friend as a way of enjoying some kind of intimacy with another man, even if it never goes further than a handshake or a clap on the shoulder. "I grew up in a very conservative, fundamentalist Christian family, and for most of my life I hated being gay," says Charles, a 27-year-old office worker in Mississippi. "Therefore I couldn't possibly have had any gay friends . . . in fact I made it a point when I was growing up to single out anyone I thought might be gay and treat them badly in school or in my neighborhood. It's something I feel very ashamed about now, but at the time that was how I was, only seeking out straight guys for company because that's how I saw myself. I realize now that I also had strong affections for those guys. It's funny though . . . it took a straight friend of mine, my best friend Jimmy, to point out what an asshole I was being to other people. He was the first person I ever came out to, he may have even saved my life. I figured if he could accept me for how I was, maybe I should start thinking about trying to do the same thing."

Adam, a 29-year-old construction engineer in Columbia, Missouri, tells me he didn't grow up having many issues with being gay, that he knew that was just the way he was, but he tells me it still took a long time for him to feel as much attraction for gay guys as he had for straight men. "I just developed an early appreciation for 'butch' guys, all the guys I grew up with were like that, and I fit in with them a lot better. Very few of the gay men I've run into fit the bill of what I like, and it's only in the last few years that I've branched out and actually dated guys that were more obvious in terms of being gay. Some of my newer gay friends have called me out on it, asking me why I spent so much time with the other side instead of hanging with men I was going get some play with. I have to tell them I don't really know, it's hard to explain what it is you find attractive sometimes."

But other men don't think it's very hard at all. They tell me it just makes sense, since there are so many more of them than there are of us, and we're surrounded by them and bombarded with their images from the time we're barely old enough to walk. Walt, a 53-year-old college professor in Florida, says it's a no-brainer why so many of our first crushes are more hetero than homo. "What are the odds that the very first boy you take a liking to in the 6th or 7th grade is going to be gay as well? Certainly that does happen, and more these days than in years past when gay men didn't identify as such until college or beyond . . . but for most of us growing up in the 50's, 60's, and 70's, we looked to the popular jocks or that good-looking but roguish boy who sat in the back row . . . we developed an attachment for the lifeguard at the beach, the kid next door who cut the grass with his shirt off, or the macho mechanic who worked on Dad's car . . . you couple that with the men you saw on television or the movies of that era, all quite decidedly heterosexual, and it's little wonder that we would form a sexual attraction to masculinity and a good physique. The world has turned a bit since then, and these days most of the gay men I know could give any of those icons a run for their money when it comes to sheer machismo; but in describing those men to others, we might still be moved to use a phrase like 'straight looking,' that's how powerful those early influences are."

A few years back the editorial staff of *The Advocate* decided to tackle the question in their August 19, 2003 "Sex Issue." They called the piece "10 Reasons Gays Chase Straights," and reasons number 1, 3, 5, and 10 sounded very much like what Walt suggests—the barrage of heterosexual culture literally everywhere we go, combined with our first exposures to other boys, the archetypes straight men represent, and their sheer numbers in the world we grow up in. The writers also touched on elements of Dave's tale above, the idea that with a little patience, almost anyone can be "had"; and they talked about a few concepts I hadn't thought that much about before, such as that on some level, many straight guys actually enjoy the attention that gets showered on them by a devoted gay guy, along with the proposition that if some gay men don't exactly actually reject their own sexual orientation, they may still be moved to seek the company of those who seem more "normal" in a mainstream context. And of course they put forth that old chestnut, the trite-but-so-very-true observation that straight men represent the "lure of the forbidden," how those "hard core heteros" present the greatest challenge to those so inclined to the pursuit. "True conquest is not about tapping the inner queer" they wrote. "It's about knocking'em dead with your wizard level sexual magic. After all, gay sex remains one of straight people's biggest taboos, so you must be All That if you snag a breeder" (p. 51).

Considering the U.S. military's historically heavy homoerotic atmosphere, it's no surprise that many of the gay/straight pursuit stories I've encountered arise from former or current soldiers, Marines, sailors, or airmen. As a former jarhead myself I can testify that few other venues offer up such a combination of youth, fitness, physicality, and lots of playful nudity. (When was the last time you showered with a dozen hot guys at the same time? That's what I'm talking about.) The guys in the barracks or the squad bay are always talking about "getting fucked up the ass" by this senior officer, or how that particular work situation "really sucks cock." For the covert gay guy it all can't help but be a little titillating, especially when those words are flying fast and furious in a room where no one is wearing more than loose boxers. You know you can't make yourself known to the barracks at large—attacks and beatings of suspected gay servicemembers are rare, but they do happen, sometimes with deadly results—and anyone who "outs" himself will find himself "out" of the military in a Chelsea minute. But somewhat perversely, that sometimes dangerous atmosphere only makes the "lure of the forbidden" all the stronger.

"I was in my first few months of the Marine Corps, stationed at Camp Lejeune in North Carolina, where I was learning how to push paper and punch computer buttons," says Tony, now a 40-year-old software designer in northern Virginia. "I'd made a really good friend in Rob, a fellow Marine at school. He was tall and wiry, and really, really sexy . . . God, I wanted him so bad. I remember lots of nights in the showers when we just washed off and talked for what seems like an hour, just two jarheads shooting the shit, and of course we're both naked. For a long time I didn't really look, I was so scared I'd get caught, if not by Rob then by someone else . . . but after awhile I was sneaking a good look here and there, and he either didn't notice or didn't care. It was pretty ballsy for me to do that, but I'd been away from home for a long time, and no action. I think the fact I wasn't supposed to have a thing for another Marine probably made me want him more, too.

"Weekends they usually let us go home, as long as we got back to base by Monday morning, so one time I invited Rob home with me to Philly. Maybe it was just the familiarity of going back to where I grew up, or the fact that even though we'd only known each other for a little while Rob already seemed like the best friend I'd ever had . . . anyway, I sucked it up, took a breath, and told him I was gay on the way up, and he didn't seem freaked out about it at all. He joked about it, like 'I was wondering why you kept staring at my package in the shower,' stuff like that.

"That weekend we got some pot, got really high in my old bedroom at home. He got up to go to the bathroom and when he came back he was butt naked, sat back down like it was just a normal thing for his cock to be hanging out like that, and we started smoking again." Tony says all that doobage they smoked makes what happened next a little hazy. "I really don't know who made the first move, but I do remember we started kissing. Then we went down on each other. I think I was too stoned to get off, but Rob wasn't, I remember that clearly. Hell, I'll remember that forever. Next day I was worried as soon as I woke up that he'd be pissed off, and accuse me of taking advantage of him, but none of that shit happened. He just called it his 'walk on the wild side,' told me he'd never really been curious about gay sex before and probably wouldn't ever do it again, and we didn't. But we stayed close until we both shipped out of school, and wrote each other for the next four or five years. Last time we touched base he had a wife and two kids. I don't know if I'm the only guy he ever hooked up with, but I sort of hope I am."

Of course, relatively few gay/straight fixations ever go quite that far, and my surveys are filled with tales of mostly unrequited lust or love. Strangely enough, for many of the men involved that actually suits them just fine. That brings us back to *The Advocate*'s article, and Reason Number 6 on their hit parade: that such crushes on straight guys are perhaps the "safest sex" of all. Notwithstanding those randy stories like Dave's and Tony's, most of the time actual sex is pretty unlikely, if the object of your crush is really playing for the other team. "Chasing after the straight ones gives us all the pleasure of fixation without the dangers of consummation . . . idolizing the unavailable is the gay and lesbian equivalent of Lisa Simpson's *Non-Threatening Boys* magazine. It's lasciviousness without follow through" (p. 49).

"I was just out of a long relationship, and my partner's leaving left a big hole in my life," says Tim, a 30-year-old bank employee in New Britain, Connecticut. "I wasn't about to jump back into gay dating scene, so I decided that the best thing I could do was just concentrate on my career, and interests that didn't have to do with other gay men. I had a lot of straight friendships that I'd let lag over the years I was 'married,' and it seemed like a good thing to put some life back into them. I was surprised to find out how much I enjoyed my old friends' company. It was a relief to spend time with men I found attractive and engaging, and not have to worry that things could ever get sexual. There were a few I can even say I had a little crush on, the kind of affection that makes you excited to see them for dinner or a movie. But aside from the occasional random thought about how good they looked in a tight shirt or pants, I behaved myself."

"When I started college it was back in the early 90's, when AIDS was at its worst and I was just this young kid from the backwoods of Kentucky," says Brian, now a 32-year-old accountant in the Cincinnati area. "I wasn't the self-loathing type, but I was really scared about the idea of having sex because of the chance of catching something. But I was 18, and like any 18-year-old I was horny all the time.

We used to get really physical back in school, and the crowd I ran with was pretty daring . . . lots of wrestling, and being naked, and talking in this really sexual way with each other, even though we didn't do anything. But it was all in a 'straight' context, which probably only makes sense if you've ever been in a situation like that. Let's just say I had crushes on half the guys who lived on my floor, and I spent a lot of time jacking off in the shower. In a way 'not' having sex with those guys, or only having sex with them in my mind, was hotter than actually 'being' with many guys I've known since."

What probably struck me the most about the *Advocate* piece was the "nod-nod, wink-wink, we've all been there" tone, since I certainly encountered men who definitely haven't been there. In fact, some tell me the very idea of a gay/straight crush is rather repulsive. "Except for the members of my family, just about every straight guy I've encountered in my life has been a real jerk," says Mike, a 36-year-old city worker in Redding, California. "It's like they say on *Queer as Folk,* there are two kinds of straight people, the ones who hate you to your face, and the ones who just hate you behind your back. I have never been the kind of guy who can be attracted to someone based on their looks alone, so even if the straight guy in question looks like a model, I still know he can't be trusted. I don't know why any self-respecting gay man would ever find himself wanting one of them."

"Not only do I find the prospect personally appalling, I think it's a sign of everything that's wrong with the gay community," avows Nathan, a 23-year-old college student in Michigan. "There's so much of this being unrealistic and disconnected from the real world, instead of dealing with life as it is and learning to appreciate what's there, and going after what's really possible. The last thing I want is someone who reminds of the kids that beat me up in middle school."

Even those men who relate their crushes on unattainable men in positive or nostalgic tones admit there are serious pitfalls when you fall—really fall—for someone you can never have, even if you do manage to find a way to, well, have him. At least for a little while. "I thought nothing would ever make me happier than getting my best friend Kelly into bed," says Bradley, a 22-year-old college student in Houston. "Totally beautiful, a really good person . . . everything you could want in a guy. He was the first person I ever told, and he'd known that I was gay for years, all through high school . . . he also knew I had a crush on him, and didn't really mind that, either. In fact we even used to joke about how we'd have to have sex one day, just to relieve the tension." Brad says he never seriously believed it could happen, or that Kelly would somehow turn out to be a secret homo. "I did not kid myself about that, I knew he was straight. He had so many girls sniffing around him all the time, and who could blame them?"

Imagine Brad's surprise then one hot summer afternoon after they graduated, when they were bored sitting around inside the house, and Kelly asked him what he was "up" for. "I said, joking around like we always did, that I could really go for sucking his dick. And Kelly said sure, ok. So I moved over beside him on the couch, and started to reach for his fly, assuming he'd knock my hand away. He didn't. So I started unzipping his pants, again assuming that at some point he was going to throw me off of him, laughing, calling me a 'fag' the way only your best friend can do it and not hurt your feelings.

"But he didn't stop me. I froze up and asked him 'Are you serious?' and he said 'Hell, why not, I'm horny and we both know you want to.' So I did, and it was just . . . wow. Better than I thought it would be." Like a lot of gay men I've interviewed Brad tells me he was immediately worried about the backlash, that Kelly would "freak out," right on the spot or later on, and that would be the end of their friendship. But that didn't happen. In fact, things turned out just the opposite. "I'm not kidding, he started asking me for it, all the time . . . especially if he'd been out on a date and the chick wouldn't put out. He would literally tap on my window in the middle of the night, climb in, and lay down beside me on my bed, then unzip . . . he said it was kind of cool to have a best friend you could get head from who could also kick your ass in basketball, and told me he wished there was a way I could teach his girlfriends how to suck dick like I did. The problem was, even though I was his best friend, for him it was still just sex and playing around . . . I on the other hand was totally in love. I loved being with him like that, don't get me wrong . . . but it made it a lot harder to ever get over him."

BILLY'S TALE

I have to stop Kelly's narrative right now, because he's giving me major flashbacks of my own seminal experience with a "totally beautiful" boy: Billy, my oft-mentioned best friend and straight next-door neighbor from my youth. I've already explained how at 16 his almost freakishly hot physique helped form my idea of what's attractive in a guy, and how it eventually inspired me to start working out and transform my own body; but long before I ever picked up a dumbbell or barbell, Billy was already affecting my body—and my heart—in lots of other ways.

Like Brad and Kelly, Billy and I were best friends, despite the very different places we came from. And just like Brad, I was totally in love; but Billy wasn't the first person I ever revealed that deep, dark secret to, even though he was a central figure in its revelation. No, the first person to find out was my "older" friend Linda who lived just down the block from my apartment—she was only 28, but to the 17-year-old me that seemed positively ancient—and she'd seen the way I looked at him when we stopped by together, or when we hung out at the pool. All that "longing," as she put it, was painted all over my pimpled face.

I didn't actually tell Linda, either, so much as I made her drag it out of me, slowly, on what really was a dark and stormy night. (There was also a lot of pot, and cheap wine, and Pink Floyd playing ominously low in the background for emphasis. What do you want? It was the 1970s, okay?) But oh, my—once I was finished and the truth was irrevocably out, to have someone else know—what a sweet feeling of freedom and release that was, and quite intoxicating and addictive as well. Before long I started telling all my close friends, actually enjoying their various reactions of shock and surprise and confusion—I loved it when they'd say something such as "Wow, like really? Um . . . how do you know for sure?" and stuff like that—until the only one left who didn't know I was gay was the one boy I wanted to be gay with more than anyone.

Finally, though, on a balmy Friday evening in May, while Billy and I were out on one of those long walk and talks we used to take, I was ready at last to spill the beans. But the words weren't coming easy; how do you look a 16-year-old straight kid in the eye and tell him not only that you're gay, but that you're also in love with him? A guy who could, if he wanted to, smash you into a bloody pulp? Not that Billy was that kind of kid, at least I didn't think so, but Jesus, who really knew what the fuck he'd do?

Without tipping my hand I'd been trying to sound him out for months about his feelings concerning gay people. Everybody at his age—then and now—uses words like "faggot" and "queer" and "homo" as handy insults, and rejoinders like "Suck my dick" or "Lick my balls" were and are pretty common, at least among the teenage jock boy set. Billy was certainly no exception; he used to smile and tell me to suck his dick all the time—usually when I'd just kicked his ass in another chess game—and I doubt he knew how I'd have given everything for such an opportunity.

But playground epithets aside, Billy was always unfailingly polite when it came to dealing with the local gay population, or rather, suspected gay population; they were older, single guys whose very passage through the apartment parking lot or laundry room inspired wild and lascivious speculation among the residents about what they might be doing and who they might be doing it with. In my braver moments I'd asked Billy what he thought about "Bruce" or "Gordon" or "Bob"; he would just shrug and say something like "They're okay," without elaborating. When it came down to it I really had no idea how he'd react.

So despite the fact I'd already told a dozen other people without anything catastrophic happening, there I was fumbling for just the right words, then giving up all at once and saying "Look, I'm gay." Almost thirty years later I can still see the slightly perplexed look on Billy's face—kind of like "Hmm, I didn't see that coming"—followed by a shrug, and then "Well as long as you don't try to jump on my dick in the middle of the night, it's cool."

And I don't think that's what I was really aiming for; like Brad, I knew my best friend was beyond my reach, though I suppose I was also thinking that if such a thing ever were to happen, however impossibly unlikely that seemed, we would have to get past that initial threshold of confession first. But him saying that, about not "jumping him" . . . that kept me from finishing up the second part, where I was going to express my undying affection and all that.

I recall saying instead something very lame, like "Are we going to be able to stay friends?" at which little thunderclouds suddenly gathered around his eyes. "It pisses me off that you would even ask that." A rather remarkable response, really, considering his age and the times we lived in. So I let the rest go, happy things had gone better than I'd hoped they would.

What I couldn't know at that moment was how much further it was going to go, and pretty damn quickly. Just two days later, sitting in a deep concrete rain gutter beside the road and buzzing on some hand-rolled joints in the twilight, Billy made something of a pass at me. Don't go thinking he'd somehow fooled me and was actually a fellow 'mo; he was just like Brad's buddy, Kelly, a horny straight boy suddenly intrigued by the idea his best friend might have some unexpected benefits. His pass, such at it was, consisted of poking my crotch with his foot, and making lewd little comments, like "You know we could have some fun," and "I bet you'd like to," without being very specific as to how or what. (I can be fairly confident I'm getting the wording right, by the way. I kept a voluminous diary in those days, and I would write down all of that spring and summer's events in exacting, excruciating adolescent detail.)

I pushed his foot off of me. It's not like I wasn't turned on, I was just a bit miffed. How dare he get my hopes up? I knew he'd only dash them, thinking he was being funny, not understanding the agony he was putting me through. But then Billy shifted position so he was sitting beside me, and now it wasn't his foot playing with my crotch, he was actually using his hand. "Somebody's getting excited," he said with that big stupid grin of his, and then he popped open my fly with his thumb and reached inside my undershorts.

It was the first time a guy ever touched me "down there," who wasn't wearing a stethoscope and a white lab coat. I think I almost passed out.

Again, I have the benefit of knowing everything that would come after that warm May night, and I can assure you despite his aggressive moves Billy really was straight as an arrow; he was only trying to do exactly what he ended up doing, which is to make me so crazy playing around with me that I'd do likewise to him. And a few moments later I had his jeans open and I was holding Little Billy in my hand—well, not so little—another first in what would be an all-too-brief but sweet season of discovery.

Brad has it so right when we talks about the difference in how a playful and horny straight guy regards such goings-on, as opposed to the gay guy he's playing with. Even though we'd get more daring and adventurous as spring turned to summer—I'll never forget the nights we went skinny dipping in the apartment pool, then crept back to my place for some very memorable sleepovers—I always knew somewhere inside that Billy would get bored eventually and go back to the cheerleaders he was used to banging. But that didn't make it any easier when it actually happened. We would even have a few more random hookups over the next few years—unpredictable little dalliances all the more exciting because of their utter unpredictability—but after the glow faded I'd always ask myself what the fuck I was doing. If I'd known more about substance abuse at the time I would have recognized the symptoms as a classic case of addiction; Billy was crack and heroin and crystal all rolled into one.

There's likely a good reason our brief intimacies left such track marks on my heart and soul. Several chapters back we talked about whether we're all born with an innate sense of desire for a particular kind of guy, or whether the guys we meet early on help shape those desires. I myself can't help but feel both forces at work, that Billy was what I wanted before I even knew what I wanted. Then over time he bent and molded that template into his own image; I fell in love with him so completely that his personality, mannerisms, and bearing became the very benchmark of what a guy is supposed to be. Once I started venturing down to the DC bar scene I was shocked and saddened to find out just how few gay guys in those days came anywhere close to the standard he'd set. (Which is not to say I didn't try to put some miles between me and those hot summer nights that lived in my memory; I just wasn't very successful at it.) It would not be until my life took the swift and sudden turn that landed me in Marine Corps boot camp that the personal hold he had on me would be broken once and for all; yet all through my military career and beyond I still found echoes of him in most of the guys I found most compelling. And the vast majority of them, I'm humbled to report, were just as heterosexual as he was. It's only in the past several years—my post-*Sissyphobia* period—that I'm really appreciating gay men of all modes and mannerisms.

But don't think for a second I am sorry that any of it happened. Every year when the weather gets warm, when you can smell the honeysuckle in the air just after dark, I find myself remembering those nights with such clarity that I'd swear they just happened yesterday, and it's hard not to smile and reminisce. These days when I'm out and about with friends I might point with approval to a hot high school or college jock passing by, and even when they're in total agreement with me, some buddy or another will invariably laugh, asking me why my mind "is always in the gutter." I try to explain to them—a gutter isn't necessarily a bad place to be. It really just depends on your company.

STRAIGHT UP NOW TELL ME

As some of you might know—if you stopped to read the author's bio—I am by trade a working journalist and TV producer. Having been born in—and now living and working in—the DC area, for me politics and the coverage thereof isn't simply second nature, it's a primary color in my constitutional palette. Therefore, I am scandalized that it took a straight buddy of mine to point out that I was about to violate the semi-sacred concept of "equal time." If I was going to have all these gay men talk about their thoughts and fantasies when it came to the het' set, he pointed out, wouldn't it behoove me to ask the object of those fantasies firsthand what they thought?

The more I considered it, the more I liked the idea. But with time growing short as the deadline for this book approached, I wasn't quite sure how to pull that off. Then I remembered an old piece I wrote for *Instinct Magazine* back in 1998, a roundtable of sorts about the ongoing importance—or lack of—of Gay Pride Day observances. With a similar deadline approaching and few takers out here in the real world, I'd gone online, gathered a half-dozen interested people I'd found lounging in various chat rooms, and then invited them into a chat I'd created for the single purpose of discussing that topic. It actually turned out rather well; they were a lively group, and all I had to do was keep copying and saving everything that was said, later editing out the parts where the fellas kept hitting on each other, asking for stats and preferred positions. (I may yet use that stuff for another project.)

So with my new straight mandate in mind I went back online, trolling about in the waters where the other side swims, various chat and cam communities, message billboards and the like. I braced myself for what I knew would be a lot of abuse—several dudes thought I was trying to pick them up, using my book as a ruse—but more often I was just ignored by guys who simply didn't respond. It took a few nights of trying, but eventually I found five guys willing to play along; the only caveats were that they had to be able to get into the

AOL chat room I created—I called it "Str8 Guys Talk Gay"—and they had to have some kind of experience with a gay friend or acquaintance who'd expressed his affection or admiration.

Now I know some purists will always question what's said and done online as opposed to, say, if I'd somehow put those guys in the same room. But as I've frequently maintained, the anonymity of the Internet is just as often a journalist's friend as it is his adversary; people who cannot see each other, and who will most likely never meet, will say the damnedest things sometimes. I was also fortunate that the willing men in question happened to represent a certain geographical diversity; they hailed from the Midwest, Northeast, South, and West Coast. As they entered the chat I had them provide their names, ages, and what they did for a living—by agreement I've deleted their actual screen names—then I threw out questions and let the conversation start. Sometimes one fellow would lag for a bit and answer a question long after we were off on another topic—don't you hate that?—so the following is edited just a smidge to take that confusion out of the mix; I've also cleaned up the grammar and spelling where it was needed. (im sure U kno what I meen if u've ben online n-e-time at ALL ☺)

So let's listen in, shall we? Here's the lineup:

- Eric, 20, auto repair worker, Passaic, New Jersey
- Benny, 31, restaurant manager, Dallas, Texas
- Ken, 38, photographer, San Diego, California
- Carlos, 25, student, Illinois
- Mikey, 28, limo driver, Tampa, Florida

TIM: And I am a 45-year-old writer in the Washington, DC, area . . . figures I am the oldest . . . ok, so my first question is, who can tell me about the gay guy in his life?

KEN: My best friend from my old neighborhood when I was growing up

MIKEY: One of my co-workers. He's not really in my life, as you put it, I just know him

BENNY: My brother is gay

CARLOS: One roomie at the private high school I went to, and one soccer teammate in college

ERIC: Some friends in high school were gay, and I think one of my co-workers at the garage is, but I don't know 100 percent for sure.

TIM: Benny, let's get right to the good stuff and hear about that brother and you. [All my "chatsters" throw in an "LOL" or a smiley face at that one; I'm pleased by the fact this does not appear to be an uptight bunch.]

BENNY: Well, I've never actually told anyone about this before so it's a little hard to just say it, but when were teenagers we used to fool around some. A lot of straight guys go through phases like that and they're still straight . . . I am, but my brother Bobby (he's 27) wasn't, and he was angry when I stopped doing it with him. About 5 years ago I asked him why he didn't have a boyfriend and he said he was still looking for someone who reminded him of the perfect guy. I asked him who that was, and he said it was me

ERIC: Wow

CARLOS: Holy shit

TIM: You can say that again

KEN: That's intense, guy . . . does it put any distance between you?

BENNY: Not as much now, no, because he does have a boyfriend these days

TIM: Benny, I may have to do a book just on you guys sometime . . . Mikey, I see you there hiding . . . what's your story?

MIKEY: Not hiding, just digesting what it would be like to have sex with a sibling

TIM: Let's not judge

MIKEY: I'm not, it's just different from anything I could ever think of . . . anyway, my story is that I have a co-worker who is pretty obviously gay, and he seems to have a thing for me

TIM: [Channeling Dr. Phil] And how's that workin' for ya?

MIKEY: At first it was just kind of funny, now it's not

TIM: Why's that?

MIKEY: Because I get enough crap as it is because I dress well, always have a good haircut, and I'm in great shape. Now there's a gay guy hitting on me all the time, so people are beginning to talk

CARLOS: People think you're gay because you look good? That makes me a big ol' queer, then

TIM: Easy on the Q word, C. Mikey, have you talked to this guy about it?

MIKEY: I've tried to be polite so far, because I've always been a live and let live guy, but I may have to take him aside and tell him to stop in stronger terms

ERIC: That's sort of what I am going through, I have a co-worker who stares at me a lot, it makes me uncomfortable

TIM: Maybe you remind him of someone he used to know

ERIC: Then why is it that he's mainly looking at my ass?

TIM: Good point. Have you said anything to him about it?

ERIC: Not yet, but if he keeps it up I'll tell him to stop, I don't want to get anyone fired over some stupid shit

TIM: But let me ask you guys, and be honest. Don't you find it at least a little flattering if someone thinks you're hot? Even if it's not someone of the female persuasion?

ERIC: Maybe in some different situation, but at work it sucks. When I was in high school I had one friend who told me he was gay, and another I always suspected but he never admitted it. I was much better friends with the guy who was open about it, that way I knew where I stood, I just let him know nothing was ever going to happen, and we were cool about it

KEN: Honesty is always best

TIM: You guys do know that it's not easy for some guys to admit it, even to themselves? People worry they might get a reputation, get harassed, even beat up. Or that they'll just lose a good friend

KEN: I think that's just sad... sounds like a horrible way to grow up

CARLOS: My soccer buddy was terrified people would find out. He told me one night when we were drunk, then tried to take it all back the next day. I kept telling him it was cool, I had gay friends before, and I was good at keeping secrets

TIM: How did you find out your private school roomie was gay?

CARLOS: I caught him beating off to gay porn on his computer

TIM: That'll do it. Did that make you feel strange, did he ever come on to you?

CARLOS: Fuck no, and I don't know how I would have handled it if he did, I was very young then. I would be a lot more chill about it now, like "thanks, but no thanks." I didn't care about the porn, that was his business, not mine. I'm sure he heard me jacking off in my bed at night from time to time

TIM: And it probably made him crazy. Ken, tell me about your neighborhood buddy

KEN: We grew up together, and I was pretty sure he was gay from like the time we were 13 or 14, but he didn't tell me until we were both 17

TIM: What made you think he was gay?

KEN: We used to hang out with girls, play strip poker and stuff, go skinny dipping at one of the girl's house . . . let's just say he tended to get aroused once he saw me naked, I caught him peeking a lot

TIM: What power you must have. How did that make you feel? Were you worried what the girls would think?

KEN: They were pretty clueless young ladies . . . they thought his woody was aimed at them, but I knew. As far as me, since I'm supposed to be honest here I can say it was flattering on some level to know he thought I was attractive. At that age when you're very awkward sometimes any validation is good

TIM: Did it ever go beyond flattery?

KEN: Again, since we're being honest, I'll admit I let him go exploring on me a time or two, usually when we were very drunk and I was very horny and those clueless girls weren't around

ERIC: I could never do that

CARLOS: Me either

TIM: C'mon guys, sometimes it happens

ERIC: If we're all supposed to be straight here I don't understand how someone who gets with a guy can consider himself straight

TIM: When I was 20 I let this girl go down on me, and I can promise you that didn't make me straight

CARLOS: Maybe you're bi and don't know it?

TIM: Far from it, I just did it to piss off her boyfriend

BENNY: LOL . . . and did it?

TIM: Better than I hoped for. So Benny, explain to Eric and Carlos how you can fool around with someone of the same sex and not be gay

BENNY: It's hard to explain, I was just a kid, curious, and it was just like jacking off to me, more like a game than sex

KEN: Lots of guys go through the experiment phase. It wasn't really like that for me, it was just this guy I was close to who would give me head if I snapped my fingers. There's an ego thing there I guess

TIM: Mikey, you're quiet

MIKEY: Just taking it all in. This is like Truth or Dare without the drinking part

TIM: Any same sex adventure you want to share?

MIKEY: Not really

KEN: Nothing? Ever?

MIKEY: A buddy of mine and I banged the same girl one night at the same time . . . I think our cocks might have touched at some point, but it wasn't intentional. We were all pretty wasted

TIM: Any regrets the day after?

MIKEY: Not from me. My buddy said he was pissed that I made his dick look small in comparison

Eric: I could never have sex with a girl if there was a dude around

TIM: What if it was Britney Spears and she said the only way she'd do you was if you tagged teamed with another guy?

ERIC: Still couldn't

TIM: Carlos? [There's a long pause]

CARLOS: Ok you got me. But I would freak out if I touched something I didn't mean to

KEN: You didn't ask me, but I'd have sex with Britney Spears with my best friend, my college roommates, with my family watching on national TV if that was the only way

TIM: Dog

KEN: Yep

TIM: Okay, quick round of questions, keep your answers short. Can you look at a guy and think "He's a good looking dude" without questioning your own masculinity?

KEN: Of course, that's what I do for a living

BENNY: I guess, but I'm not going to say it to his face

ERIC: I don't look at guys like that, I only check out females

MIKEY: I have no problem with it

CARLOS: I don't see guys that way, sorry. I might check out his clothes or the way he cuts his hair and think "that works," or "that sucks"

TIM: Hope I never run into you on the street, C. you'll probably rip my wardrobe up. Next question: what is it about high school and college age straight boys, and that empty seat they have to leave between them when they go see a movie together? Are you guys really that insecure? Not picking on you Eric, but you're the youngest, so you start.

ERIC: I never thought about it before, I just like the extra room I guess

KEN: I think it is insecurity, to tell the truth. We didn't do that when I was that age and going to movies, but I've noticed it a lot these days

BENNY: I think straight guys at that age are just getting out of the house and finding their own way, and they really worry what things look like, so maybe they don't want to look they're on a "date"

MIKEY: I usually only go to see movies with women, I don't remember doing that much if at all

CARLOS: I'm like Eric, I never really thought about it, but Benny's right, guys a little younger than me are really tied up in appearances, and there's always pressure to be hard looking or tough . . . so staking out that space is like marking your territory I suppose

TIM: Ok. You're at the gym and getting ready to hit the shower. You see a guy who seems to you might be gay walk in there before you. Do you still go in, or do you wait around until he's done?

CARLOS: Probably wait, to be honest. I know if I was able to go into a ladies' shower I'd be looking all over the place

KEN: That's silly of course I'd go in

BENNY: I'd go in, sure

ERIC: I don't go to a gym, and if I did I wouldn't shower there

MIKEY: I've caught guys checking me out in the shower before. I just ignore them. If they approached me when I was naked I might have a major problem with that

TIM: Fair enough, though I find myself wondering about Eric and his hygiene

ERIC: Hey

TIM: Kidding. Next question, keep the answers short. If two gay guys (or gals) want to get married, should they be able to legally just like straight people?

MIKEY: Sure

KEN: No problem with that

BENNY: If I said no my brother would kill me, so yes

ERIC: It seems weird to me, but if they want to, I guess

CARLOS: Fine by me

TIM: This one has nothing to do with my book, but I'm just curious . . . what about the idea of gays serving openly in the military?

ERIC: If they want to, why not? Seems stupid to make us do all the work

CARLOS: If he doesn't mind getting his ass shot off more power to him

MIKEY: Better him than me. I'm pretty antiwar, sorry

KEN: Me too, but there's no reason for a ban on gays at all, it's just people's ignorance and prejudice. All right wing assholes piss me off

Benny: I'm not that political, but if my brother wanted to join he should be able to. I hope he never does though

TIM: Wow, you guys are like a George W. Bush nightmare . . . it's so good to feel hope again. Thanks guys.

PORN AGAIN

I'm sitting with my friend Greg in his bedroom. He's got his computer fired up, and he's showing me pictures and videos of some his favorite guys, the men he calls "the hottest guys" in the world. "That one there, I just love his tatts . . . makes me wish I had the guts to get some, not that they'd ever look good on this body." He clicks his mouse a few more times. "This guy here, even hotter," he says, as the video plays. "Look at his face and body, the way he just grabs the lens, and makes you look at him . . . he's like a superhero or a movie star." I point out to Greg that he's obviously already in a movie, albeit one without any dialogue, just a really awful electronic soundtrack and the occasional dubbed-in groan. "You know what I mean, a real film. Not that I mind seeing him this way. They'd never let you see his stuff like that on a big screen."

Seeing a hot guy's "stuff" is the name of the game when it comes to many gay men and their love of pornography, whether they're a postcollege 20-something like Greg, a just-coming-out teen—they're not supposed to be able to get their hands on it, but of course thousands do—all the way up to middle-aged gay men and seniors. I regret I didn't include a specific question or two about porn in my original surveys or polls; it's hard when you're first embarking on a book like this to know all the little alleys and side streets you'll be traveling down. But it's pretty clear porn is a big-ticket item when it comes to your average gay man's fantasy life; when I asked them to talk about their visions of Adonis or their perfect idea of a man, I was surprised by how often the men I interviewed used porn production houses—Bel Ami, Falcon, Titan Media, Colt, to name just a few—to try to illustrate that personal vision of perfection.

"My fantasy guy is usually wearing a uniform of some type—I love those videos where the actors are dressed up like macho cops or soldiers," says Ben, a 33-year-old sales manager in Rockford, Illinois. "I have always enjoyed being with men like that for real, so that's one thing I look for when I'm shopping. I wouldn't say I have the biggest collection in the world but I do own several tapes and DVDs. It gets you through the dry spells, that's for sure." Sam, a 29-year-old hospital worker in Parkersburg, West Virginia, tells me his porn preference runs toward the "mountain man" type, the kind of "big burly man you might see driving an 18-wheeler or working on a construction site." Sam says his job keeps him so busy he doesn't have a lot of time right now for a social life. "But a man has his needs, you know. You have to take care of them somehow."

In the spirit of full disclosure, let me admit from the outset that I myself am a big fan of a little good porn from time to time, as are most gay guys I know. And if you're like us—and like Greg, and Ben, and Sam—you've probably been there: It's been a long day, you've gotten home late, you don't feel much like going back out and dealing with traffic or even other people, but still there's that, as Sam puts it, need down there . . . and mentally replaying some of your personal greatest hits for the 20th time—like that long-ago afternoon when you hooked up with the cabana boy in South Beach, or that first and only date with the hunky guy you spotted in the gym, then invited home for a "drink"—isn't going to quite cut it. That's when you find yourself reaching for the DVD or video, or booting up your computer for a little downloadable action.

For what it's worth though—just so you can see where I'm coming from here—I don't embrace or endorse anything illegal, nor do I find the really kinky or "out there" stuff very appealing. If *Fisting Weekend Part III* or *Bondage in Bonn* trips your trigger, that's fine by me, and more power to you. Those aren't exactly my scene. They're not even close to my scene. But show me some classic confection where various well-built young lads are cavorting on the beach, in the woods, or off in some sun-dappled field, and I'm off on my own personal Frisky Summer, applauding—vigorously—with one hand.

In this affection for the naughty bits as recorded on film and video, and as digitized information spewed—quite literally—all over the Internet, my horny buds and I are just a few of many, many men of all sexual stripes. The numbers alone tell the story; though estimates vary widely, some experts put the annual porn profit in the United States alone at something close to $10 billion. How much of that market caters exclusively to the man-on-man variety is hard to put a handle on—so to speak—but when you consider the sexual nature of many gay men, who sometimes live in situations where actual physical contact is hard come by—the puns fly fast and furious, now, sorry—it only figures that we must represent a sizeable chunk of the business.

In my latest interviews for this book, conducted long after my surveys and polls were put to bed, I've been asking gay men just what kind of role porn and the enjoyment thereof plays in their lives. Dozens tell me they find it every bit the enjoyable release that I do; most don't go out to video or bookstores to find it, preferring instead to use the privacy of the Internet and either download it or have it delivered to their doorstep. Others belong to Web sites where they find new movies and images waiting for them a few times a week, and many of them talk about belonging to informal groups that collect and trade those memorable scenes online, or by recording videos and CDs to exchange by mail—defying the strict copyright laws that make that a definite no-no.

"It's just one of those little bright spots I look forward to once in awhile," says Bryan, a 28-year-old county employee in the Portland, Oregon, area. "I still go out on dates, and I have a 'real' life I'm happy about. But it's fun to toss that DVD into the machine once in awhile, and place yourself in the scene with the big hairy trucker who makes 'friends' with the skinny blonde kid who's somehow all alone out there in the wilderness. It's a harmless fantasy. Once in awhile I get some good ideas about what to do in bed, too."

Steve is a 26-year-old waiter in suburban Pittsburgh who tells me his taste runs to the "gay for pay" sites he finds on the Net. "I don't know if the guys on the sites or in the movies are really straight, but lots of them at least look like they are, and I have always had that thing for straight guys. This one site I belong to has new movies every couple of days, sometimes it's just one guy jacking off, sometimes it's a couple of guys really going at it. I've belonged to it for two years now I guess, and I've seen the same guys go from being nervous just playing with themselves to being part of a great big group orgy. I almost feel like I know them. Of course I don't, but that's how powerful the fantasy is for me, and as far as stimulation goes it is really reliable."

"I think you could safely call me a fan, even a big fan," says Mason, a 38-year-old financial consultant in Vermont. "Some men are big into sports, and they spend hours a week glued to the television watching some guy try to get a ball past another guy and into a net or a hole or across some line. Society says that's perfectly legitimate. I, on the other hand, spend hours each week watching attractive guys get physical with each other in a totally different way, and they use the balls and the holes, sometimes even a net . . . and they get just as sweaty on the way to scoring. Is it all that different, when you really think about it?"

Preaching to the choir here, Mason. But while most of the men I've gotten with recently have no trouble admitting to their fondness for erotica, I have encountered several who are highly critical of the whole enterprise, from the folks who create it on both sides of the camera, to those who sell it; but they reserve their harshest criticism for those who buy it. "It's just like the hideous drugs that threaten our society," says Ted, a 43-year-old Los Angeles resident. "I wish men—and boys, you know they're all not 18—wouldn't demean themselves by performing such intimate acts on video, and I dearly wish it was illegal for someone to make such videos possible. None of that would matter though, if, like the sale of illegal drugs, there wasn't such a huge market. The gay men who buy that trash are the ones that make the industry so profitable. They should be ashamed of themselves."

"I used to enjoy porn when I was younger," says Kurt, a 39-year-old living in Tampa, Florida. "But I haven't watched a movie like that in a long time. Why? Because one night I rented a video, and in it I saw this sweet-faced young man just brutalized by a whole horde of larger, muscular men. Even though he was supposed to be enjoying himself in the context of the film, it was obvious he wasn't. There was one scene where he was virtually gang-raped, and I suddenly found myself thinking 'That's somebody's kid, there, maybe somebody's little brother. Look what they're doing to him, what would his family think if they ever saw this?' It was so disturbing that I've been turned off by the very idea of porn ever since."

I have to admit that last comment does give me pause, though again for what it's worth the brand of video I find most enticing rarely if ever contains such brutality; in my favorite scenes it really does appear that most of the fellows are largely enjoying themselves, at least while the camera is rolling. But there are certain undeniably exploitative aspects to porn—indeed, for some that's part of the its forbidden allure—and the critics I talk to also cite its addictive potential, as well as the way it glorifies the physical aspects of sex over the spiritual, minimizing any notion of real romance in favor of raw, carnivorous action.

I decided to put some questions to some guys I know who have a rather intimate acquaintance with the industry, though most have since left the business; they also don't want their real names used, not because they're personally ashamed of the association, but rather because they're just realistic about how other people tend to react to the Big P.

The first fellow I'll call "John"; he used to run a small video production company and has taken part in a couple of dozen films. "First off, let's eject that bullshit about 'exploitation' right away," he says, and pretty forcefully. "There's not a swinging dick among us who isn't exploited by someone in one way or another every day . . . your boss may treat you like shit and pay you at the same rate, you might work for a company where the clients you have basically make you kiss their ass, exploitation is everywhere. The difference here is that everyone knows the score going in, a lot of the young guys are pretty damn savvy."

I ask John about the ones who aren't so smart, though, the desperate kids who might need the money to make their rent or pay their bills, and haven't really considered the fact that their naked and engorged images might well live forever on some stranger's crowded disk drive or in his treasured video/DVD collection. "I can't tell you that every production company explains that to them, but I always did. I always checked and double checked their proof of age, I'd explain that at some point a future boyfriend or girlfriend might find out they'd done erotic features or photography and have a problem with it, that I'd be happy to hire them, but only if they thought it all through. I have to live with myself, you know."

John shares an unexpectedly moving story with me; it seems to strain credulity, but he swears it's true. "We had this one kid come in, really good looking, tall and athletic, a straight boy he said, but he had some gay friends who were always telling him he should do porn, because he had this nice big dick. They weren't lying, either . . . once he said that, I had to see it, and he wasn't shy about whipping that thing out." John says he sat the boy down, explained all the caveats to him, gave him his card, and told him to call him back in a week. "So he calls back, and tells me he's decided that it's too risky, because he's going to join the Army. I wish him the best, tell him to be careful.

"Six or eight months later I'm watching the local news, and I see this kid who's been wounded in Iraq and they're talking to him in a military hospital. I was fucking floored, man, because it was the same kid who turned me down! Thank God he was just wounded, not dead . . . and that he wasn't one of those poor bastards who have to learn to live without an arm or leg. But after seeing him I got to thinking how things might have turned out a lot different for him . . . it's hard not to think that if he had done the scenes he might have liked the money, and stuck with it awhile, maybe tell the Army to wait, or maybe change his mind and not enlist. I guess what I am getting at is this, that everything is risky in some way. Doing porn is pretty far down on the list.

"Now as far as romance goes, that's not really what we're about . . . our job is to get you excited and get you off . . . but I can tell you I've seen a lot of films that actually had some character to them, that had some sweet love stories in there besides the sex."

"Tom" tells me he never performed in any such "romantic" endeavor in the dozen or so flicks he was part of. "All my scenes were pretty cut and dry for the most part, not much set up or story, and what stories we had were pretty lame," he says. "I did this one movie where we were all supposed to be life guards at some pool, and it was mostly just a lot of sucking and fucking, some three ways, stuff like that. In another we were dressed up like football players, and we celebrated our big win with this orgy in the locker room and shower."

Tom says he started doing scenes when he was 19 and continued on until he was around 22. "I'll always have that story to tell people if I want to, how I helped pay for college by getting my rocks off. I can't speak for anyone else in the business. I only know what my experience was like for me. But no one ever asked me to do anything I might not have done for fun on my own." I ask him what it's like to get naked and aroused with so many bright lights on, to have sex with guys he hardly knows, surrounded by a production crew and a director calling for better angles or more action. "To be honest I was pretty turned on when I first got into it, I hadn't had a lot of sex yet, and suddenly there's this guy paying me to go down on some big muscle man or fuck the hell out of some young twink, and I got off on the fact that people were watching me do it. There were times I was really into it, less and less of that though as I did more films. Later it just got to a point where I was done with school, and I felt like doing other things."

"Chester," as he wants to be called, is a lot older than Tom; he's in his mid-forties now, but back in his late twenties and early thirties he took several turns rolling about in the sheets—and out in the woods, and the occasional barn—during his six-year stint in gay porn. He's still in great shape, and with his shaved head and salt-and-pepper goatee he still turns heads when he hits the clubs. But no one ever recognizes him from his "glory hole" days. "Back then I was a bleach-blond-long-haired-surfer-beach-bum kind of guy, always had the tan going . . . I hardly ever get tan now except in the summer. Once in a very great while I take a look at those movies, and scan through the photos, and it's like looking at someone else. I really don't miss doing porn, but I do miss that hair . . . once I started getting a little gray and thin though I had to ditch it."

Chester says he started doing scenes after he lost his first postcollege job and was having trouble finding a new gig in the Los Angeles area. "I was pretty strapped for cash, and just bumming around on the beach, trying to decide if I needed to go back home to

Georgia. This guy saw me and gave me his card. I thought it was a modeling job, which it was, sort of, just with no clothes. I thought, 'Why the hell not, it'll pay the rent.' Then I realized I liked doing it. That led to a few stripping jobs, and eventually some videos. Nothing too weird or wild, just your standard j/o, some one-on-ones, the occasional trio or group. I think I did like two or three a year."

I ask Chester if he found the "performance" as much of a turn on as Tom did. "You know I don't think I ever really thought about that when I was in a movie. I actually got more turned on when I was dancing for someone up on a bar, and you could only get down to a g-string in the clubs where I worked. I used to get offers to 'show more' for some extra cash, and if the guy was hot enough I'd give him a flash. Doing videos and photo shoots felt more like work, even if that work meant I was humping some guy. Sometimes the guy I had to hump wasn't someone I'd choose to hump in a million years, but that's one reason why they pay you. It's about someone else's fantasy, not yours."

Speaking of fantasy, I put some questions to "Dylan," a 22-year-old college student who's still making the occasional video for an on-line production company. Dylan's biggest attraction, besides his hunky-smooth-jock build and handsome face, is that he is billed as a straight guy, albeit a straight guy who has jacked off on cam, been massaged and blown by a few eager male companions, and has even plowed a few men's asses in his day. "I was working in a hotel part time, and there was a guy who was booking rooms there once or twice a month, always coming in with these guys half his age. I clocked him for a gay dude, thought he must be paying these guys for sex. One time when he was leaving he gave me his card, and explained he was shooting videos, and asked me to be in one."

Dylan says at first he was taken aback by the proposal. "I told him I wasn't gay, wasn't interested. He said he was only looking for straight guys, that that was what he was all about. He wrote down what he'd pay me, told me to think about it. I liked those dollar signs, that's for sure, but still wasn't too crazy about the idea. I didn't even know if I could get naked on cam, let alone get hard with some guy watching me jack it."

But those dollar signs were hard to forget. "I called him back, told him I'd try it. It was really weird at first, just like I thought it would be. But he had some good straight porn playing off to the side, and I just focused on that, and nature took its course. And the money was really good." Eventually he grew comfortable enough that in later sessions he would let other guys get in on the act, submitting to their happy hands and mouths, and in his latest videos, giving a few of them a good poke in the rear.

I tell him that I have to know what that was like for him; even the sexual adventurer in me can't quite picture putting myself in such a situation with a woman, even though I know it would do nothing to make me think I was in any way heterosexual. (Not that there's anything wrong with it.) "I guess it's not easy to convince some people that I'm having sex with guys but I'm not gay," Dylan says. "Not to sound like a whore but I really am just doing it for the money. A guy can suck a dick better than a woman usually can, but it's still a guy, so that's a little strange for me. [His boss] says that's why the guys who buy the videos get so turned on, to know it's a real straight guy getting his dick sucked, or fucking some other guy's ass." Recently Dylan says the boss has started to up the ante. "He's bugging me to try sucking a dick myself, and maybe getting fucked. Who knows, if he pays me enough I might go for it. The fucking thing I think I could do . . . putting my face in another dude's crotch, that'll take some psyching up."

That brings me back to the "live forever" aspect of porn, especially how it applies in a digital age when most videos don't just rest on dusty shelves or inside a locked cabinet, but are also traded and retraded at light speed around the world, one hard drive to another. How does Dylan, for instance, feel about the idea that one of his college buddies might find his pictures or videos online, or that some family member or future employer might stumble across them?

"My buddies all know already, some of them say they want in on the action. People who really know me know I'm straight, anyone else I don't give a shit about," Dylan replies. "One of my buds is gay, and tells me he has every one of my videos and likes the jack off to them, that's kind of special, I guess. He knows me well enough not to try and make a pass at me, 'cause that ain't happening. I guess it would be weird if my Dad or one of my brothers found them, that would mean they were looking for stuff like that. Same thing goes for any job I might get or not get. Never really thought about it, I'll let you know someday if it happens, you can put that in your book, too."

I ask Tom and Chester the same question, about the chance that some future partner might be horrified to find out what they'd done in their younger days, if they worry that their brief porn dabble might be a turn off. "Gay men are a lot less judgmental when it comes to porn than straight guys or women are, since most of us like watching it and are less hung up about sex in general," Tom says. "I probably wouldn't date anyone who had an issue about it, so that's not going to be a problem for me anyway."

"I don't think you can even find any of my videos anymore, I may have the only copies left," says Chester. "The company I made them for went out of business a long time ago. I doubt the original films or tapes even exist at this point. I should probably get off my ass and get them transferred to a DVD or something before they disintegrate, it might be fun to pull them out when I turn 60 and show my geriatric friends what a hunk I was then. My partner already knows, he's cool about it."

I'm also curious to know what all of them think about the men who bought their films, who might be "enjoying" them to this day. "If I help some lonely or horny guy to get off, great, it's an ego boost I guess to know people want to see my body and fantasize about it," says Tom. "I've been recognized a few times when I've gone out to a club, it's never bothered me . . . usually it was worth a few drinks, and a couple of dates here and there. You might not think people can get star struck when it comes to a porn actor, but they do . . . most of them realize that there's a difference between what happens in that video and what I might really be like." Chester has a similar take. "That really was a younger me, not the 'me' I am now. If some guy still has one of my tapes and he's still getting off, I say God bless him. But he really should be getting some of the newer offerings out there, the lighting and production value is a lot better. So are the plots."

Finally I ask my porn stars about the idea that working in the industry might have some kind of detrimental effect on the psyche or the soul, if not for any of them specifically, then perhaps other porn actors that they've known. "Oh, there were lots of fucked up guys on the set, sure, druggies hustlers and head cases, you name it," replies Tom. "That's one reason why I refused to ever do anything raw [sex without a condom] because God knows what you could catch. But you get to talk to those guys, and you realize that they'd be fucked up no matter what they did, their damage happened a long time before they ever got on a movie set."

"I don't think it ever got into my head the way you hear it does to some people," says Chester. 'It's just something I did once, like the dancing and photo shoots. Trust me I've done a lot of other things I regret a lot more." As for Dylan, who tells me he's still intent on making some more "easy money" before he gives it up, he says he doesn't think the experience has damaged him at all. In fact, he happens to believe just the opposite. "I was kind of timid and scared about a lot of things before, and I didn't think of myself as all that good looking. Now [his boss] tells me people like my vids more than any of the other ones on his site. It doesn't turn me on or anything, but it does make me feel like I'm kind of 'hot,' which gives my self-confidence a boost. Sometimes I wish girls got off on porn the way gay dudes do, I could probably find a way to make it work for me. Most chicks I know just think it's nasty."

However you feel about his actions or attitudes, Dylan certainly seems to have that last point right, how gay men are more accepting of porn than heterosexuals on both sides of the sexual divide, especially females. Sexual renegades that we are, gay men have always been a lot more comfortable accepting erotic imagery within our own mainstream; like it or not, it just seems to go with the territory of our bars and bar rags. Can you imagine walking into a straight club and finding nearly naked—and sometimes, fully naked—images of men and women scattered about the way one does upon entering some gay venue? All members of the same team, most of us just aren't ashamed or embarrassed by the sights. In fact, most of us find them enjoyable and titillating.

With a few notable exceptions—like Dylan himself—most straight men I know have a hard time even admitting that they jerk off at all, let alone that they do it while they watch porn; that's an attitude that starts in junior high or high school I guess, when a teen who admits he likes to slam his own salmon seems to be admitting he can't find a girl to do it for him. Straight guys, even the occasional straitlaced straight guy, will confess that they've seen an X-rated flick or two in their day, but never out in the open and shamelessly the way your average gay man will. And far fewer will admit that they regularly surf the Net or order up a pay-per-view movie when the girlfriend or wife's away, with the clear intention of pumping their gas in the self-service lane.

    I used to wonder if gay men were just more highly sexed than straight guys, right up until the day I stashed my little gay light under a bushel and joined the Marines. That's where for the first time it was acknowledged, and rather matter-of-factly, that this was something we all did. Late-night barracks gabfests often lingered on the topic to much comic effect; we talked about personal bests in times-per-day, or the weirdest places we found ourselves fondling ourselves. I remember my buddy Jay, who used to drive home to Ohio every weekend; he told us how he used to wait until he got out on the freeway far outside the city lights . . . that's when he'd just reach down, unzip, and go for it, sometimes two or three times during his eight-hour drive. (Savoring that visual, I always wanted to ask him where he put the proceeds of those little sessions, but considering my molelike status as an undercover 'mo, it wasn't safe to appear too curious.) Another buddy, Kenny, explained how he'd wait until everyone was asleep in the barracks, then roll over in his bunk and grab a sock, using it just like a cotton condom. (He also explained the rude surprise he gave his bunkmate one morning, who picked up that sock in error and put it on with a little squish.)

    My favorite story though belonged to Ricky, who told us all how the "hornies" always seemed to hit him about 3 p.m. every afternoon, which happened to be the same time each day he was alone in the supply office. Ricky said he would pull the trashcan over with one foot and place it strategically between his knees, take care of business without even getting up, then kick the can back to its place and get back to work. I remember it was Ricky who used to avow that there are two kinds of guys: the ones who jerk off, and those who lie and say they don't.

    If only all of us could be so frank and unembarrassed about indulging the sexual side of ourselves. The few straight men I know these days who will admit to owning some porn for a little self-service from time to time also tell me how they have to keep their stash "in the closet" so to speak, or at least under the bed, lest they offend their wives or girlfriends. But that doesn't always work. One young lady I know told me how she was "crushed" when she hopped on her boyfriend's computer one day to send an e-mail—he was in the shower at the time, the poor slob—only to find links to a dozen porn sites he had bookmarked. "It's just so . . . so dirty. I felt like I must not be good enough for him," she cried to me, and broke up with her boyfriend not much later.

Contrast that sad little tale with the story of a gay guy I know who jumped on his boyfriend's PC while he was taking a shower, and found hundreds of movies and pics on his man's hard drive, becoming completely livid with each new discovery. "He'd been holding out on me," my buddy said. "This was like the mother lode of porn, and he never shared. What an asshole." His boyfriend apologized, and now they often watch their favorite scenes together as a sort of virtual warm up to their own real-world canoodling.

It was a little surprising to find that virtually all of my psychological and relationship experts were somewhat indulgent of gay men's interests in porn; analyst Bill from Chicago pointed to the fact that such imagery can indeed be enjoyed jointly by couples, and provide some "variety" even in the context of a monogamous relationship. "It's important that such adult material be viewed in an 'adult,' manner; I know one case where a man got jealous because his partner seemed more interested in what was happening on the screen than what was going on in their bed, even though the partner was the one who suggested they 'take in' the movie in the first place. I think fantasy is a wonderful thing, and couples who can use that within their relationships to enrich their sexual experiences probably have a lot going for them in the long haul."

But Bill and all the other experts I talked with do acknowledge that porn can have its addictive aspects. "Fantasy is powerful, and some people will overdo it to the point where it replaces reality," he tells me. "Like any other addiction, you start having a 'problem' when you reach the point where the addictive agent starts to take over . . . you find yourself being late to work, or missing work altogether . . . or you find that you're spending more and more of your hard-earned cash on your stash of porn." Bill tells me he had one client who nearly bankrupted himself because of his "habit," not to mention just about losing most of his "real world" friends. "This was a fellow who had only a moderate income, which came from a job that required him to be mentally sharp. But he was getting less and less sharp all the time, because he was staying up late joining more and more porn sites and downloading videos. He used to tell me he had hours of hours of stuff saved up, movies he hadn't even watched yet, but still there he was night after night, putting ever-greater charges on his credit card until he was pretty much maxed out."

Bill says his client told him that even as he was sinking into deeper and deeper trouble, he discovered he was actually enjoying porn less and less all the time. Yet those diminishing returns didn't keep him from eventually tapping his monthly rent fund on a regular basis . . . this as he was called on the carpet by his boss for his habitual lateness and mediocre work efforts. "It took that double whammy—getting threatened with unemployment, and eviction—to snap him out of the spiral he was in. That's when we started working with him. As is usually the case he had a lot of other issues he had to resolve along with his fixation on pornography. That was the just the tip of a very big iceberg."

But Bill cautions that even with the experience he relates about his client—and he points out there are thousands and thousands of folks like him out there—it's important to remember that an addiction shouldn't necessarily cast a complete shadow over the subject of that addiction. "Lots of us like to have a cocktail now and again, that doesn't make us all alcoholics. Some people love to bet on football or basketball games, and that doesn't make them a 'gambleholic.' I don't happen to take that simplistic approach that says alcohol and gambling are de facto evil, simply because some people can't manage their impulses in a healthy fashion. Similarly, when I hear people rail against pornography or erotic imagery—especially that of the same-sex variety—one might pause to remember the millions who view it without any negative consequences at all, as opposed to the much smaller numbers of people who have a real and definable problem."

Bill reminds me how earlier we'd talked about rejection and the issues many people have about their self-image. "I'd never advise anyone to use porn as a replacement for a real relationship, but everybody likes to take a 'vacation' now and again from the real world they have to live in. Porn can help you escape from that world, just for a little while, when you feel it's judging you too harshly. You have to come back from a vacation eventually, but there's nothing wrong with having a good time while you're there."

Mason, our big porn fan from Vermont, puts it more succinctly. "Your porn star is never going to be anything more than a fantasy, but one thing you can count on, he's never going to reject you. And he doesn't give a shit what you look like."

CANDID CAMERAS

There must have been, oh, 20 guys watching me wank it, maybe more; I wasn't really paying attention to who was coming into or leaving the room . . . I was staring at the three dudes who were wanking it right along with me. As luck would have it we all finished at roughly the same time, to general applause and congratulations from the group for another fine "show."

Before you get the wrong idea, let me assure you this wasn't a suburban sex party, or some same-sex re-enactment of Caligula. None of the guys—be they watchers or wankers—were even in the same area code, let alone inside the same room; this little soiree took place in cyberspace, with the main event broadcast live and in living color on the Internet. What's more, none of the participants were, shall we say, professional performers . . . we were all just a bunch of regular, horny Joes, doing what an ever-increasing number of regular, horny Joes are doing these days.

If they have access to computer and a webcam, at any rate.

That's a little snippet from an article I wrote for the April 2001 issue of *Instinct Magazine*—we called it "I'll Be Watching You"—and it dealt with what was then a fairly new phenomenon: the proliferation of webcams and the increasing willingness of gay men—including yours truly—to use them for fun and frolic. Wherever you stand in terms of approval or disapproval of such goings on as I described then, one really does have to marvel at the technology that makes this all possible, and that's especially so these days, with the growing numbers of folks who have high-speed Net access, and even higher-quality webcams. Just the other day I heard a technologically challenged chap at work remark that he's still waiting to see if we'll ever really have those futuristic video phones like we used to see in all the old sci-fi flicks; he didn't seem to know that for lots of us, those "phones" have been here for years already, as part of our basic home computer equipment.

Gay men being, well, gay men, we were among the first to realize that having such a hook up in the bedroom makes virtual "hooking up" as easy as booting up your hard drive. As I explained in the article, the same webcam technology that lets Daddy see his kid's first step from a thousand miles away also lets a thousand gay Daddies peep in on one another, either as a pure observer—there are hundreds upon hundreds of webcam sites where guys like to put on a show, sometimes for free, but more often for a fee—or in a more "interactive" fashion. Sometimes that interactivity happens in webcam "communities," where members can browse lists of other members' cameras, view their profiles, and make contact; other times it's a more personal setup, where one guy simply finds out that a guy he's interested in has a webcam that's accessed by a messenger program. Links are exchanged, and fun generally ensues.

"I've had a membership to ICUII [it's supposed to sound like "I see you, too"; you can find it at www.icuii.com] for several years," says Jeff, a 25-year-old receptionist in Harrisburg, Pennsylvania. "I don't use it as much as I used to because I don't have the time I did in college, but back then it really helped open my eyes to all the thousands and thousands of gay guys out there. I could spend hours on that thing every night, meeting people just to talk and make friends, or get really, really sexual with. I remember one night I jacked off on cam with a guy who had a 10-inch dick. That doesn't happen everyday." Jon, a 19-year-old college student in Akron, Ohio, says the similar cam service he belongs to lets him meet and converse with a host of people he'd never encounter in the real world. "How else could I get to know and see a farm boy from Wisconsin, a surfer from California, and a cute banker in Sydney, Australia, all in one night?"

"Talking to cam-to-cam is definitely a lot better than just chatting with people you meet in some random chat room," says Kevin, a 30-year-old writer in Grand Junction, Colorado. "So many people you meet online are liars, and that 'cute' guy you've been chatting with all night might be someone who doesn't think twice about sending you somebody else's picture. [We'll be talking about that hot topic a little later on.] But when you meet someone who has a webcam, and that cute guy you're chatting with is moving around and talking and laughing at your dumb jokes, well, that's really him you're seeing. The cam helps cut through the bullshit fast . . . and if things get sexual, that's awesome. I've had a lot of fun with guys right in my room, even when there was four feet of snow piled up outside and I couldn't go anywhere."

"Whether you're an observer or an active participant, hanging out one-on-one or putting on a show for a whole group of people, fast computers and faster connections have created a new wrinkle in the age-old face of sex play, tailor-made for the New Millennium," I wrote back then in *Instinct.* "There are no invitations to send out, no coats piled high on the bed, none of that wear and tear on the carpet, certainly none of those nasty little STD's to worry about. Hell, you never even have to get up from your chair" (p. 31).

I first stumbled on the whole webcam craze the way most guys do; I was surfing the Net one day, probably researching some long-forgotten article, when I happened upon something rather amazing. This attractive young man had set up various webcams around his apartment that would catch him doing just about everything we all do in our daily lives, including sleeping, getting dressed and undressed, eating, watching TV, or chatting on the computer . . . and once in a while, masturbating for all he was worth or having some carnal company over for the evening. By current standards the site was rather primitive; the camera image wasn't the best, and the picture would update only every thirty seconds. I learned to my chagrin that a hell of a lot can happen in that short space of time it took the new picture to download; it was simultaneously addictive and infuriating. (These days that kind of problem is largely a relic of the past, and it's easy to find a site where the "cam op" in question has full-motion video, and full audio to boot.)

Over the next few years I encountered more and more such sites, some of them elaborate affairs with fancy graphics and intricate menus that allowed one to access weblogs—now simply called "blogs"—photo galleries, stored videos of previous goings on, message boards, and chat rooms. (Others were little more than a single page with a camera, usually with a link that allowed the viewer to chat with the cam op via the AIM, Yahoo, or MSN messenger services.) Eventually I got so intrigued I decided I had to have my own site, but virtual sex wasn't the main thing I had in mind, at least not at first. I just thought it would be cool to have a place my friends could come and chat with me live, and where I might make some new friends along the way.

Then a funny thing happened. I discovered that being peeped at on cam can be every bit as addictive as peeping in. Lots of us are exhibitionists at heart in one way or another, and when you have a few dozen people logging on every night to see you and say hello—even tuning in overnight to watch you sleep—it's a mighty blast to the ego. It wasn't long before I found myself indulging the occasional polite "request," and I couldn't help but notice that the attendance in my chat room swelled in direct proportion to the swelling in my boxers. Like a lot of other guys with webcams, I learned it can actually be a lot more fun to indulge yourself when you're also indulging the fantasies of untold folks out there in the great unknown.

"I know it sounds awfully creepy to some people," admits Danny, a 19-year-old college student in Texas. "I didn't start out to have a 'hot cam' site either. It was mainly a way for my friends and me to chat with each other. When other people started watching us get silly with each other, you know, flashing our dicks and whatnot, my friends kind of freaked out. But I was kind of turned on by it, to tell you the truth. If my hard drive hadn't crashed I'd still be playing around on cam. When I get my new computer the first thing I'm going to do is get that webcam back up and running. I miss it a lot!"

Which is to say, he misses that ego stroking that comes with the territory, and lots of other cam boys echo that sentiment. "Just knowing there are guys out there who want to watch me makes me feel better about myself," says Michael, a 24-year-old cam op from Ohio. "I love getting naked on cam for guys. It just turns me on greatly to know that people are watching me and are turned on by me in return."

Robbie, a 19-year-old in Milwaukee, doesn't mind the ego stroking, but when it comes to that other kind of stroking, it's still a relative rarity. "I didn't want to have a cam site where I just beat off my cock all day." He created his site after spending a lot of time in online chat rooms; he says he thought it would be "neat if people could see who they were talking to." Like a lot of personal site owners, Robbie provides gallery pictures, along with his various musings and thoughts, message boards, and links to his own favorite sites. "I wanted to give people the opportunity to see the whole picture . . . my camera is there for observation and surveillance of anything I may be doing at any given time."

And he means that. "It doesn't happen all that much, but if I get excited at my desk for some reason I won't hesitate to take my boxers off and jerk off in front of the camera," Robbie says. "It's another part of being candid and just letting people watch . . . whatever may happen, whenever it happens."

Sure beats *Survivor,* doesn't it? In fact it's often occurred to me that the explosion of so-called "reality TV" programs back in the day may have owed much to the sense and sensibilities of the Net-viewing public, since at any given moment of the day one can dial up any one of countless webcams, Big Brother–like, and peep in on the lives of total strangers. You may not get to know them as well as you did, say, Richard Hatch—remember him?—but if you're looking for "fat naked fags" they're out there . . . along with skinny naked fags, smooth fags, hairy fags, old fags, young fags, you name it. Some of them show it all, while some of them just tease you silly.

Mike is a 20-year-old cam op who lives near Littleton, Colorado. Like most of the guys I've talked to, he says it "feels good" that so many guys like to watch him get completely naked and aroused, then "perform" on his cam; he also records videos of some of his hotter sessions and makes them available for his fans to download for anywhere from $25 to $100. The twist here is that Mike tells me he's straight. "It doesn't turn me on so much as it is nice to know that people think I'm worth that money they spend, that they think I have a nice body," he says. "I'm not shy about being naked and hard on video, and I'm not afraid to show my face like some guys on cam are. People want to give me money to watch me do something I'm going to do two or three times a day anyway, that's a great job to have."

Jonny is a 21-year-old cam op on a large group site made up of several well-built and incredibly photogenic young men, all of them listed as "straight college guys," but unlike Mike, none of them are about to give their fans a look at their full Monty. "We know it's 99 percent gay men who watch, and we know that that's what they would really like to see, but we don't do it, not even when we give our 'private sessions,'" he tells me. "Once they've seen that, most guys will lose interest and go on to somewhere else. But if you hold that back, they're stuck, hoping they'll catch you live the day you decide to go crazy." Jonny says most of his time on cam is spent flexing, lifting weights, modeling different kinds of underwear, swimsuits, and wrestling gear. When he first started with the site he rarely did more than pose in his shorts or sweats, his smooth and toned athletic body oiled up so it would look even better in the light of his dorm room. (He swears he really does live in a dorm at the Midwest college he's attending, and on cam it looks just right . . . which is to say it's a total pig sty.)

Once he'd been on the site a while Jonny says he started getting bolder. "I never used to show my ass unless I had underwear or a swimsuit on. Now I get completely naked except I'll wear a jock, or

I'll put a sock on my dick, or I'll hold a hat over it or even a shoe. [That must be for the foot fetish guys.] You might see the very top of it right below the pubes, or you might see my balls swinging from behind, but you never really see 'it,'" he explains. I ask him if he's ever been tempted to just drop the sock or the hat. "There was one night some girl was in the chat, saying these really sexy things, and I almost did it . . . I was actually getting hard and that almost never happens, believe it or not I get kind of embarrassed if I start bulging . . . anyway I started thinking 'what if it's not a girl?' and was just some guy who was doing a good acting job. That would have been weird even for me . . . besides we can get kicked off the site if we show anything, that's the rule, even in the private chats we're supposed to keep it covered."

I tell him such rules seem oddly puritanical, considering that the fans who foot the bill are, as he points out, "99 percent gay." Why not give the people what they want? "I just work here, and the money really helps with school and other expenses," Jonny says. "The guy who runs the site tells us what we can do, and he will kick somebody off. One guy who used to be on the site came home drunk from a football game, got in his chat, and did the whole thing naked, started stroking it, the whole deal. He was gone the next day. It's just the rules we have. I could probably make a lot more money if I did go all the way in the privates, but letting some guy look at my body or my butt is one thing, letting him see my dick feels like I'm crossing a line or something. Trust me I've been offered hundreds of dollars for that, and I'm not going to do it."

Jonny may not need the cash, but most other cam ops do, since maintaining a decent webcam site is most often an individual and frequently expensive affair, what with all the hosting and design costs, access fees, and the equipment involved. That's why so many cam sites come and go so fast, and the ones that stick around the longest usually charge anywhere from $15 to $30 a month for their members, on top of whatever they make from those private sessions. But that money hardly frightens the cam fans away, far from it; there are thousands out there quite willing to whip out their credit cards, even if that means they'll only be "teased" by a Jonny—or any other cam op—who isn't whipping out much of anything at all.

As with the porn we talked about earlier, the whole webcam phenomenon certainly has its critics. I've talked with some men who tell me they'd just as likely run down the street butt-naked as they would ever appear on an Internet cam in the same state of dress. And they have some pretty strong opinions about the men who do, whether they're on an established site like Jonny or Robbie, or simply interested in chatting one on one. "We've just taken all the mystery and innocence away from the manner in which we meet or communicate with each other," says Lowell, a 37-year-old account manager in St. Joseph, Missouri. "Before two guys even meet in person for the first time, they may have already seen each other completely naked, doing the sort of intimate things that some of us used to build up to after we got to know each other. It was bad enough when people were sending each other naked pics . . . now it's a long-distance hook up, and it's just based on sex. I just think it's so sterile."

"I don't have a problem with people who meet and chat and maybe fool around on their personal cameras with someone they like," says Rob, a 28-year-old postgrad student in New Jersey. "I do have a problem when guys turn themselves into webcam whores, a lot of them not even in high school yet. I find that pretty distressing, and shame on those perverts who egg them on. But lots of guys who are old enough to know better do the same thing . . . I used to chat with a guy who lived down south somewhere, and over a year or so I really built up a kind of fondness for him, I was even hoping that one day we might meet in person. I'd sent a friend of mine his picture once, and he emailed me a link a few months later, telling me that my 'friend' appeared to have a new hobby. It was appalling what he was doing on camera for strangers for little more than pocket change. I called him on it . . . he told me to stop being so uptight, that he was just having fun and making money doing it. We haven't spoken since. I'm glad I found out about him before I invested any more emotions in him."

"I hear stories like that and I think the guy on cam was the lucky one to find out how uptight that other guy was," says Derek, a 24-year-old waiter in New York who used to appear on a few group sites and still makes a little "money on the side" when he puts on the occasional "show" on his private webcam. "It's one way I like to express myself, I like being the center of attention and commanding an audience, even if it's just a few regular 'fans' of mine. I would never want to date anyone who had so many issues with that side of my personality, which is very sensual and sexual . . . and there are thousands of guys out there who appreciate it, and enjoy it."

"I regularly check out about 20 cam sites," says Jason, a "middle-aged" cam fan in California. "Most of them are the real life 'voyeur' cams, and they hardly ever show anything. To tell you the truth guys like that are a hell of a lot hotter to watch than any porn site, because if they finally do slip those boxers off the payoff is so much greater than it is when a guy just yanks it all the time like it's his job. I don't always join up, because I'm not made of money, but I've been a member here and there . . . cams are always better than some pre-packaged porn, because most of the time you're watching it all happen live, it's more exciting and immediate."

George is a 33-year-old cam fan from Indiana who also loves the "immediacy" that his favorite cam sites provide. "There's certainly that aspect of it, that 'anything could happen' feel, and often it has. I was watching one of my favorite sites one night, a dorm cam, and the guy on the camera was having a party or something, with all these young jock types going in and out. Mind you this was a guy I'd been watching for a few months . . . he always said he was straight, and there were always a lot of girls in his room, some that he 'made out' with. (Never any sex on camera though, and he never took all his clothes off.) But he was soooo cute, and very nice and upbeat in his chat room, it was a nice distraction from the work I have to do on my computer at all hours of the day and night.

"So he's having this party, and I'm checking it out here and there as I work. I must have got caught up in my facts and figures for a bit, because when I glanced back over to the corner of my screen I suddenly saw they all had their shirts off, and they were sitting on the bed, everyone with a beer in hand, laughing and having a good time. I felt like I was right there with them, it was really a flashback to my own college days. Then one of them came over to the keyboard, typed in something, and gave the camera a thumbs up . . . I loaded the chat real quick-like, and asked the people in there what was going on. One of them typed 'just wait, you'll see,' and that's what I did . . . a few moments later everyone in the dorm room was naked, and the 'straight' cam guy was blowing all of his friends, one by one. Now you tell me . . . is that better than some canned porn, or what? It was all happening, right in front of me, so to speak. Had to be one of the hottest things I have ever seen. He hasn't done anything like that since, but I keep watching, hoping he will."

Between the unexpected "hotness" that shows up on cam from time to time, and the fact that cam fans tune in so regularly that they begin to feel like they "know" the guy they're watching, it's little wonder that so many guys get "attached," sometimes emotionally, strange as that may sound to the uninitiated. "I just totally fell in love with this one boy on cam," says Jerry, a 35-year-old webcam enthusiast from Kansas. "He might have been the hottest guy I've ever seen, anywhere. Like a lot of young guys who have sites he claimed he was straight, but that he just liked to get off with people watching. And talk about horny . . . it seemed like every night he came home, beat off and blew his load in about two minutes. I got so used to seeing him, and it wasn't just his face or his body or the fact he was so generous with his physicality . . . it was like he was someone I actually knew. Then poof, he was gone, and I haven't seen him since. I miss him."

"That sort of stuff happens all the time," says one site administrator I'll call Reggie, since he doesn't want his name used. He handles about a dozen webcam ops and their sites, something he calls about as easy as "riding herd on a bunch of cats," in that so many of them start out eager and excited to be on cam, then get bored quickly like a kid who tires of a new toy. "Other times the guys on cam get burned out, or they get involved in school or something in their personal lives," Reggie tells me. "But what [the cam ops] never seem to realize is that there are a lot of lonely guys out there, many of them deeply closeted or living in really remote areas where they have no chance of ever meeting another gay guy, who come to depend on those cam sites as an outlet for their sexual fantasies. When the cam op pulls the plug, for whatever reason, it can leave a real hole in people's lives."

I actually experienced some of that myself. I too had admired the occasional random cam boy and made him the object of my harmless personal fantasies, and missed him a bit when he "unplugged" and vanished for parts unknown. But once I had my own site it was I that suddenly became a fantasy object for others. I discovered that people I didn't know and would likely never meet were suddenly intrigued with my intimate details. That interest increased a dozen-fold when I met my young and hunky ex-boyfriend Andy, and he redesigned the site to make it a joint affair; we would routinely get e-mails, literally from around the world, from folks telling us what hope we gave them that two gay guys of such different ages could actually meet, fall in love, and share that experience on camera, in pictures, and in the videos we made for the site. When we broke up a little more than a year later and I took the site down—without Andy it just wasn't that much fun for me anymore—I was deluged with even more e-mails; there were notes of condolence, telling me to keep my chin up, e-mails berating me for letting such a "great guy get away" (really appreciated those, thanks), and e-mails from guys who were offering to "fill the void" that Andy had left, if not in my heart, then perhaps in my bed. (All politely declined, but thanks again.)

It really didn't surprise me that people who only thought they knew me were willing to be so bold with their advances; I'd already heard a number of stories from my favorite cam boys about their own obsessive fan base. It doesn't happen very often, but sometimes a fan's enthusiasm crosses the line into out-and-out stalking. "I had a convicted armed robber make threats on my life and send slanderous e-mails to my former employer," Robbie tells me from Milwaukee. "Some 19-year-old loser made comments about my new car and my exact whereabouts. He told me he'd be 'watching' me. Two days later, the lug nuts on all four of my wheels were loosened and my front tire started wobbling on the interstate." Robbie says in both cases he called the police, but he doesn't know if they ever took any action. "It makes me feel kind of vulnerable at times," he admits. "I won't be doing this for the rest of my life, but I'm not ready to quit just yet."

"I think the threat of being seen by someone who knows you or recognizes where you are is always in the back of my mind," says Matt, a 24-year-old college student in Arizona who used to be appear regularly on a group site. "I actually had someone who lived in the same building as me talk to me in a chat room one night, it was very disturbing to think that even with the Internet being so massive and anonymous that this one person had stumbled onto me." Webmaster Reggie says the potential "stalker element" is one reason he advises his cam boys to be "very careful about any personal information they reveal" to their fans. "I discuss a number of things with every model, including the possibility of a Jeffrey Dahmer-type of stalker who might just take an interest in them . . . not so much as to scare them, but to make them aware that the 'Net is a large place, and likely puts them in front of more psychologically-disturbed people than they'd encounter otherwise."

The biggest complaints that most cam ops have don't involve the "boil your bunny" crowd—such stalking really is an extreme rarity—

but rather about the fans that come to feel that they "own" them, or at the very least, have carte blanche to order them around. "Take your shirt off. Show me your cock. Can I see your butt? Roll over. Play dead. Sit. Fetch. Good boy," says Robbie derisively about the messages he's gotten once he's turned his cam on for the evening. "Sometimes I wonder when I became a 'gigapet.' My responses have ranged from: 'I have a better idea, why don't you play hide-and-go-fuck-yourself?' to 'Sure . . . you watching now?' But I really don't have a lot of patience for guys that beg me for a show. If I'm not in the mood for sexual exhibitionism, I won't do it. Period. Which is one reason my site is free. If you start charging, people think you owe them something, and in a way, they're right. But my site is free, so it's all pot luck. You get what you get."

With all the potential negativity you might wonder why anyone would put himself "out there" for the world to see. But even those cam ops who admit they get burned out a little from time to time are quick to point out the good times they've had with their sites, some good friends they've made, and some unexpected bonuses. "I was lucky, I never had too many obnoxious fans and no one who knows me ever emailed me a pic from one of my jack off sessions, demanding to know 'was this YOU??'" says Dave, now a 28-year-old fitness trainer living in the Houston area. "I was a young cocky college kid in great shape, and I loved to show off. I'd say it was about 99 percent fun." Dave says he never made a ton of money from his site, usually it was just a little more each month than it cost to keep it running. But once in a while he'd get a very nice surprise. "I guess a lot of the people who were watching must have had a lot of cash . . . some of them used to tell me I should raise the price on my site (I only charged about half of what people usually do) but I would tell them 'it's ok, I'm doing just fine.' The next day I would check my [he gives the name of an online banking service] account, and there would be a $100, $200, one time even a $500 donation. That kind of thing happened once or twice a month. I would write them back, thanking them, telling them I hoped they could really afford it. It just shocked me to think that my little time on cam a few nights a week could end up meaning that much to so many people."

THE CLUB AT THE END OF THE STREET

The voice, loud and brassy and commanding, calls out over the thump-thump-thump of canned club music, the steady din of a couple of hundred voices, mostly male—there's but a giggle of young women here tonight—and the haze of cigarette smoke wafting through the triangular glare of dozens of spotlights.

"Good evening and welcome to the House of Wet! Everybody having a good time?" The response is about a six on a scale of one to ten, so I know what's coming next. "Oh no, that's just not going to do it . . . I said is everyone having a GOOD TIME?" This time the cry back registers a good eight, sufficient for our host to start the show.

Or make that "hostess"; you would not call "her" a host, at least not to her face, as she towers above you on five-inch heels, wrapped in a shimmering silver dress and sporting a frosted blond wig that reaches nearly a foot toward the tall ceiling. "I am the Queen of the House, LaTroya. Y'all ready for a contest?" This time the cry reaches an ear-splitting nine-point-five, and now that she's satisfied that the crowd is paying sufficient attention, she motions for the paid dancers to leave their perches, for the deejay to lower the volume, and turn up the lights that illuminate a platform-like stage that runs the length of the room.

Within the next quarter-hour that stage will be filled with a half-dozen or so contestants in this Wednesday Night's Amateur Contest; for more than 30 minutes up there they'll pose, prance and dance their collective booties off, each hoping to win enough mass approval by the time all is said and done that he can take home the coveted $200 first prize, plus whatever tips he can get in the meantime. Those usually come in the form of a $1, $5, or even $10 bill that their admirers will stuff in their socks in appreciation for their efforts.

That's the only place to put them after all, since socks are the only thing tonight's contestants will be wearing.

It may come as a surprise to some to learn that the nation's capital, famously buttoned-down and all-business from 9-to-5, gets more than a little bawdy once the sun goes down. And few places in town have been bawdier over the years than the club called Wet, one of four gay male strip joints that sit just blocks away from the U.S. Capitol, virtually in the shadow of the sainted dome itself. Sadly, for those who love to stop by a place where free-flowing alcohol and even freer male nudity pretty much guarantee them a good time, all four may soon go the way of the dinosaurs; by the time you read this those same city blocks may be plowed under to make way for an entirely different field of dreams, a stadium for the city's new baseball team (As if there wasn't a lot of pitching, catching, and trying to get to second base going on around there already.) At this writing the plans are still in flux, and it's not clear yet if any provision will be made for new DC locales where the boys will be allowed to strut their stuff. For although there are several other such clubs scattered in cities across the country where hunky dancers can ply their trade wearing little more than a smile, the DC strip scene is rightfully famous for its longevity, and its sheer diversity of fine male bodies; for years they've come here to dance, literally from all over the world, in all colors, shapes, and sizes. It'll be a shame to see it all go.

But I haven't come to Wet on this night to talk about the imminent approach of any wrecking ball. I'm here to take in a scene that's very much in the spirit of fantasy we've been talking about in this chapter, to talk about a place where men of all ages can show up to admire the taut bodies and handsome faces of fit young men dancing naked in bright lights. Yet it wasn't that long ago that a club like Wet was generally frowned upon and disparaged, and some gay men still have the same reaction when they hear the words "strip club"; they picture a dark and seedy space, filled with desperate, unattractive, or unwanted men, hoping to get close to the sort of guy they can only dream of having, to maybe cop a quick feel or pick up a trick for their money. To be brutally honest, that assessment isn't too far off the mark when it comes to some of the other clubs in town, and that went for Wet too when it first opened its doors as a go-go club in the early 1990s; I remember popping my head in there out of curiosity and popping right the hell back out again, feeling like I needed a shower. (And not the one they've installed up there on the bar that gives the place its name.) There was more groping and feeling-up than you find in a backseat after prom night, and most of the dancers looked like the kind of smack-addled rough trade you see only in bad porn flicks, circa 1977.

Then something shifted, somehow. I went back to Wet with a couple of friends from out of town a few years later; they said they wanted to take in a "really sleazy place" just for the hell of it, and being pretty drunk at the time, I said "Why not?" No place was sleazier than Wet, I thought, so imagine how surprised I was to find the crowd that night to be rather young and hip, the vibe surprisingly mellow and not in the least bit sleazy, and the dancers shockingly clean-cut and wholesome-looking, even as they jiggled their johnsons and bubble butts for the guys bellied up to the bar beneath them. "How long were you going to keep this a secret?" one of my friends demanded, giving me a shot in the arm for emphasis. I don't remember what I answered. I was too transfixed by the sights.

Soon Wet became a regular stomping ground for my friends and me, and by the looks of the ever-increasing crowd, most of gay DC at some time or another as well; it's not hard to spot the same lawyers, doctors, college professors, and journalists you normally see in the city's more upscale environs . . . not to mention all the college kids in town working to become the lawyers, doctors, college professors, and journalists of tomorrow. There's nothing like bunch of naked guys dancing and a couple of cheap, stiff drinks to bring everyone down to the same basic, hound dog level, even if some men still prefer to hang back in the shadows, so as not to appear to be enjoying themselves too much.

By far the most popular night is Wednesday, when hundreds show up for the amateur contest, and it's not hard to figure out why. You just never know who's going to enter, or chicken out at the last minute, and that suspense is part of the fun. One takes a walk around the bar as the midnight hour approaches, trying to spot the hopefuls. I talk to a nervous young straight guy sitting with his girlfriend in a dark corner; his name is Nick, and he's from just up the road in Baltimore . . . with dark wavy hair and a muscular athletic build he's a total knockout. "I really need the money, and this seems like an easy way to get it. But I don't know if I can actually get up there and take all my clothes off in front of a bunch of guys."

Joey is a 20-year-old college student who goes to Georgetown; he's slim and tight, with short blond hair and what appear to be green or blue eyes. (It's dark where he's standing.) "I was here last week and I saw this really hot guy, then all of a sudden he's up there dancing. He should have won but he didn't . . . anyway I thought it was really gutsy for him to enter. So I thought I'd give it a shot, see if I have the nerve." A dozen or so feet away from Joey I find Steve, a 23-year-old from northern Virginia, tall and lanky and fair skinned, with a short shock of punky black hair; it turns out just about all the girls in the room are part of the "cheering section" he's brought along with him. "They've never seen me naked, so that's going to be a little wild," he confides. "But it's my birthday, and this seemed like a great way to celebrate. In my birthday suit."

Whether it's easy money, showing their "guts," or being out with friends looking for something "wild" to do, the guys who decide to "bare all" on this night "all have their reasons," explains the "Queen of the House," LaTroya. Most contestants are between 18 and 30, she tells me, usually on the lower side of 24 or 25, and for a young guy like that the prize money is nothing to sneeze at. But she points to other motivations as well. "Some guys just like to show themselves off, they want the crowd to see they're one of the 'beautiful people,' or they see the paid dancers we have and think 'I can do better than that!' Sometimes they're visitors from out of town, and since nobody knows them here, they figure they'll give it a shot. Some people just want to do something 'out of the normal' for them, or their friends talk them into it. And some people just let the drinks take control, and go with the flow!"

Indeed, I notice that Steve is getting pretty tipsy with his girlfriends, and I mention he might want to dial it back a little, lest he risk toppling off the platform and into the crowd. He puts his arm around me flirtatiously and says "as long as you're going to catch me" before breaking out into laughter and spinning back to his friends. That reminds me of one of Wet's biggest selling points, the sexual vibe it creates in the crowd, even if anything approaching actual sex—or even simulated sex—is officially frowned upon. There are several signs posted reminding patrons not to touch the dancers below their shoulders or above the knees, and reminding the dancers, be they paid or amateurs, not to give themselves more than a glancing touch . . . at least not where anyone will notice. Like the other DC clubs, Wet has been shut down a time or two in the past, when local authorities got wind of such behavior. The staff here even checks the restroom periodically, to make there's no hanky-panky going on in the stalls.

Still, the presence of the working dancers "working it" up on the bars and platforms, and the imminent appearance of the night's contestants, always tends to work a certain magic on the crowd, encouraging folks here to check their regular "attitudes" at the door. "I can talk to people here who won't give me the time of day at other clubs," one guy tells me. "It's like everybody is here for a good time. If someone does pitch me an attitude I can just walk away and look at the nearest naked guy, so it's all good."

I spot one of my favorite dancers walking through the crowd—he uses a stage name when he dances, his real name is Brian—and get his attention for a few moments. (That's all the time he can spend with me; when they're off the stage the dancers are supposed to "mingle" and flirt, and pump up the good-time vibe, paying special attention to the men who might not always find a hunky boy draped shirtless all over them.) "This is all about the fantasy," he explains to me. "I'm not really selling my body when I'm up there, trust me, I'm worth a lot more than $8 an hour and a few bucks in my sock. I sell them the illusion of sex"—he draws the word out for emphasis—"and I have some regulars who like to come and watch me when I work. I try and show them something they'll remember." It's not hard to believe him, either; earlier in the evening I spotted him swinging upside down from the steel bar riveted to the ceiling . . . I have no doubt that the four or five guys I saw staring up at him will recall that sight quite lovingly.

Brian says he really "gets off" on being naked in front of people, and he almost means that literally; he's well-known for becoming quite physically aroused up there on occasion, especially if he spots a guy watching him that he happens to find attractive. "I just kind of close my eyes a little, and wham, there it goes. The guys love it, and I get bigger tips." But even Brian says he can get tired of the stripping scene. "Sure it gets old, sometimes. When it gets too old, I'll just quit."

Those sentiments are echoed by a friend of mine named Matt—that's his real name, not his stage name—a 19-year-old from Fort Washington, Maryland, who entered the amateur contest one night a few years back after he got drunk and his friends "dared" him to do it. "I placed third out of four people and was offered a job. I figured 'I'm broke so I might as well do this until I can find something better,'" he tells me. "Little did I know that the longer you dance the harder it is to quit. I ended up working as a stripper for the next year."

Matt says when he first started "it was very exciting and new. I had the most fun that I had ever had at a job." He says it made him feel "amazing" that so many guys would look up at him and stuff money in his sock. "It made me feel hot to be such a sexual object . . . but as time went by it wasn't that much fun anymore." Matt says being a stripper conflicted with his conservative, religious background, and caused him a lot of sleepless nights.

"To put it bluntly, I started to feel like a slut . . . we had customers that would sit there and actually tell us exactly what to do and how to dance for them. They'd say 'turn around,' or 'squat down I want to see that ass,' and lots of other disgusting things. It makes a person feel worthless. Like all you are is someone's sex toy . . . I started to hate to look down, and think about the fact that the people looking up at me are only interested in my dick. They have no concept of who I am or what I believe. Sometimes I wondered if the customers would even notice if stopped showing up."

But Matt hastens to add that he has no regrets at all about his twelve months at Wet, since during that time he fell in love with one of his fellow dancers, a young man he calls the love of his life. "I'm not bitter at all, I just think I should be honest. This isn't for everyone."

With that somewhat sober reality check in mind I pull aside another of my favorite dancers for a quick chat; he still works at Wet as I write this and doesn't want his real name or his stage name used. "No, it's not for everyone, but look . . . we're getting naked in front of people and getting paid for it," he points out. "If you don't want people staring at your ass and your dick, you shouldn't be a stripper . . . I mean, come on, get real already. No one is making you do it, right? You can always work at McDonald's."

True enough, I suppose, pondering how often I've enjoyed looking at his golden arches up there on the platform. Like most of the guys who work here regularly, he seems rather blasé about being naked in public, which calls to mind a criticism I've heard voiced by men who tell me they would never be caught dead in a strip joint. "It takes all the 'specialness' away, if that's even a word," says Jay, a 28-year-old office-worker friend of mine from DC who says he's never even been "tempted" to check out Wet or any other such club. "When I see a guy naked it means he's there for me, and only me, and I am not about to share him with a crowd." Mark is a 40-year-old DC attorney who also tells me he's happy to stay away. "Debasing, dirty, disgusting, and that's just the D's," he tells me. "I'm sure I can think of a lot more words, but you get the idea . . . I can't imagine why anyone would want to get naked in front of a crowd, and I can't imagine going to watch someone make such a spectacle of himself, either. I can't see the appeal."

Obviously lots of men do, however, and I am surrounded by them tonight. "It's the guys dancing sensually above them, the movement of their bodies, the play of their muscles when they move, just the admiration of the body parts they find most attractive," says LaTroya as we huddle at the end of the bar, looking down its length to where it trails off into shadowy bobbing heads and bodies. "People want what they are not, if they're heavy and don't have a perfect body then they often tend to look for a thin or very built guy . . . if they're older they frequently want to look for someone younger . . . if they're young and skinny they look up to the older, muscular dancers." She points down to where one of her dancers, a handsome young jock type with a buzz cut, squats near the edge of the bar, smiling and laughing with a guy about his same age. The only difference between them, she says, is that one is stark naked and bathed in light, the other fully clothed, hands in his pockets and smiling, yet still a bit bashful and a little self-conscious.

"That right there is part of the appeal," she explains. "That's a total fantasy, having a conversation with a beautiful guy, to be near him physically when he's totally naked, and out in public, too." That sort of appeal is multiplied several times on Amateur Night, she tells me, when the guy you've been talking to all night, or maybe just eyeing from afar, suddenly decides to throw caution to the wind and enters the contest.

Speaking of which . . . the show is about to start. At her invitation I follow LaTroya to the inner sanctum backstage, where tonight's contestants have been summoned for their pregame pep talk, which is a primer of sorts on what they can and cannot do up on stage, and what they can and cannot allow others to do. There are six guys back here tonight—LaTroya says seven in all signed up, but one seems to be missing. "Oh child, that happens all the time," she explains. "Some get cold feet when we call them back." I can see from the faces around me that nerves are in fact taking hold on almost everyone; Nick, the young straight boy, is nearly white as a ghost. "I can't believe I'm going to do this, man," he says, and he barely seems able to unfasten his jeans. He's also worried the crowd won't cheer for him if they know he's not gay. At that Joey and Steve start laughing. "I just hope they don't figure it out," says Joey, explaining to Nick that naked straight guys are such a staple of gay men's fantasies that it would probably give him the edge. That seems to make Nick feel better. Steve meanwhile has taken off everything but his briefs, and he starts doing pushups to pump himself up. "Hey, good idea," says Nick, and soon they're side by side, puffing away.

As for the other contestants, they're not doing much talking; one already has everything off, and he's working to get himself aroused before slipping on a cock ring. He and the two others have the clipped and too-mannered look of "professionals," i.e., dancers who work at other clubs in DC or Baltimore and enter such amateur contests as a way of supplementing their incomes. They're also putting on a light coating of baby oil, so that their muscles will shine under the lights. "Do any of us have a chance?" muses Joey, glancing in the presumed pros' direction. At that I lightheartedly tell my trio to line up for inspection, and I get a very odd and quite incongruous flashback to my days as a Marine sergeant as I look their bodies up and down. Handsome Nick is by far the most muscular of the three, but Joey is just a little bit "cuter," with a very round butt to his credit; tall, lanky Steve, quite cute in his own way with that great big flirtatious smile, appears to be packing a major-caliber weapon in his briefs. "I think you all will do fine," I say, though to be honest the Wet crowd is famously unpredictable, and sometimes those pros do win, just because they have the "moves" down pat. (They don't need to know that, though.)

Still, it's a sweet sight to watch Steve, Joey, and Nick backstage as we hear LaTroya starting to pump up the crowd outside; they're like a team in the locker room before the big game, trying to get each other psyched, even though they're going to be competing with one another in a few minutes. Nick nudges Steve, secretly pointing to the pros across the room, two of whom have their tools out and are stroking furiously. "Should we be doing that?" he asks behind his hand, to which Steve responds, "If you do, I won't need to." Nick just shakes his head and smiles. "It's too fucking weird, but what the hell . . ." and out comes Nick's dick. "Holy shit," says Joey, looking down at him. "I am so going to not win."

Sad to say that's the point where I have to make my leave; I dash out of the back room and elbow my way through the now-packed bar, all the way up to the front of the stage where LaTroya sees me and gives me a wink. "Did you behave yourself?" she asks, making sure her stick microphone is off. I assure her that I am a professional and that any enjoyment would be purely incidental. Her response is a roll of the eyes, a "Yeah, right" toss of her wig, and a light bat on the head with the clipboard she's been cradling in her non-microphone hand.

Soon she's calling for the paid dancers' exits, for those lights to be brought up, and the dance music turned down a few notches. One by one she calls tonight's contestants out on stage; each gets a burst of applause as he takes his place beside the others and starts shimmying to the music. . . . all six have taken their spots when Diego, that cute skinny boy we met a few chapters back, dashes up to LaTroya, says a few inaudible words into her wig, then bounds up on stage. She looks at me with a little shrug; I see her mouth the word "bathroom." (I hope he was just taking a leak, and not throwing up from nerves. I've seen it happen, and it's not pretty.)

As is her custom once she has her boys in place, LaTroya instructs them to "turn around and face the wall," telling them that all she wants to see is "tail structure," and by that she doesn't mean through their briefs or boxers. "Here at Wet it ALL has to come off," she advises them to the cheers and whistles of the crowd, then pauses behind each dancer as he strips down to nakedness, commanding him to "work it, baby." And work it they do, each in his own individual way; Joey turns out to be a really good dancer, very fluid and sensual in his moves . . . Steve isn't half bad either, and his girl-crowd is almost beside itself with delight . . . Nick does his best, but he still looks ready to faint. Diego's well-rounded soccer butt is already drawing raves from the several guys standing behind me—one swears "you could bounce a quarter off that thing, and it would land in Miami," which really doesn't make any sense to me, but his friends all laugh in agreement—and as for the ringers up there, they're obviously well built and very able dancers, but mainly they just look bored by the whole affair. (I swear the one closest to me looks like he's standing in line at the post office.)

"Y'all ready to see what's up front?" comes the cry from LaTroya after a few minutes of this display, and the cry back is deafening. But as always she cries out a second time. "I said Y'ALL READY TO SEE WHAT'S UP FRONT?" and now the response is so loud I hear my ears buzz. "Turn around and face the crowd," she commands her contestants. "Show'em what you're working with!" That's when seven bodies spin away from the wall, and the already wild crowd goes just a bit wilder.

As a writer I can put myself in the heads of guys like Jay and Mark, who would in all likelihood condemn this scene, and the players in it. As a journalist I can report that I am now looking at seven naked guys, dancing away for all their worth in front of a crowd that closely resembles a pack of dogs that haven't been fed for, oh, a week or so, and is watching them as if they're cuts of meat, not actual people. I can see how some guys might find this display, if not actually dirty, then at least a bit debasing in many respects.

But as an unabashed fan of good-looking guys, and as someone who admires anyone who has the cojones to get up and get naked in public, whatever his motivation might be, I have to think instead that wow, this is pretty fucking cool. I've seen lots of other Amateur Nights at Wet, probably too many to count, but as LaTroya calls for the music to be restored to its full level, and reminds the crowd that they're encouraged to tip these contestants generously, that it's "not easy to get up here in front of you," I'm struck that this has to be one of the best ever. Clearly the crowd agrees, and before the "queen" has even gotten all the way off the stage, several guys are already lining up in front of each contestant, exchanging a few words with him before stuffing a bill into his sock and returning to the throng. I'm pleased to see that for once the pros aren't getting much attention, that it's my little quartet getting the lion's share, Joey in particular; he's really commanding the stage, moving all over the place like a little hottie boy possessed... Diego spots me, flexes his cute little skinny boy muscle, then turns around to shake his major asset... and maybe the oddest, and sexiest thing of all... Steve and Nick are nearly face to face, not really looking at the crowd... it's as if they're dancing with each other, or maybe for each other, big smiles lighting up their faces. (If Nick is doing that to hide his hetero nature, well, it's pretty convincing.) Steve's girlfriends are certainly eating it all up; they're hootin' and hollerin' away, and it's clear from the way they're mock-fanning themselves that they have a lot more than a sisterly affection for his naked bod. Nick's girlfriend, on the other hand, does not appear to be having such a good time; she's standing at the lip of the platform off to the side, her arms crossed tightly across her chest, her mouth pursed like she just bit into one large and particularly sour lemon. I try to speak to her and she just spins away from me, making a beeline for the exit. (Poor Nick. He's going to have a lot of explaining to do, assuming she'll even speak to him later.)

Maybe ten minutes go by before I remember that I want to find out firsthand how they're doing up there, so I reach in my pocket for a handful of singles. I motion first to Diego, and he leans down so he can hear me as I stuff a dollar bill in his sock. "What's it like?" I almost have to shout over the music and crowd noise. He stands up and tosses his head back laughing. "I love it!" he fairly screams. I manage to get Joey the whirling dervish to stop momentarily. "Do I look okay?" he asks anxiously, apparently unaware that with his slim toned body, bubble butt, and slick dance moves he's an early crowd favorite. "Hot," is all I say, tipping him, then move down to the dynamic duo, still dancing face to face, and occasionally, back to front; Nick and Steve have got the folks here going wild, and they know it. It takes me a few minutes to get their attention. Nick stoops down first, no longer looking scared in the least, and with his jock-boy build it's hard to keep just eye contact with him. "The hardest part was turning around that first time, after that I stopped thinking," he shouts at me. "Steve is really helping me out!" (I can see that pretty clearly myself, and I notice he does not ask me where his girlfriend went, in fact he never even looks over to her last known position. That's interesting.) He gives me a clap on the shoulder and stands back up as I shift down toward Steve, weaving and bobbing there with his hands doing this little finger snap thing above his head, twirling his dick around so that it looks like a propeller on a small plane ready to taxi down a runway. He looks down at me, over at Nick, then back at me, and I see him—rather than hear him—say, "I think I'm in love."

Standing back now to take in all four at once—the other three dancers really do appear to be just going through the motions, they're hardly into the "fun" vibe at all—I'm struck by how much they resemble a naked boy band up there, eliciting something of a boy band response from the guys and gals crammed up next to the platform. Then I hear LaTroya's voice ringing out above the music. "Have y'all picked a winner yet?" she bellows, and the crowd roars back, though I honestly don't know how this is going to turn out. I'm just glad I don't have to choose.

LaTroya commands the crowd to give everyone a round of applause, and the dancers all return to their original spots, now just kind of bopping along in place and looking out over the crowd, and I can see some nervousness returning to my Fab Four's perspiring faces. As one former contestant once told me, this is the part where they really begin to feel the "most" naked, feeling every eye on them individually as LaTroya singles them out in turn, and the audience gives each a round of cheers.

Contest night has just three prizes; the first-prize winner gets his $200, the second-place winner gets five free admissions to the bar, and the third-place contestant gets a ticket for five free drinks. Everyone else goes home empty-handed, except for the tips he's gotten during that 30-minute dance session. I'm glad to see my guys all have bulging socks, so they'll have at least a little something to show for their trouble. But fortunately for them, the first round of judging sees all four getting much louder cheers than the ringers—even Steve's girls are screaming loudly for Nick and Joey, and Diego has that loud male cheering section close by—it's like everyone can see who the true amateurs are tonight. LaTroya makes it official by asking them politely to leave the stage. (They don't even look like they care very much, as they slip their cheesy bikini briefs back on and step down into the shadows.)

Now comes the hardest part, and strangely enough, this is where something akin to strategy comes in, according my former contestant friend. "You never want to be the first guy they call, because the crowd always cheers louder for the second, third, and fourth guy." The judges, usually some contest night regulars that LaTroya has tapped for the job, are sitting in the back of the bar, faced away from the stage; she'll approach each of the sweating, panting guys on the platform, point at him, and yell "How much do I hear for this contestant?" and the judges have to somehow gauge and measure the responses against one another, without knowing exactly who they're for. "It's kind of brutal, when you think of it," my friend says. "I mean picture it . . . you're standing there naked, balls out and swinging, not really dancing anymore so you have nothing to focus on, and now someone else is getting louder cheers, it's a great big group of people saying, 'Not you, sweetie.'" My friend has actually won a few of these Amateur Nights in his time, but he's lost a couple, too, which he seems to remember more. "I can tell you I was pretty pissed the nights I didn't win. It's a big time, public rejection. As soon as I won another contest I stopped doing it. Better to go out on top."

Which one will be on top tonight is still way up in the air; there seems to be a little problem with the judging—they're really having a hard time back there. LaTroya's taken the crowd through two more rounds already; the first time Joey got louder cheers, the second time it was Steve, and it looks like Nick and Diego might be battling it out for third and fourth. It's such a strange and silly exercise when you really think about it, but totally engrossing in a sort of American Idol way.

I can tell by her body language that the queen tonight is not amused as her judges finally approach her with the results . . . she simply snatches the clipboard away from them, and they quickly scurry away from her withering glare. "Y'all didn't make it easy," she scolds the crowd—or was that aimed at the judges?—"but we have a winner." She milks the suspense for a few more moments, pacing back and forth in front of the stage, flipping her blond tresses with her gloved hands. "Third prize . . . third prize goes to . . . Diego, give it up for Diego!" It's cheers and boos at that announcement; Diego's half-dozen most vociferous fans are screaming "He was robbed!" but LaTroya ignores them, pressing on. To his credit Diego still flashes a big smile and gives the place a "thumbs up" as he grabs his boxers, slips them back on, and exits stage left, hopping back down to stand beside the platform.

"Now this was the hard part . . . apparently," the queen confides, and somewhere in the shadows I'm sure her judges are squirming. "We have a tie for second place" she starts to say, and the crowd volume goes up instantly so that she has to shout even louder. "Second place prize . . . second place goes to . . . Nick and Steve!" And that's when two quite charming sights occur; first Nick reaches out to shake Steve's hand, and gets pulled into a full-body-contact naked hug—which he doesn't resist, and God, do I wish I had a photo of that—and then Joey, standing there alone in the center of the platform, realizing he's actually won, has this shocked little "O" expression pasted on his face, his hands grabbing the back of his head.

LaTroya hands him his little certificate—he'll get his cash from a bartender before he leaves—then he whispers something in her ear; she laughs and nods, then calls for the paid dancers to get back up on the bar and stages as the music pumps back up to full volume. But Joey doesn't step down like the winners usually do when the contest is over. He stays up there, doing a victory dance of sorts, and won't come down again for the better part of an hour.

It's getting on past 1 am, and although the crowd doesn't exactly empty out, this being a work night it does begin to thin out a bit. Presently I find Diego—he's got his pants back on but he's still sans shirt—getting a series of free drinks by way of consolation from his boisterous fans up front. I give him a hug, but he's not at all down in the dumps; as often happens he's been offered a job to dance here three or four nights a week. "Don't know if I'll take it, but it was good to be asked." I ask him if he minds telling me how much he made in tips. "Dude!" he says laughing, "I almost forgot." He sits down on a nearby stool and pulls each long leg up, taking the crumpled bills out of his socks and spreading them on the bar. "Looks like maybe $60, cool," he says smiling widely. (I also spot more than a few phone numbers scrawled on matchbook covers, which he pulls out and stuffs in his pocket, grinning sheepishly.)

Suddenly I feel a body leaning on me from behind, and I turn around and find myself face to face with Nick, just inches from his full lips, in fact. "Nice pile, D," he says to Diego. Then to me, "Here ya go," and hands me his free bar admission slip. "I won't need this."

"Yeah, I guess this isn't your kind of place," I say. Then he surprises me. "Well . . . I am going to start working here, so I get in free, I guess." Steve appears behind him and taps him on the shoulder. Seems somebody needs a ride home. Nick runs to get his jacket from the back. "Is he . . . ?" I start to ask Steve, who quickly presses my lips shut with his finger. "I don't know, and I don't care," he says. "But this has got to be the best birthday ever, man."

IDENTITY THEFT

"Maybe ten years ago, when the whole Internet chat thing was just getting going, I started having long late-night conversations with a young man who told me how 'intrigued' he was by older men who had kept themselves in good shape," says Arnie, a 59-year-old retired executive in suburban Pittsburgh. "Around here we always joke that everyone's garage is sunk six inches lower than ground level, because so many people have a lot of weights and weight benches and lots of folks are really into lifting, and I am no different. So when he sent me a picture of him shirtless, all pumped up from a workout, I was excited and I had no problem believing it could be him. (Back then it could take a few minutes for a picture to fully load on your computer, and I remember how turned on I got as his picture scanned lower and lower, revealing his handsome face, his beefy shoulders and chest, and finally his midsection which was very ripped and toned.)

"By the language he used when we chatted, it was, again, very easy to believe he was genuine. He'd talk about how he was glad to be out of high school and finally starting college, how he was getting comfortable with the idea of being gay. He said all the things you would expect. I gave him my home phone number, because I was anxious to advance the relationship past the computer . . . he gave me several reasons why we couldn't talk on the phone, such as the fact he always had roommates around, or he couldn't call me from the place he said he worked. (Before everyone had a cell phone it wasn't completely unreasonable.) In any case, he was very flattering about the pictures I had had scanned and sent to him, and late one night he seemed like he was getting very, very horny and his chat got very sexual. I said we should meet immediately (I was a lot bolder then) and after a few moments he agreed. He gave me a street corner not far from the college where he said he was studying. So I got cleaned up, shaved, and drove down there and waited. Several minutes went by and he hadn't shown yet, and I was beginning to get annoyed when someone rapped on my window, scaring the daylights out of me. I thought it might be the police. But it wasn't. It was a homely fellow who looked only a few years younger than me. I rolled the window down a little, asked him what he wanted, and he said 'Arnie, it's me, Robby.' Needless to say he was not a handsome college-aged jock with bulging biceps. It seems very funny now, but I was actually shocked that anyone would seek to meet me, under such incredibly false pretenses."

Sound familiar? If you're like several men surveyed and polled for this book, then at some point you've been sitting right there—at least figuratively—in the front seat of Arnie's car. Or maybe you're more like Teddy, a 24-year-old bank employee in Rochester, New York. "I came from a very closeted background, so when I was growing up the only gay people I knew were on the Internet," he says. "When I was 18 I made friends with someone I thought was just like me, same age and background, same likes and dislikes, you name it. It got to be so I was excited just to see his name pop on my Buddy List, because this was someone I could pour my heart out to. The pictures he sent me didn't hurt either, because he was very attractive and at 18 it's very easy to build up a fantasy based on the way you chat with someone and the pictures that they send you.

"He didn't live near me so meeting him was never going to happen, but we really seemed to have a kind of 'relationship' after a few weeks of talking," Teddy recalls. "Then one night he told me he'd just taken a bunch of new pictures that he was sure I would like. He said they were very 'hot,' but before he showed me he wanted me to take some digital pictures of myself that were 'just as hot,' so we could trade. 'Young and innocent' me had never done anything like that before, and I told him I didn't know if I could ever show myself like that. Then he sent me one of his 'hot' pics to try and get me excited, and it worked . . . I took out my digital camera, took off my shirt and dropped my pants, and took about two or three pictures. I saved them to my computer and I was about to send them . . . that's when I noticed something 'funny' in the pic he'd sent me. I had been so fixated on all the skin he was showing that I had missed a little logo down in the corner that he hadn't completely cropped out. Turns out he'd sent me a picture from a porn site! (I was young, but not that dumb, I already knew all about the porn sites.) Since the face and body from the site pic were the same as the guy in all the photos he'd sent in the past few weeks, I realized he had been playing me for a fool the whole time. I asked him what the hell was going on, and he tried to deny it all, then he signed off and I have not seen him online since. Thank God I never sent him anything."

Literally every other survey or interview I collected for this book had a story at least similar in some respects to those above; in my *Chasing Adonis* poll 54 percent of my respondents say they've gotten at least one "fake pic" from someone they'd chatted with online, and most of the men I talked with say it happens to them "all the time." Others tell me how they constantly spot men with fraudulent photos posted along with their profiles on the numerous Internet communities used by gay men; still others relate to me how often they've contacted—or been contacted by—someone who eventually turned out to be a lot less than the sum of the "parts" he was claiming as his own. Most times the scam is simply noted and frowned upon; other times a guy can end up like Teddy, feeling angry and hurt . . . and occasionally you can find yourself in Arnie's shoes, who showed up to meet a young man he'd come to like, only to find out that he did not actually exist.

With so many gay men using the Internet as a frequent or even primary venue in which to meet others, such dishonest Johns represent the worst kind of betrayal; they're the fantasy men who prey on our deepest desires, leading us on to believe that they are exactly what we want, apparently unburdened by any sense of conscience or propriety. They clip and steal pictures from Web sites—often using porn sites, but frequently a "model" site, or simply someone else's online photo album, will do just as well—or they goad others into sending them photos that they in turn send out or display as their own. (A lesser sin, but still a sin in my book, is committed by men who use actual photos of themselves from days long gone by, before age and weight accumulated, or most of their hair departed the scene.) In many cases such men create wild and flattering profiles of themselves to go along with those images, looking to light a spark of interest in the too-trusting or simply unsuspecting.

"I was chatting with a guy on Manhunt [that's a popular nationwide gay male hook up site] and he was getting me really intrigued by the idea of meeting up with him some night," says Jeff, a 33-year-old restaurant worker in Baton Rouge, Louisiana. "His pics were really hot, and he was into all the same stuff I was into. He said he was a jock, a mountain biker, liked to go hiking, real outdoorsy stuff. His stats were good, too. [Those are age/height/weight measurements, and lots of men will throw in the cock sizes as well.] He only had two pictures posted on the site and you couldn't see his face very clearly, so I asked him to email me some more, just to see what I might be getting into. So he sent me an email, pics attached, and those pictures didn't look like the ones he had posted, and I told him that. That's when he started getting kind of bitchy with me, finally saying something like 'what does it matter what I look like anyway, we're only going to fuck.' Good thing I realized what a total asshole that guy was before it went any farther."

"When I first got online I was as gullible as anyone else when it comes to believing people," says Jerry, a 30-year-old visual merchandiser in Columbia, South Carolina. "Since I would never send anyone a fake picture (I don't have to!) it just didn't occur to me that anyone else would. But after getting fooled over and over again, I finally learned how to spot the signs, the most obvious being that it's a professional picture like you'd find on a porn site or if he sends several that appear to be different people. [That's happened to me several times.] If I have the slightest doubt about someone's honesty I stop talking with them, and I definitely won't go and meet them."

Ed, 24-year-old college student at U Conn, says the same sort of thing "happens constantly" to him; he's been on the Internet for years and traded with thousands of people. "It's easy to see dozens of people a day just sitting in an AOL chat for a couple of hours. A lot of them are obvious, the guys that send out pictures of famous porn stars, or even scans from A & F catalogs . . . then there are the guys that just use some poor regular (though physically beautiful) guy's pictures. Either way, these people never admit it's not them." Ed tells me he saves pictures from just about everyone he talks to. "That way if I see them more than once, I can look up who it was that sent me a certain picture the first time . . . if I ask to see another picture and he says he doesn't have one, and I happen to have a folder that has a lot more of that particular guy in there, then I know the guy is lying to me."

"Fake pic traders should just die," says Andrew, a 24-year-old nursing student in Iowa City, Iowa. "Sometimes you can tell right away that someone is lying to you, but sometimes you can't . . . I have had dozens of people contact me telling me they liked my profile, and we would strike up a kind of 'relationship' on line, chatting a lot at night, maybe even talking on the phone. They would look and sound exactly like the kind of guy I'd most like to get to know better . . . then later I'd find the same pics on someone else's profile. How do you ever know for sure who's telling the truth? It just sucks that anyone would lead another guy on like that."

Amen to that Andrew, and I speak as one who's fallen for the ruses just as often as the next guy. On the wall next to my computer I keep a framed picture that many visitors have remarked is "really hot," and it certainly is; it's a candid and nonprofessionally snapped image of a very muscular young man of perfect proportions, standing in what looks to be a bedroom, and he's wearing tight white boxer briefs that he's pulling down to reveal his pubic hair and half of what appears to be a very large dick. (I'm not a size queen by any stretch, but some things do command at least a measure of admiration.) His face is tilted downward, but what features you can make out look to be quite handsome, and he has longish hair that falls to his shoulders.

I keep it posted there next to this machine for two principal reasons. First because, well, it's a very hot pic and deserves to be displayed. But the main reason is that I have gotten that picture from at least five different guys over the years, all of whom swore on their sainted mother's graves that it was really them. I believed the first guy, as I was new to the Net at the time and hadn't realized yet that when some men put "VGL" on their profiles it just as likely means "very good liar" as opposed to "very good looking," and those are the men most likely to be all about the fakery. (I would also learn in short order that when a fellow's profile says he's "hung" he's often leaving out the phrase " . . . like a light switch" . . . that when he says he's "husky" it means he's shaped like a Butterball turkey . . . if he's "got a great personality" it's a good bet he's ugly as a mud fence . . . and if he mentions that he's "into commitment" it's a neon sign flashing "stalker, stalker, stalker.") By the time I got that pic for the second or third time I was becoming lamentably well versed in the treachery abroad in Net Land, and simply ceased all contact with anyone I suspected of being dishonest.

But still I've been fooled, and fooled again, because like a lot of other gay men I want to believe the fellow on the other keyboard is legit. Maybe it's because my very first Net dates went so well . . . like that memorable young man who didn't look like his pictures, he looked better, was hornier than a rabbit, and quite talented in the sack. Or the time I met a guy online who didn't have a pic to share—these days that's a red flag, early on it wasn't that unusual—but he did have a very sexy voice on the phone; when we finally met in person I was shocked and pleased to find out he was utterly adorable, and a really, really good lay.

Most times I've been hoodwinked it's been a case very much like Teddy's, when someone had a large number of photos available to send. I remember striking up a chat-type relationship with an apparently well-built young man; like Arnie's friend "Robby," he claimed he was a college jock, but fortunately for me he also said he lived hundreds of miles away, so that a personal meeting wasn't in the offing. Still, he was someone I enjoyed chatting with—he had dozens of extremely erotic pictures he said he'd taken using one of the digital cameras that were just coming into general use—and since he seemed to be the total package—smart and sexy—I'd come to like him quite a lot. One night he asked to see an article I'd been writing—it was among the very first I would submit to *Genre Magazine,* in fact—so I sent it to him. A few days later he sent me an e-mail, critiquing the piece rather harshly . . . except now his language wasn't that of a college kid at all, but rather more like a college professor.

And that's just what he turned out to be—he made the confession at the end of his e-mail—adding a small coda in which he briefly apologized for his trickery, yet expressing his confidence that we "could remain good friends." I was so stunned I don't think I even sent him a reply, and I never heard from him again. (Besides, he didn't think I was a very good writer, so fuck him and the horse he rode in on.)

Thank God he didn't live any closer, else I may have been moved, like Arnie, to try to meet him in person. I've only had that Arnie-type experience once, when I made a date with someone who'd sent me pictures of a tall, thin young man who was very attractive. And it really was him in the photos . . . the trouble is they'd been taken about 10 years and 50 pounds before we ever met online. I can still recall that look of wonderment in his eyes that I would turn around and leave the bar, and I saved the e-mail he sent me later by way of explanation: "You just seemed like a really nice and sensitive guy, not someone who would be all wrapped up in exteriors. The pictures I sent may be a little dated [a little!] but I am still the same guy inside. I was hoping we could still be friends." You keep hoping there, dude.

Patrick, a 23-year-old college student from San Luis Obispo, California, tells me he knows exactly how I feel, maybe more so. "John was my best friend from the Internet, we'd been chatting for like six months on the computer, and finally I was going to get to meet him in person," Patrick tells me. "He'd sent me his pics, I'd sent him mine, we'd talked on the phone for hours, and I had finally talked him into driving down from where he lived so we could hang out." Patrick says he wasn't worried about meeting John at his apartment—"We'd had so many phone conversations I felt like I knew him, inside and out, and I trusted him," he says—but John suggested they meet first at the mall. "That was fine with me, so I drove over there, parked, and went to where he said he would be. I was so excited, I was almost shaking. But when I got there, I didn't see him, and I got worried that maybe I'd gone to the wrong place. After looking around for a few minutes I remembered I had my cell on me, so I called. Right away I heard a phone ring a few feet away from me, and I turned just as I heard him say 'Hello?' in the phone. It was John's voice all right, but the guy talking wasn't the guy I had come to meet. John, or whatever his name really was, had sent me pictures of a really cute guy the same age as me. This guy was about my age, but he was the farthest thing from cute . . . he was tall and skinny with stringy hair and really bad skin. He stood up and looked at me, and said 'Patrick?' but I ran away."

Patrick says "John" kept calling him back on his cell phone, but he didn't answer. "I checked my messages later, and he'd actually had the nerve to leave me one telling me that I had hurt his feelings, and that I was just a 'shallow little pretty boy faggot' like all the other guys. I wonder how many he's scammed into meeting them, and I just can't understand why anyone would do something like that. If you're going to be a liar, fine, be a liar, but don't get mad at me when I bust you."

"I met a guy who said he was an 'Adonis,' 32 years old, six-feet one, and a muscle-bound 190-pounds with a nine-inch penis," says Edwin, the video news photographer in Arlington, Virginia, that we first heard from back in Chapter 3. "Oh, dear God, I don't know if I even want to talk about it . . . when he opened the door, there stood a 'smurf.' He was maybe five-feet-five, about 300-pounds, and bald as all hell. He was standing there naked, because he said he wanted to meet me that way, so I looked down and saw that he had maybe two-inches of manhood, and he was already hard! I should have gotten angry, but instead I just busted out laughing, turned around, and went home . . . I don't know why men do this shit, especially when they are going to meet you in person."

That is the pertinent question, isn't it? For men with any kind of self-confidence or healthy self-esteem, it can be hard to put yourself in the shoes of someone who can so casually perpetrate a fraud, even if they don't intend to physically hook up. "Look, we all have our good days and bad days," says Don, a 41-year-old mortgage banker in Springdale, Ohio. "I know when I am having a good day, like when I'm all pumped up from the gym and my abs are tighter than normal and the haircut is looking just right, that I might grab my digital camera and take a lot of pictures, and use those pictures to update my profiles or just save them to send to someone sometime. I'm not going to necessarily point out that I don't always look that good if I am talking to someone online. I think it's a given that we try to present our best sides as often as we can. But when you talk about men who blatantly lie, use old pics or someone else's, that's a sign they have a lot of issues. It's pretty anti-social, when you get right down to it."

"At the very least, they're dishonest people," says Brian, a 20-year-old college student in Massachusetts. "They could be some old or unattractive guy that no one would ever talk to, and the only way they can get you to talk to them is to pretend to be someone else. I know for a fact that one guy got in touch with me three or four different times, each time pretending to be someone else. But the weirdest thing ever was the time this guy sent me my own picture, then still claimed it was him even after I showed him who he was talking to. I guess these guys are so pathological that they figure everyone is a liar like they are."

That's actually happened to me a few times, too, back when chat rooms were new and there were a lot fewer people online. And that is one weird conversation to have, having to explain to someone how it's not cool to steal your identity. (Just as it happened with Brian I found myself having this surreal argument with the guy, who was reluctant to let go of his little fiction even though he'd been so clearly busted.) I've also found pictures culled from my old webcam site and posted on some strange guy's profile; I usually send them a severely worded e-mail, with a copy to that particular site's administrator, and the profile is gone in a day or two. I suppose it's flattering, after a fashion, to have a face or body someone would want to claim as their own, especially when he says he's in his late twenties or early thirties, and here I am staring at 50 in a few years. Still, I'm not all that crazy about being used as just so much chum for another fellow's fishing expedition. I'll hook my hotties, you hook yours, use your own damn bait, thank you very much.

In my polling I actually posed the question "Have you ever sent someone a fake picture, and claimed it was you?" Only 8 percent of my respondents answered that yes, they had; either that is a very busy 8 percent to be responsible for all the nefariousness on the Net, or lots of folks weren't being honest with me. In my surveys and interviews I asked the same question so the men involved might respond at length; again, not many did, but I did get a few responses I can share with you. "Yes, I have sent out fake pictures," says Scott, a 49-year-old who doesn't list an occupation, but says he lives in Canada. "I'm not a bad-looking chap, but I can't compete with guys half my age in the looks department. That's the kind of guy I am attracted to. So if I want to have his picture and talk to him, I have to pretend we're on the same level when it comes to age and appearance."

I ask Scott if he ever feels guilty "leading someone on" in such a way. "I just use the chats as a hobby or a recreation, and I never let it get so far that anyone would grow attached to me. If I sense that's happening I either stop responding, or I will tell him that the pictures I sent aren't really me. Either way, the other guy usually stops talking to me, which reminds me why I started faking in the first place."

Alex from Michigan—we'll get to his age in a moment—says he's really into "older, muscular, hairy guys," and has similar pictures to trade whenever he gets into one of those "muscle men" chat rooms or Web sites. "Those guys are my fantasy . . . that's the kind of guy I would love to get to know and have him come sweep me off my feet and take me into his arms. Most of the time the kind of guy they like is the same type they are, so that's the kind of picture and profile I have." But Alex explains to me that he is neither muscular nor hairy—nor is he "older." As a matter of fact, he's not even "legal," per se. "I'm 16, so if I tell them my age most of them freak out," he explains. "I'm also really skinny so even if they were into guys my age they wouldn't want me. The only way to talk to them is pretending to be just like they are." Alex says only a few times has someone wanted to set up a "meeting" and he has an answer ready if that happens. "I tell them I have a really jealous boyfriend who would kill us both if I tried to do anything with somebody. It's funny that some of them have said the same thing to me, which makes me wonder how many other skinny 16-year-olds are pretending to be muscle men, and we're all online, trading other people's pictures."

Dennis, a 23-year-old college student in Dededo, Guam, has an interesting take as both a victim and perpetrator of photo fraud. "I once chatted with a man who had a beautiful picture," he tells me. "We chatted for a while to see if we could mentally connect before exchanging numbers . . . then we talked on the phone and I liked the way he sounded and what his morals were. A few more phone conversations later, we agreed to meet. To my dismay I found that he wasn't at all like he claimed to be, and didn't look like he said he did. To be nice, I hung out with him for awhile to make him feel that it was not all lost." But Dennis says he's also created false profiles, and posted fake pictures, too, though he hastens to add he never tried to set up a meeting with any of the men he was chatting with under those false pretenses. "I wanted to find out why men are more responsive to attractive men, and why the anonymity of the Internet releases inhibitions in men that they can't release in a real social setting." Dennis says his "experiment" convinced him that too many men are caught up in "fantasy" when it comes to deciding who their "ideal mate" might be.

"The Internet is all about fantasy and shouldn't be taken seriously," avows Pablo, a 32-year-old in Astoria, New York. "I'm a fat guy that likes 'in shape' guys, and it usually doesn't go the other way, so I get off 'collecting' friends online who are 'in shape.' Only way I can do that is using someone else's pictures." Pablo says he found a really cute guy's Yahoo photo album online "several years ago," a guy he has never spoken with who doesn't even know he exists. "I think he lives way out West somewhere, like Wyoming or Colorado." Pablo says his unknown benefactor has been a "mad picture taker," and updates his album a couple times a month. "He always has new pics in there, so I just grab the best ones and save them then send them out to my 'buddies.' This guy isn't shy, even though he looks like he's only 18 or 19, and he even puts nudes in there, so I send those out too. He's got them up on the Internet already, so it's not like I am violating his privacy or anything." Pablo says he was "amused" once when he got an e-mail from one of his deluded friends, when he found one of "Pablo's" pics posted on a porn site. "He thought he was doing me a favor, letting me know about it. He has no idea that's not really me, but I thanked him anyway."

I ask him what he would do if the "owner" of those photos ever gets wise to him and drops him an e-mail. "That's an interesting question. I guess I would just tell him to fuck off. I have too many hot friends now that I like to talk with who think I'm a young stud. I would hate to lose them."

Pablo doesn't seem to have the slightest amount of guilt or remorse, but at least he's honest—in his own peculiar way—about why he does what he does. I've gotten in touch with several other "fakers" I've found skulking about on Web sites such as RateMyBody.com or FaceTheJury.com—those are sites that generally skew to the teen- and-twenty-something crowd of all sexual orientations—and very few ever respond. (I know they're fakers, by the way, because they're using pictures I recognize from porn sites, or pictures I've been sent dozens of times by others over the years; one guy I spotted recently who claimed he was "an 18-year-old hottie" was using a photo I was first sent back in 1994, an image of a fellow that has to pushing at least 30 by now.) Most ended up "blocking" me to prevent any further contact. But some did respond, and they had the same cornucopia of reasons.

"I'm not an ugly guy, or an old guy trying to get some hot boy to send him nude pictures," says one 20-year-old fellow who lives in Florida. "To tell you the truth I am pretty good-looking guy. But I am also very closeted, and if I am going to put the word 'gay' in a profile I just can't afford to have my real face or body 'out there' for anyone to see and possibly recognize." Closet Boy tells me the pictures he uses at least resemble him in most respects. "I found these photos of a tall blond guy with a great body who looks a lot like me, so trust me no one who meets me is going to be disappointed." I ask him if anyone else has ever called him on the fact his photo wasn't real. "Not very often, and usually if they do it's some older guy I wouldn't want to meet anyway."

One guy who won't tell me his real name, age, or location is using a picture on RateMyBody.com that belongs to another member of that very site. (I know this is guy is faking it, because like a lot of the newer sites RMB encourages its members to post at least one photo where they're holding up a handwritten sign that has their member name on it; this fellow has appropriated some choice photos of a young man I happen to know well.) "I just liked the way he looked, and since I posted those pictures I've gotten a lot of very nice messages and offers." I explain that I told my friend about him. "Oh he's written me several times, and I expect I'll get kicked off at some point. But until then I'll just enjoy the attention I am getting." (That little sign trick is one I started using myself by the way, especially if the guy I was chatting with mentioned he had a digital camera; it takes only a few minutes to take such a picture and e-mail it, and since so many people have been affected by the fake pic traders, no one who's legit ever seems to mind.)

This last guy tells me he would never contemplate trying to arrange a meeting offline with any of the men who make him the "offers" he speaks of. "I would be lucky to escape with my life, I think," is all he says by way of response, and from that I gather he's most likely a lot older and nowhere near as buff as my good-looking young friend. Yet as we've already seen, lots of men using fake photos and profiles have set up such a rendezvous; so what drives a faker like Arnie's "Robby" or Edwin's "Adonis" to go all the way, knowing they'll be found out in the end?

"I do it all the time," says a guy I can identify only as "Gym Hottie"; I spotted him on Manhunt lurking about in the LA area, and on his profile he says he's a "well preserved 39, 6-1, black hair, brown eyes, hard gym bod with silky smooth skin." But since he happens to be using a string of photos that, once again, I recognize from a popular porn site, I ask him how true any of that description actually is. (It takes a lot of cajoling on my part, but finally he 'fesses up.) "No, that is not me in the pictures. No, I am not 39, I am 47. I am 5-feet-9 inches tall." He even admits he's not particularly "well preserved," and actually has a bit of a skin problem, and is pretty hairy. "But you'd be surprised how many guys will come over, see what I really look like, and still have sex with me especially if it's late at night, 'cause that's when guys usually get horny and let their dicks do their thinking for them."

Another false photo user on Manhunt is "Swimming Stud," who lists his age as 19, says he's 6-feet-4-inches tall, and only into "real and genuine" guys in the Baltimore area. Of course Mr. Stud is also using photos of a certain Olympic champion swimmer that lots of gay men tend to drool over; he's just cropped the famously boyish face off the photos. (It's a wonder he didn't also use the pictures with the eight medals dangling over that delicious chest.) "Some guys get really excited, because they think it might really be Michael Phelps," SS tells me. "Even when I say I'm not, over and over, some guys still seem to believe it, and they ask me to come over or ask if they can visit me." So what happens, I ask him, when that door opens and they find out the truth? "Well if they're mad I'm not him, that's their fault, because I said I wasn't, even though I am using his pictures." I ask him how old he really is, and what he really looks like. "I'm just under six-feet, not in the best shape, and I'm 24. Some guys have slammed the door in my face, but most will just go through with it. I get action all the time, a lot more than I did when I used my real pictures. If you get a guy boned up enough he'll want to get off, even if you're not what he was expecting."

Therein, I suppose, lies the answer, and sure enough, more than a few men I've gotten with admit—if somewhat sheepishly—that they "followed through" in their encounters, even when their online contact was an utter liar. "What can I say, I was a horny 20-year-old and I wanted to get off with another guy," recalls Pat, a 30-year-old in Miami who says he "knows better" now. "It probably happened a half dozen times . . . I'd get there or he'd get to my place, and he wasn't who he said he'd be. I usually went ahead and had sex, because in some strange way I felt like I'd 'made a bargain' with him and it would be rude not to."

"Most gay men, and especially young gay men, are very sexual creatures," says Jess, who's now, ironically enough, a 34-year-old photographer in Anaheim, California. "When I was young I sent out fake pictures all the time just to get laid, and most times no one ever even said anything to me about the fact I wasn't the guy they were waiting for. We'd just get inside and fuck, and that was that. But maybe the funniest thing was the time I invited someone over I'd sent a fake picture to, and he wasn't who I was expecting either. I looked at him and he looked at me, and we both started laughing. He really didn't think I was very attractive, and I told him the same thing. But it was really good sex, so who cares?"

Chapter 7

Survey Says!

> Our opinions do not really blossom into fruition
> until we have expressed them to someone else
>
> Mark Twain

Not long ago I talked about the marvels of webcam technology that allow us to make a live video "connection" with somebody across the vastness of cyberspace, and it truly is a wonder. Yet equally impressive, and much more invaluable to this book—if perhaps not quite as much fun—is the more low-tech ability to post a survey and a poll online (or send them out directly via e-mail) and in the end have hundreds of people take part over a year-long period. In the end, 995 gay men of all ages took the poll, and 215 answered the surveys or sat for interviews. Without the Internet there's just no way I could have crossed paths with so many guys in so many places, in a relatively short amount of time.

But as I've related here and there, it's not easy when you're first starting a project like this to know all of the subject matter your respondents are going address, even as they answer your questions and provide you with their opinions. In designing the survey and polls—which I will one more time concede don't constitute a classic "scientific" inquiry, they're just snapshots taken of willing participants—I had lots of informal discussions with friends, colleagues, and random people I would meet online and during various social outings and book appearances. I would ask folks: if they were going to read a book about gay men and body image/relationship/desire issues, what topics they would like to see covered? And if they were writing such a book, what questions might they ask?

Many of their suggestions were fairly obvious topics to tackle, such as the effect of popular imagery on what we find attractive, how much our first crushes affect us for the rest of our lives, favorite body parts, the use of steroids, and body image disorders; all those subjects we've gone over here were among those most often pitched at me. But as I went through the survey and interview results—those taken online, through e-mails, and in person—sometimes it was the topics we hadn't thought of before we started that sparked my interest just as much; for instance, the year-long online poll didn't ask gay men how often they enjoyed pornography, if at all, or what kind of porn they liked best. I didn't ask men if they'd ever been stalked by someone who didn't want to give up the chase, nor did I ask them how often they'd found themselves attracted to straight men. Those were all subjects that many of my respondents brought up themselves, which required me to get back to work with a new set of questions so I could do a better job exploring those areas with anyone interested enough to give me a response. Trust me, I dearly wish I had included questions about porn and stalkers and straight men, especially in the online poll—I would have loved to see where those numbers ended up—and I hope you don't feel like I let you down, just because I had that little brain fart. (If I ever do an updated version of this book at some future date, you can bet your ass I won't leave anything out.)

And it's funny how I also experienced something of the opposite reaction with some of the topics I did include, which is to say that some people weren't shy at all about telling me that "this is a really dumb question," or "why the hell does that matter to anyone?" One fellow, upon seeing a question about how some men seem to prefer to have friends who don't "look as hot as they do" (so they appear to shine just a little bit more) just had to tell me that "the author of this survey needs to stop hanging out with so many freaks." Notwithstanding the fact that he may be onto something there—lord, but I do have some freaky friends—it wasn't me or my friends who suggested that particular question. It was a subject thread I found on an online bulletin board, and as it happens, there were actually a lot of spirited responses. Another guy took the survey to task when I started one question with the premise that "studies show Americans are by and large getting larger." His comment? "Why do you think people are getting fatter? Where I live and work everyone is in shape, everyone is hot, where the hell did you get that idea?" Of course, this particular gent happens to live—wait for it—in sunny South Beach, so I'm guessing he's never taken a stroll through a mall in Appalachia or parts of the Midwest.

Truth is Americans are getting fatter—like it or not—and at much younger ages than in years past. How much that might eventually shape our sense of what's hot and what's not is awfully hard to tell. Some men tell me they welcome the trend. "It just means I won't have to work out as hard as I do now," says one fellow wryly. "I think we might be on the edge of a change toward seeing larger guys as sexier than we do now," says another, pointing out how society in general and painters such as Reubens in particular—once delighted in full-figured female bodies, a far cry from today's "thin is in" paradigm. But probably as many as half of the men I got with simply refuse to believe that obesity is anywhere close to epidemic, or even a significant health issue, and they weren't shy about telling me I was "full of it."

Another critique—and this came from maybe 10 percent of those who responded—was that nowhere in my questioning did I make any specific inquiry regarding race or ethnicity. That was actually by design, because I wanted to see how often people brought that topic up themselves when I asked them to describe their "ideal man." Though I did touch on it here and there, I have to tell you it just wasn't something most men dwelt on in their responses for *Chasing Adonis*. Of course, gay men and the way they handle racial/ethnic issues is a hot-button topic; maybe it's just possible that some author you know is already working on a book dealing with that topic, and that topic alone, for publication at some future date.

One area I asked several questions about—but decided against using most of the answers in the text—was the whole topic of makeovers and plastic surgery and hair replacement, i.e., those strategies some gay men use to give themselves a new look and perhaps improve their self-image. I did get some good material in response—I used a little bit of it here and there—but then I realized as I was going along that this was ground I'd already plowed pretty thoroughly in *Reeling in the Years,* in the chapter titled "Forever Young?" and the poll data which conclude that book. So that's not so much an omission on my part, as an admission that this journey was beginning to get a little lengthier than I thought it would be.

In all I think the survey and interview responses I received and made use of—and like my last two books, I had to leave lots of good stuff on the cutting-room floor—gave me a pretty good idea of where a lot of gay men's heads are when it comes to what they like, and why they like it. And the following poll graphics—along with some choice quotes—paint an intriguing picture as well.

So let me shut up here, so you can see what they had to say.

THE RESULTS

True or False: If a guy has a great face, I don't care what his body looks like.

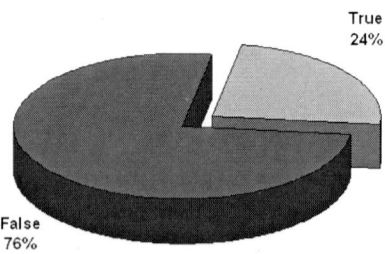

"Well, I would rather have someone with an average face and an average body than be unsatisfactory in the other categories, but no one is perfect and if I got along with the person, then it wouldn't matter. But, I have come to realize, that if a guy has a nice body and a bad face, he is still pretty hot, and there's always paper bags."

Jeff, 16, Student, Richmond, Virginia

"I like a guy who has a decent-looking face and a decent-looking body. If his face is awful, I could care less what his body looks like, and vice-versa. He's got to be at least decent-looking."

Jesus, 23, Advertising, Miami

"I have to admit that I once slept with a man that I thought had the perfect body but the perfect face. So I would have to say I can forgive that face but not the body."

Mark, 38, Houston, Texas

True or False: If a guy has a great face/body, but a so-so personality, I will still consider having sex with him.

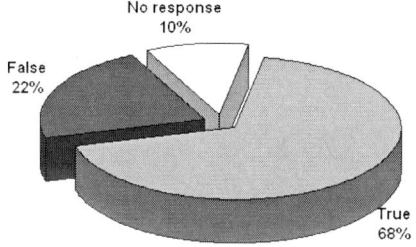

I also asked the exact same question in the opposite way, but got a much different response percentage, which just goes to show you how cognitively dissonant people are when it comes to polls, and how they will answer questions differently, based on how they're phrased. You may note that phenomenon throughout, and when you do, don't blame me, I just asked the questions.

True or False: If a guy has a so-so face/body, but a great personality, I will still consider having sex with him.

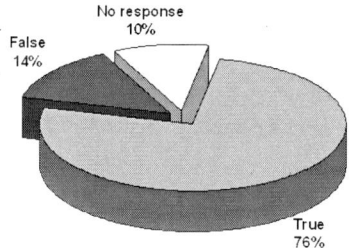

"The intellect is most important. I've been turned down more because of my appearance, and won't do that to others. I really look for intelligence, interests, and the person inside the package."

Sal, 44, Educator, Philadelphia

"I bet most people say they'll take the personality every time, but men are such liars, and they really only think with their dicks 95 percent of the time. If we're going to talk, fine, have a personality. If we're going to fuck, just shut the hell up and roll over already."

Barry, 30, dancer, New York City

"Without a personality, what good is a body or a face?"
Robert, 47, Warehouse Manager, Cambridge, Ontario

What is your favorite body part on a guy?

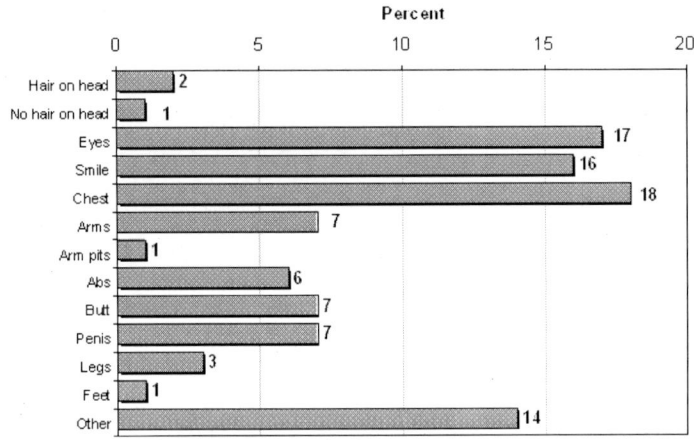

"Eyes. I want cobalt blue eyes that pierce through my own and make a maze out of themselves for me to get lost in every time. I want fire within those eyes that burns of passion and lust and feeling and hate and love. I want eyes that speak, yell, scream, chant, holler, and call out to me in every glance."

Greggie, 18, Sales Associate, Lake Ridge, Virginia

"The best way to draw my immediate attention is to offer a confident, witty greeting and a sincere smile. There are millions of people who are too self-absorbed or too bored to pay attention to social basics. Being intimidated, unfocused or insincere when you meet me is fastest way to ensure that I won't be interested."

Rick, 32, Software Developer, Omaha, Nebraska

"You want to make me hungry, you better be packing some meat!"
Dave, 22, Student, Boston

True or False: I like guys with smooth bodies, with little or no body hair.

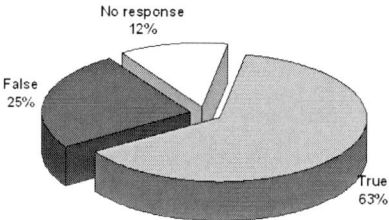

True or False: I like guys with moderate body hair.

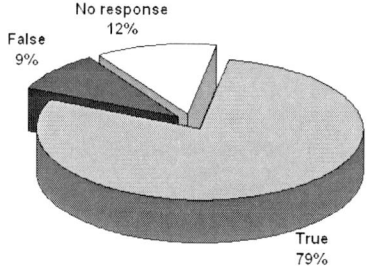

True or False: I like guys with fuzzy bodies, lots of body hair.

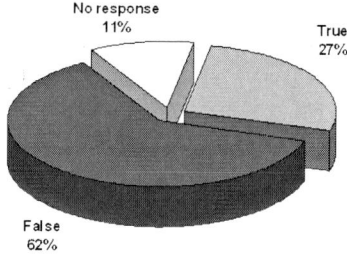

"I am drawn to hairy men. I like bears, but sometimes they can get too heavy. So, I like hairy men, especially muscular ones."

                Little Bear, 39, Massachusetts, In the Military

"Give me smooth abs, every time. I can't stand chest hair of any kind. It's not attractive to me and honestly, though it's a strong word to use, I find it downright repulsive."

                John, 30, Paramedic, Los Angeles

"It's so much if he's hairy, it's where he's hairy. I like a nice head of hair, but no beard or mustache (soul patches are ok, though.) I like the chest smooth, then maybe a bit of a happy trail, leading down to a nicely trimmed bush. And I said trimmed, not de-forested. Guys who shave it all off down there are just freaky to me."

Benjamin, 29, Nurse, Fort Worth, Texas

True or False: I like thin guys the best.

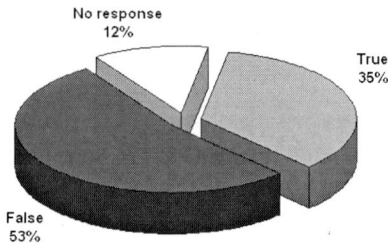

True or False: I like chubby guys the best.

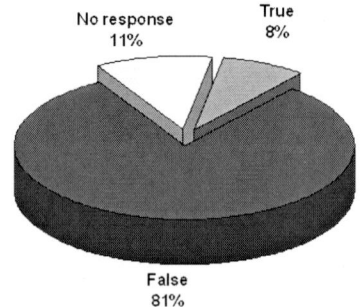

True or False: I like guys with a little bit of muscle.

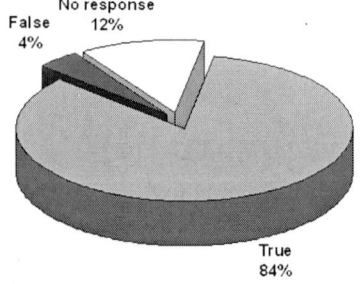

True or False: I like guys with a LOT of muscle.

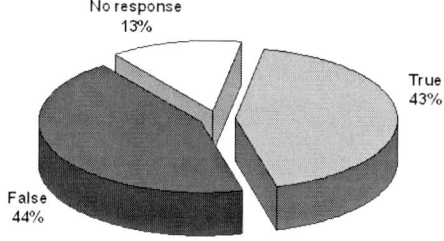

"I find a big chest a six-pack most attractive. Everyone I socialize with is a gym rat."

Chuck, 39, Human Resources, Miami

"You can tell a lot about a guy by his smile and by looking into his eyes. But then again, a tight stomach and a killer chest don't hurt either."

Stephen, 20, Student, Oklahoma

"When I was a teenager I always thought tall slim guys were where it's at. Forty years later I still think tall thin guys of any age are the hottest, and muscle queens are a total turnoff. In this I would imagine I am somewhat in the minority."

Grover, 59, Retired, South Dakota

"I kinda like a guy that's got some meat on him. I'm not looking for obese, but a bit of a beer belly goes nicely with big arms, a rugged jaw and large arms. I absolutely believe that a guy has a right to go with what he finds appealing. (I'm also all for guys that go for guys that have money, as long as they're up front about it. Rich ugly people need a good time too.)"

Darren, No Age Given, Lindenhurst, NY

"Don't want them too big, don't want them too small, give me a hot boy with a medium-sized build, a little jock-type maybe, someone I can wrap myself around in bed, and I will be in Heaven."

John, 27, Computer Professional, Seattle

What category describes you best?

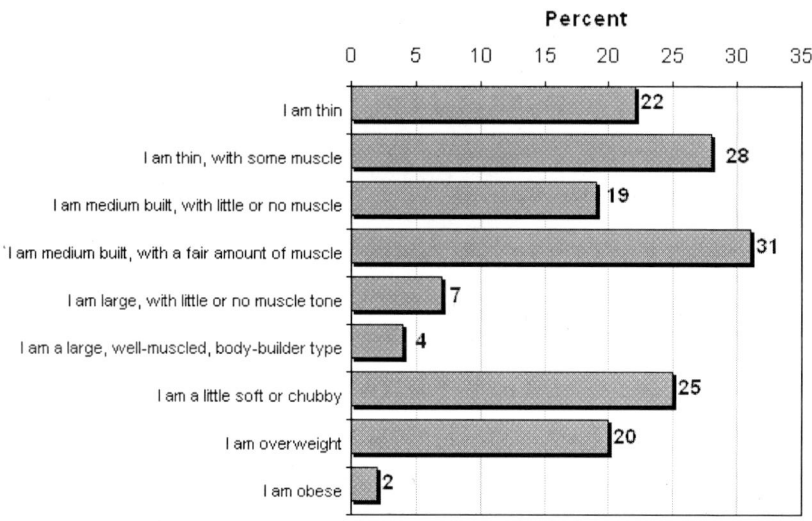

Yes, I know those response percentages add up to 158 percent; I suspect some people saw themselves as "overlapping" when it came to some of those categories and chose both. I would also note here something that I've encountered quite a bit in this book and in my own life, that many people simply do not have a realistic self-image. I talked with lots of guys, especially younger college-age guys, who'd been thin for most of their lives and still regarded themselves as such; they didn't seem to realize that they'd put on that famous "freshman 15" and were actually pretty chubby in their midsections. I also met men who were once fat but had started exercising seriously, and looked to me to be a great shape; I found that many of them were *still* seeing those pounds when they looked in the mirror, as if they were haunted by ghosts that only they could see.

True or False: I was fat once, then lost weight.

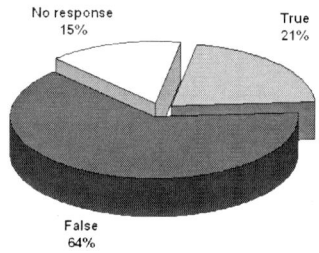

"I was a big fat turd. I worked my ass off to lose that fat. Now I hate it when I hear fat guys whine about being fat. Drop your cupcakes and get your ass in the gym."
Russell, 37, Office Worker, Des Moines, Iowa

"My weight and are lifelong foes. Right now I have the 'fat guy inside' on the run, but I know I can't stop and congratulate myself too long. He's always waiting around for me to slip back to my old lazy ways."
Larry, 43, Teacher, Long Island

"I'm not fat. I've never been fat. Can't imagine living life like that, especially as a gay man. I've seen how we treat fat guys, and it ain't pretty."
Brian, 27, Accountant, Tennessee

True or False: I was skinny once, then put on weight.

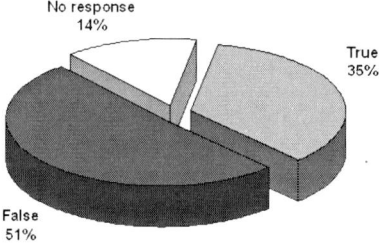

"Skinny as a rail, thin as a pencil, that was me in high school. Thank God my metabolism finally slowed down enough for the food to start sticking to me in my mid-20's. I know some people think thin is sexy, but I fucking hated being thin."

Tom, 30, Construction, Kansas

"I've been all over the map. Thin as a child, got chubby as a teen and twenty-year old, nearly obese when I was about 30, said 'fuck it' and started lifting weights and running. Now at 40 people tell me I look like a body-builder. I have a wall in my house with pictures of me from each of those eras in my life. The other night I had company, this woman from work who pointed to the wall and said 'Who are all these people?'"

Ronald, 40, writer, San Diego

"I was too skinny, now I am very muscular. It's much better on this side of the fence."

Steve, 39, Attorney, New York City

True or False: I like to see hot guys in advertising/magazines.

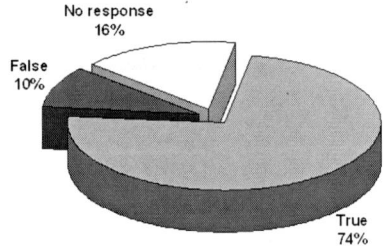

"Gay men in general are very stuck on image, and that's not necessarily a bad thing in and of itself. I mean, hey, we're a lot better looking as a whole than straight men. At least we care to take care of ourselves! Ads don't tell people how to look, but if some gay guys get inspiration to look better—and be healthier in terms of weight—then that's a good thing."

Max, 20, Student, Montreal

"I think they are nice to look at, but I also think we may have a bit too much of that stuff plastered around. Let's be real, there are fewer of us that look like that than are those that do. In some ways I'd say it might even be harmful, that it gives people an idea that they have to be 'perfect.' Who is to say that some men are not perfect in their ruggedness?"

Al, No Age Given, Interior Designer, Calgary, Alberta

"Ads are all about being hot and sexy. Hot and sexy sells. You sure wouldn't get any business with my ass up on a billboard."

Chris, 22, Retail, Upstate New York

True or False: Hot guys in ads make me feel bad about myself.

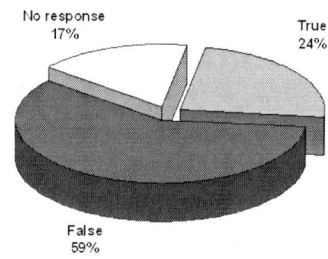

"I find them sexy and appealing. I never compare myself to them since I do not try to look like them."

Vasile, 42, Software Engineer, Alexandria, Virginia

"I don't understand the slick young hairless images, I don't find young guys very attractive, and they need to have more hair on them. But somehow those ads do make me feel inferior, and motivate me to work out harder. I think gay men, like all men, are visually oriented and beauty and fitness are paramount. And if those images make me—a moderately good-looking man—feel bad, I can't imagine how they make homely or fat men feel. It's probably pretty harmful."

Andrew, Law Student, No Age or Location Given

"We all have different bodies and the key is to take what we have and make the best of it. So by looking at magazine models, one guy who looks totally hot—that's well and good, but then I realize he is shorter than I and has a different body type. So I can admire him, but I cannot compare my body to his. But he can still motivate me to stay focused and keep the workouts fresh."

Howard, 40, Government Accountant, Alexandria, Virginia

True or False: The gay community is way too hung up on the way guys look.

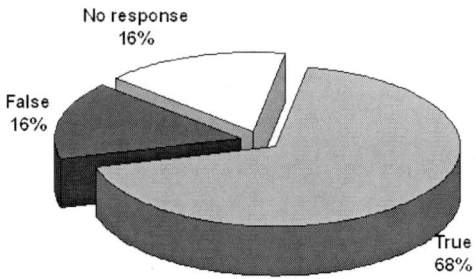

"The gay male is obsessed with beauty and youth, and we objectify and deify muscles and looks over all else. There is no way that brains will ever win out over beauty in today's gay culture."

Bill, No Age, Occupation, or Location Given

"Gay men are all about physical appearance, which is pretty harmful because we'll all get old, sick, and die. It is impossible to expect youth and physical beauty as a constant, from any living creature. Time is the gay man's worst enemy, and being that age is inevitable, our attitudes are extremely harmful and self destructive."

Chad, 23, Fashion Designer/Artist, New York City

"The gay community is more 'body fascist' than any other. The prissy skinny queens bitch if you carry an extra ounce, the gym bunnies look at you like you're something they've trod in if you are not toned at the least, the bears don't want to know you unless you're covered in thick fur, and the chubs and chasers demand you be at three stone overweight. And if like most men you're not a perfect example of one of their extreme stereotypes, you get ostracized."

H, 35, Records Manager, Amsterdam

True or False: I like guys who look like me.

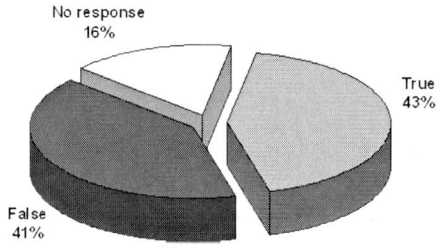

"I never really thought about it before, but I guess every one of my serious boyfriends over the last few years did look a lot me in some or most respects. I don't know if that makes me a narcissist, but that's the honest answer."

Stuart, 25, Musician, Georgia

"Why would I want to roll over and see myself lying there? Life is about making different parts fit together, not falling out of a cookie-cutter."

Dennis, 50, Physician, Eugene, Oregon

"I do tend to pick mates who resemble me somewhat. I don't usually think about it, but I have noticed it on one or two occasions."

Jeff, 43, Writer, Cincinnati

True or False: I like my friends to be good-looking.

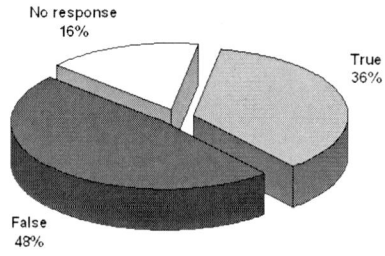

"When it comes to the guys that I go out to the bar or club with, I prefer a large group of attractive men. That way you get more attention. For close personal friends, it isn't much of a question . . . but if a guy was extremely good looking . . . well, it would be uncomfortable."
Jason, 27, Political Consultant, DC/LA

"I'll be honest. It's nice to have friends that are less-attractive than me, I shine better and people notice me a lot more. Just another evil queen, I guess."
Eric, 24, Student, New Hampshire

"It's nice to be around beautiful guys, sometimes it even makes me feel prettier, but I don't really give it much thought. A friend is a friend regardless of 'beauty'."
Jon, 41, Realtor, No Location Given

True or False: I do not exercise.

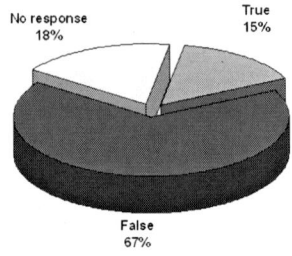

True or False: I exercise, but don't belong to any gym.

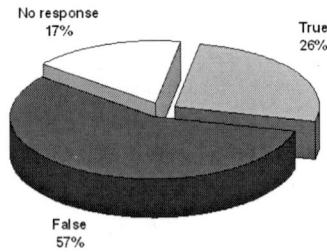

True or False: I go to a gym to work out.

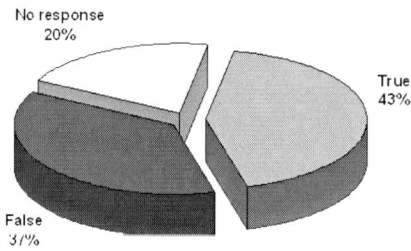

True or False: I go to a gym to check out other guys.

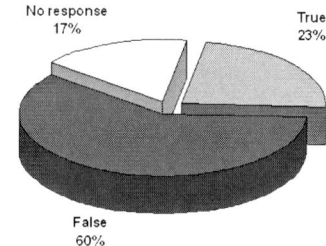

True or False: I go to a gym to work out, and to check out other guys.

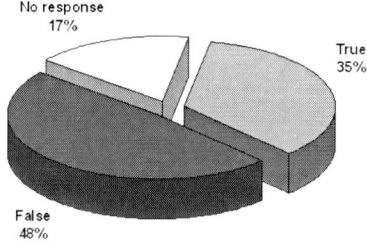

"Working out is like a way of life for me, almost an addiction. I get depressed if I miss one workout, and a panic attack if I miss more than that. Some people say I am way too obsessed, but a lot more are always telling me how much they would like to feel my chest and biceps. I listen more to that second group."

John, 26, Model, Hawaii

"Hate the gym, hate the guys who go to gyms, hate the whole body Nazi gay culture thing. If you're not already naturally muscular, then you're not supposed to be."

Fred, 37, Librarian, Minneapolis

"My gym is so 'cruisy' that I'm waiting for them to put up a big disco ball, and pay a half-naked 'shooter' boy to walk around between the free weights and machines. (That's actually not a bad idea.) Seriously, if you're gay in this town you don't have to go out at night . . . all the action is here already."

Josh, 28, Starving Actor, West Hollywood

"I'm not very muscular, but I love muscular men. I like to watch them undress and take showers and steam baths. I spend more time in the locker room than I do working out. I don't like to sweat."

George, 60, Retired, Fort Lauderdale, Florida

True or False: I like the way I look.

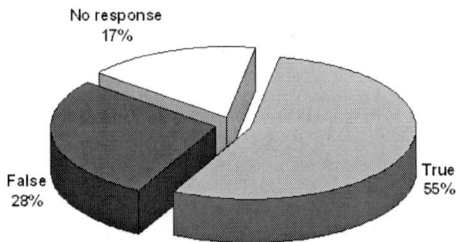

"I am very fortunate, I suppose, in that I've grown into my looks as I've gotten older. I feel bad for those who bloomed or blossomed too early, and don't know how to deal with others now that all their petals have fallen off."

Frank, 47, Travel Agent, Orlando

"I find I am constantly questioning myself on everything I eat. Whenever I take a shower I find myself looking at my reflection and saying to myself 'you're fat you need to look better.' I find that I fall into a negative cycle about how I look, which then affects the way I feel."
Anthony, 18, Student, Australia

"I started off medium with some muscle and now I am extra large and a little soft and chubby. I don't care what other people think. I like myself better this way."
John, 44, Computer Specialist, Washington

True or False: I have been rejected solely because of my physical appearance.

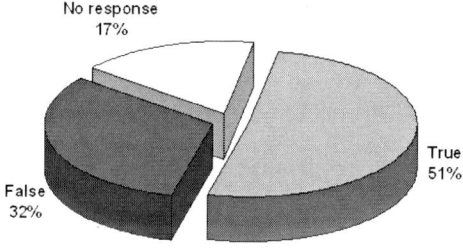

"Is there anyone out there who hasn't been rejected? No one is everybody's type."
Charlie, 31, Artist, Provincetown, Massachusetts

"I only felt rejected by the muscular type of men that I was most attracted too, before I started working out and becoming muscular myself. Now those same types of men are hitting on me."
Chase, 40, Horse Trainer, No Location Given

"Sometimes guys have said they don't fancy me, and I take it in stride. I treat others as I'd like to be treated myself, I've taken a lot of blows in life and it's taken all my life to gain the self-acceptance I should have always had. I love who and what I represent, I don't need others to justify my desirability. Different strokes for different folks!"
Andrew, 33, Unemployed, London

True or False: I have rejected someone else, solely because of his physical appearance.

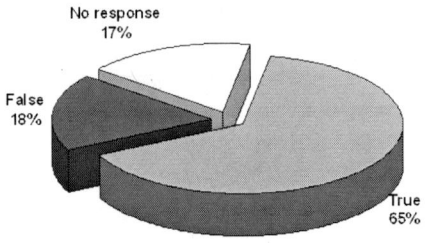

"I've never rejected anyone socially because of appearance, but I have had to decline when offered one-night stands or dates. I view every offer as a compliment, though, whether coming from a really hot guy or a true troll. No one can help what they are or aren't attracted to."
Scott, 35, Sales, Baltimore

"I consider myself to be the ultimate diplomat in life. I can turn someone else away and make them feel very good about it. People often say that I should run for President!"
Anonymous

"One night I was getting hit on by this nasty old fat man who just didn't seem to be getting the message. Finally he went away and started in on someone else, this super hot guy I'd been checking out for an hour. They left together, don't ask me how he did it. But that has always bothered me for some reason, and I'm not sure why."
Billy, 24, Student, Tempe, Arizona

True or False: I have been treated well, socially and otherwise, because of how I look.

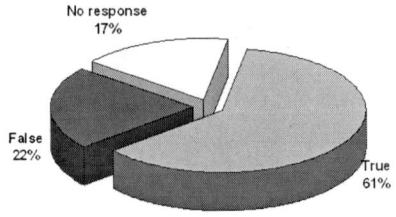

"Usually just when I'm out at the clubs. I get in free, and people buy me drinks, give me their phone numbers, etc. It's nice to feel wanted."
Davey, 19, Student, Vancouver, British Columbia

"In my younger days it happened constantly, I was quite the looker back then. Even today I will find myself getting stared at occasionally, and my partner of 30 years will shoot me an elbow or a withering glance."
Glenn, 60, Retired, Palm Springs, California

"People have always treated me well, but I don't really know how much of that is based on how I look. I'm told I am very attractive, but I don't take it that seriously. Of course that may be just something that's easy for me to say, simply because I am attractive. If I am. This is a hard question."
Jake, 30, Flight Attendant, Atlanta

True or False: I have been treated badly, socially and otherwise, because of how I look.

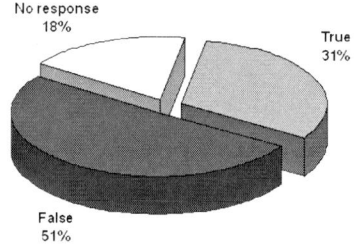

"It happens all the time. Gay men are pigs like that, you can't get the time of day from them if you're not someone they'd like to get in bed with them."
Leon, 38, Dentist, Akron, Ohio

"I'm older, and I'm fatter than most guys want. So I am either the butt of their jokes, or I am simply ignored, usually the latter. Can't tell you which is worse."
Neal, 51, Office Manager, Harrisburg, Pennsylvania

"I used to be good-looking, before an accident left me with several ugly scars on my face. Now I know how guys who've been ugly all their lives feel, and it fucking sucks."

Drew, 27, Grad Student, New Jersey

True or False: I've gotten a fake or misleading picture from someone on the Internet.

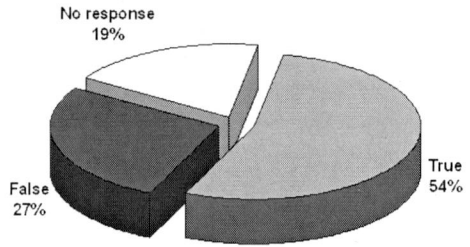

"More times than I probably realize, I'm way too trusting of people. I don't even want to think about all the ugly old men who've lied to me just so they could see my naked pictures and get their rocks off. But at least some people are still honest."

Steven, 21, Student, Illinois

"He swore to me his pics were the real deal, and said I wouldn't be sorry when I met him at the hotel. Boy was he wrong, on both counts."

Devin, 30, Mechanic, Nashville

"Ugh! So many people send pics that are three or four-years old and their bodies have become way fatter than the pic they sent. Fortunately I've been in a relationship for the past 5 years so haven't had to deal with this."

Dave, 34, Personal Trainer, Washington, DC

True or False: I've sent other people fake or misleading pictures.

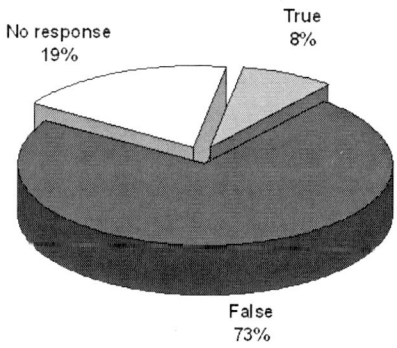

"Look, it's not something I do all the time, and it's not like I'm ever going to hook up with someone I trade pictures with. I just like looking at cute boys, and no cute boy would ever send me his pics if he knew who he was really talking to."

Identity Withheld

"It really is me in that picture. It's just not up to date. I had more hair then, and I was in much better shape. I am still the same man inside, doesn't that count for something?"

Rick, 49, Professor, Midwest

Afterword

Letters. I get letters. Not so much of the actual paper and ink variety—though I do still get those on occasion—they are usually the electronic kind: e-mails sent to my various Internet accounts, or long messages left on my Web site at www.timbergling.com.

Usually when someone bothers to write me it's because the person really liked—or really *didn't* like—something I've written in one of my books, or perhaps in some piece I've penned for the *Washington Blade, The Advocate,* or some other gay publication. Sometimes the contacts have seen something I've posted on my current Web site and feel compelled to give me a holler, or they might be one of the few lingering fans of that old webcam site I used to have a few years back. The vast majority of the contacts are extremely positive, and it's humbling to hear someone tell me that I managed to touch them somehow with my meager peck-peck-peckings on this keyboard. A middle-aged mother wrote me once to explain how reading *Sissyphobia* helped her get a little bit closer to her flamboyant teenage son; an *Advocate* piece I wrote on gay veterans of World War II had several such vets—and many of their family members—thanking me for remembering them and their service. (No thanks necessary there, gentlemen. I think we all need to be thanking *you*.)

Even when someone is taking me to task for something, most times their messages are respectful, or at least restrained. Commentaries I've written for the *Blade*—on everything from pornography, to coming out and staying out, to oxymoronic gay Republicans—have generated more than a few indignant Letters to the Editor, and the writers thereof usually copy me via e-mail, so that I won't miss out on one syllable of their indignity. But again, politeness and civility usually reign. (Even when a *Republican* is calling me a son-of-a-bitch, for instance, he usually does it with style and a certain degree of panache.)

So imagine my surprise when the following e-bomb detonated in my mailbox a year or so ago, from someone who said he was surfing the Net one day and stumbled upon my presence. (I've cleaned up his numerous typos and somewhat mangled diction best I can, and I edited out some extraneous asides that frankly made no sense, but overall I think his meaning will be very clear.)

"Guy, I am totally awed by you," he starts off promisingly enough, before hurtling over the cliff and into the abyss. "And not by your pics, your books, or your profile . . . I am awed by your self-centeredness and self-perpetuating idea that you are some gift to men and we all should be worshipping you for your body and your books."

He goes on. "What is it with gay guys like you? You preach about being one of the good guys yet you're exactly the type of guy that gives gay men a bad name. You're a wolf in sheep's clothing, only I have learned to spot those types a mile away. You honestly think you're a better guy than most don't you? Why else would you promote yourself the way you do? You're so full of yourself I am surprised you ever need to shit."

Certainly after reading up to this point of his e-mail I *was* feeling the need, but he was just warming up. "Your profile is a riot and your websites are just hysterical. I know why you're single, you're way over 40, and you're so self-centered and vain that it's going to be hard to find someone who would actually put up with you. Then there is the fact that 'like attracts like,' and so most likely you're looking for someone similar to yourself, but therein lies the paradox. That person will end up being as shallow and vain as you, and it won't work. You need to pause for a moment and realize that there is more to life than money, looks, fame, whatever. No wonder there was that debacle with the young guy you tried to have a relationship with.

"It's sad that you want to be accepted as professional, yet you feel the need to publish photos of yourself trying to act like a 25-year-old running around with his shirt off and bleached hair. Got news for ya, those years of your life are coming to an end. Nice body or not, not many hot guys are looking to date or trick with a 50-something guy. Tick tock, tick tock. You might want to think about being a real person rather than a really hot or wealthy person. Besides, my friends and I make fun of guys like you trying to act 20 years younger. You're 44 and you're bleaching your hair? Oh my God, you're too much. I bet you wear A&F and American Eagle, and J-Crew too, no? Who are you, Norma Desmond? All the money or muscles in the world doesn't change who you are . . .

"Get a clue, guy, get a life, and get over yourself. There are more important things in the world than you writing about gay men's pursuit of Adonis, when you yourself are the exact type of guy that book should be written about. Maybe it makes you feel better about yourself, because it makes you feel above the common problems you write about, when in fact they stem from inside you. Normally I don't write emails like this but somewhere I came across your websites and I just can't believe guys like you are out there. It's flabbergasting, almost comical."

I think we can all be thankful this fellow doesn't "normally" write many e-mails—God help anyone *else* he aims to savage—but believe it or not I was actually rather pleased he wrote me this one, because he managed to touch on some themes I was thinking of kicking around in this closing section, themes my friend Greg Herren also touched on in his Foreword. This fellow knows me only through the words and images he's seen published or put up on the Web; as far as I know we have never met in person, and he knows none of my friends. Yet look at all the presumptions about me that he makes, most of them rather false and far off the mark. I am not rich, for one. Nor am I materialistic; if I were I'd have tried to be a stockbroker or a lawyer or doctor or any one of a dozen fields where people can actually *make* money, as opposed to being a writer and television news producer barely getting by. I *will* plead guilty to owning lots of A&F and American Eagle clothing, mainly because it's relatively inexpensive—see "not rich" above—for some reason it fits me well in terms of personal style; and although I did bleach my hair for a few years back on the other side of the millennium, it made my scalp itch too much, so I stopped. (I kind of miss it though, and people's reactions to my "lemon head.") As far as being a "wolf in sheep's clothing," that one is really amusing, as I have never thought of myself as anything other than a wolf in *wolf's* clothing.

But take a moment or two and read back over that e-mail; note the ageist asides, with six separate references in one paragraph alone. There's his belief that one can't be a "professional" and have a good build *and* dare to show it off, along with his attempt to buttress his opinions by linking himself to a group which supposedly *all* feels the same way about guys like me. There's also a clear intent to personally wound me—when he mentions my ex-boyfriend Andy, my apparently limited romantic prospects, or compares me to Norma Desmond of *Sunset Boulevard* fame—and constant allusions to my vanity, self-centeredness, shallowness, and my alleged requirement to be worshipped. Then there's his stated supposition that one can't be a "real" person if one is really hot or wealthy, neither of which describes me anyway. (Jesus, if only!)

Where do you suppose all this is coming from? Clearly my unhappy little e-bomber has so many issues with this own lack of self-esteem that he has to project, pulling the pin on each of his smoldering insecurities then lobbing them at me like hand grenades. But the main reason I've brought you his two-page cry for help isn't just to remind you of the loonies loose in the world; crazy or not, and however he overstates his case, he actually provides a pretty good example of how some people react when they see someone who's even moderately attractive, or someone that even they have to begrudgingly admit is "hot." (Especially when that "hot" person is presenting himself in a bold and confident manner.) Instead of allowing themselves to feel attraction, admiration, or just a positive motivation to improve themselves, they feel rage, or envy, or scorn. An older guy who appears youthful? He's pathetic, kidding himself; he needs to act his age. A well-muscled or attractive guy? He's vain, shallow, self-centered, or brainless. In their worldview, he *must* be; the idea that someone who's hot on the outside might also be intelligent and a worthwhile person *on the inside* is too much for their fragile egos to bear. So they strike out, belittle, make assumptions, and send severely worded e-mails, "not recognizing or understanding," as Greg Herren so thoughtfully writes in the Foreword, "that such attacks tell more about the attacker than the subject."

My e-bomb thrower does make one interesting observation, however, that part about when it comes to writing a book like *Chasing Adonis,* I am "the exact type of guy that book should be written about." (You don't think he meant to let slip a compliment in there, do you?) Inasmuch as this book *was* targeted at men who are fascinated by the concepts of beauty and desire—whether they see themselves as beautiful and desirable or not—then yes, this book is about me, just as it is about most other gay men, whether they are young or old, thin, medium, or chubby, or colored in shades of chocolate, caramel, or vanilla.

Whether we like it or not, men in general—and gay men in particular—are drawn to what it is they find beautiful, for whatever reason they find it so. As Greg writes, "There are no specific rules of attraction. People are attracted to what they are attracted to, whether it's smooth young boys with slim bodies, guys with huge muscles, Bears, daddies, whatever." I wasn't born beautiful, or even moderately good-looking, but through a lot of hard work, a bit of luck—and the occasional, strategic use of good lighting—I've managed to create a reasonable facsimile of what some people might find a passable handsomeness, one that's most likely equal parts physicality and personality. I happened to be a skinny gay kid with bad acne and glasses who decided he didn't want to be that kid anymore and decided to change the way he looked. But that's just my story, and it's not much different from tales told to me by countless other gay men as well, men who didn't like being skinny, or fat, or having crooked teeth or a nose that was too big or oddly shaped, and took some steps to remake themselves. As we've already seen that transformation wasn't always enough to make them *completely* content, but the overwhelming majority of men were still happy they made the change.

I'm certainly glad I did, but just like several of the men we heard from earlier, even now I'm occasionally haunted by the memories of what it felt like to be excluded from the club because of the way I looked; sometimes it really *does* feel like there's a sign posted outside our little gay amusement parks, a notice which reads "You must be THIS hot to take this ride," and nowhere in the fine print does it say anything about how smart or witty you are. As someone who often wonders how it is he found his way inside the gates and still feels like an imposter from time to time, I have nothing but compassion for those who feel left out or marginalized.

Reading back over my e-bomber's message, the idea that I think I'm a "better guy than most" is laughable, especially on those days when I look in my mirror and can't help but notice my thinning and graying hair and my eyes going all crinkly with the passing years; truth be told, I hear that "tick tock, tick tock" my correspondent warns me about; he doesn't have to remind me that the clock is moving on. Any trip out to a gay club these days is a vastly humbling experience, as I note the sheer tonnage of beautiful and sexy men of all ages, guys whose faces and bodies far outshine the wattage I'm able to generate, or was *ever* able to generate, for that matter. But trust me, I'm not complaining. For whatever reason, I've had more than my share of attention in my time, and strangely enough, more attention these days than ever. Is that going to last forever? Of course not; even now I may be near or at the top of the proverbial hill, ready to start that long slow trip down the other side, but that's really just fine with me. We get two choices in life—get older, or die—and the former seems infinitely more attractive than the latter. I can only hope I do it gracefully, without surrendering to bitterness and attacking those who are better-looking or more confident than I am or was.

Reading back through all the survey and interview responses, I find lots of plaintive—and often bitter—words from gay men who worry that, since they never were, nor ever will be, a 9, 8, or even a 7 on most people's sexy scale of 1 to 10, this big gay parade of ours is passing them by. I can only hope they read the words of those men who happily testify how their idea of true beauty falls far outside that which the predominant imagery we see in magazines and newspapers might say is "hot." I hope they pay attention to the tales of men who tell me that although no one would ever mistake *them* for anyone's male model, they've managed to live rather worthwhile and fulfilled lives, surrounded by friends and lovers who have appreciated them for everything they are, inside and out.

There are men that I've spoken with—too many, really—who seem convinced that a perfect smile or body will unlock every door that leads to happiness; in that, they are much like those poor folks who are absolutely convinced that if they just had a little more money, virtually all of their troubles would disappear. Yet I would hope that such men will take to heart the stories of those who *are* considered beautiful yet worry constantly that their good looks will be held against them, that they will be dismissed as mindless pretty boys or shallow playthings. There's that famous quote attributed to Gertrude Stein—"I've been rich and I've been poor; rich is better"—and just like anyone with money, few of the good-looking men I've interviewed or surveyed would trade away what they have. In this gay world we live in, it is beauty that is often the coin of the realm, and having it is "better" than not having it. The cute guys know that. Still that doesn't mean they get a free ride. An easier ride, sometimes, sure. But not free.

As with my two previous books, researching and writing *Chasing Adonis* was something of a revelation for me. When I set about putting *Sissyphobia* together I suspected I would find some hostility and bewilderment aimed at effeminate men; indeed, that was part of the inspiration for writing it. But I didn't realize how *deeply* those feelings ran or the reasons behind them until I started my research. Similarly, it wasn't exactly breaking new ground to talk about the tension that often exists between younger and older gay men in *Reeling in the Years*; generations have clashed since time immemorial. But getting into the heads of younger and older gay men, to see what they *really* believe and say about each other, to tell the stories of underage gay kids and gay senior citizens, and the guys sort of stuck in the middle, that was a wild journey through time, literally.

Chasing Adonis was a different sort of trip, but no less revelatory. I tried to be as upfront and honest about my own concepts of beauty, so as to make it clear at all times where I was coming from—I hope my own stories and personal histories didn't strike you as indulgent—but how wonderful and eye-opening it was to find so many other men who approach beauty and desire from totally different places and perspectives, who have so many stories of their own, and have differing ideas about why they find some men desirable and others not so.

Like many men you've heard from here I'm a big fan of our so-called "prevailing imagery"—the kind you see in A&F and Calvin Klein ads, and most of the illustrations and photo layouts you find in the mainstream gay mags—and I'm not ashamed to confess my admiration for all those smooth, young, and muscular bodies; such images have often helped me get off my ass from time to time and hit the gym, not so much because I've felt any pressure to keep up, but because they're a gentle reminder that with a bit of effort I can have the same sort of build, one I've come to enjoy having. It wasn't a surprise to find out how many others disagreed with that entire mind-set—truly there is a fine line to be walked between maintaining a healthy physique and succumbing to "body fascism"—but the vehemence and intensity of those with other viewpoints was still a little shocking, if nonetheless informative.

I'm thankful this book gave me a chance to walk among those men I might not otherwise have ever spent much time with; I'm not *physically* attracted to Bears or the girth and mirth fellows, but I have to tell you that of all of the people I surveyed and interviewed, I never found people more personally engaging than those great big large-hearted guys. Their sheer gregariousness and sense of inclusion would be a welcome addition to the rest of the gay community, if only such an attitude transplant were possible. How often I heard gay men lament that the men they found most physically attractive were sometimes lacking in simple human warmth, or the ability to connect one-on-one without keeping an eye on the door for the next guy to walk in, someone who might be just a little bit hotter. That's not meant to grant any legitimacy to the whines of those who claim that all "pretty boys" or "muscle queens" are more self-centered or vain than the rest of us; combing over all the responses and stories of the past two years, I think it's fair to say we're *all* a bit like rivers and oceans, with unsuspected depths, uncharted shallows and shoals, possessed of sudden and dangerously shifting currents and undertows.

How else does one explain how gay men looking to achieve a "healthy" physique would choose some of the unhealthiest methods to get it? What about those tales of unhappy men, constantly rejected for the way they look or for being too old or too young for the men they were chasing after, who find themselves rejecting *other* men on the same rationale? What accounts for men who meet other men, set up a date or an intimate rendezvous, then find reasons not to show up, bail out at the first opportunity, or turn out to be someone entirely false in his representations? What other explanation can you find for otherwise sensible or reasonable fellows who throw their good sense to the wind and pursue men who simply aren't interested, or may be unattainable for a variety of reasons? One of the counselors I talked with confessed his belief that, when it gets down to it, "we're all just a little bit crazy, in one way or another." Not a surprising verdict, especially for the millions of gay men who've been forced to deal with bigotry, hazing, abuse, or getting marginalized from near-infancy, sometimes within the bosom of what should be a nurturing home environment. Honest to God, I don't know how any of us get through it all, with any of our sanity intact. But when you throw desire into the mix . . . well, that's when things can get volatile, and very unpredictable. Desire is a terrible seductress, after all. It can take more strength than many of us possess to keep her in check sometimes; some guys just can't handle their own, or being the object of someone else's, wants and needs.

Little wonder then that so many men live out their most erotic desires safely within the realm of their fantasy lives, and in this book's longest section it was utterly fascinating to take a look behind the curtain and see how those fantasies play out. I had no idea that my early "straight-boy fixation" was nearly as widespread, really almost universal, as it turned out to be, at least among the people I interviewed and surveyed. (I also wonder how many of the self-avowed straight men who cater to the desires of gay guys are actually as straight as they claim to be, but that's a question only they can answer.) There may be thousands, or even millions, of gay men out there who don't have anything close to a positive opinion about pornography, erotic Internet sites, strip clubs, and the like, but those men in large part didn't participate in my surveys. I'll have to leave it to you, the reader, to look at your own tastes and experiences to figure out where you stand, and how harshly you might choose to judge those who *do* indulge themselves with their "dream lover" of choice.

It's fitting that I find this journey ending in the same season it began for me; as I write these words, spring is abroad in the land and the sap is quite definitely running. A few days ago the temperatures crossed the 80-degree threshold for the first time in more than six months, and following as they did a particularly long and cold East Coast winter, those temperatures made for some stirring visuals; everywhere you look there are younger and older men, gay and straight, small, medium, and large, doffing their cold-weather gear in favor of loose-buttoned shirts and shorts . . . tank tops and T-shirts once again rule the day. The gyms are filled with the "oh shit, I have to get back in shape" crowd, and the running paths and biking trails are likewise packed with folks enjoying the feel of sun and wind on naked skin, as they puff and grind the miles out under their tires, or their tired feet.

I find myself moved to return to those same playing fields where my "impending fagdom" made its first appearance more than 30 years ago. When I get there I discover I'm not the only one who's undergone a transformation in that time; with the 1960s baby boom over, my old elementary school was apparently converted ages ago to a strange compendium of library and local police substation. There are still green and grassy places where children play, but the kids kicking a soccer ball here today are far fewer in number and less organized than my old PE class was. Truth is, I hardly recognize the place, and I don't linger very long; I can only imagine what would happen if some cop approached me, asking what I'm doing here. I don't think he'd care much for the honest—if somewhat misleading—answer: "I saw some really cute and shirtless 12-year-olds playing ball around here once, and I was thinking about them today."

I decide to take a quick drive around my old hometown. There's the house I lived in when I discovered the "quality time" a teenage boy can have all on his own, with the help of some lusty mental images. I spot a fit young lad of maybe 17 or 18 out mowing the lawn of a neighboring home; in his board shorts and wife-beater he's someone both the teenager I was and "middle-ager" I am could very much agree on, lusty-image-wise. Not too far away is the high school I went to, where I saw the first few guys who began to cement the image for me of what a male body should or could be; on this day and hour it appears deserted, but that's okay . . . I remember well enough what went on inside those walls, all the good *and* the bad.

Here I find the old apartment complex—and apartment pool—where I met Billy and took several huge steps down the road to where I am now. Today there's a group of kids gathered near the same steps where I poured my heart out to him; as they scream and shout and ride their skateboards in the parking lot it's a curious thought to wonder how many of those youngsters, if any, might be looking at their own best friends the way I once did. It's all very familiar yet strangely alien to me now. I imagine any gay man taking the same physical journey down memory lane experiences pretty much the same thing. We grow so far away from our hometowns, and they change a lot after we're gone . . . but parts of them always stay inside of us, unchanging.

So I guess it is with the making and remaking of our physical selves, the first people we meet who help shape what it is we find attractive, and the echoes of them we perceive—or don't perceive—in everyone that follows after. We carry a lot of where we're from with us, and many of us do tend to return and return again to the familiar—or run like hell from anything that reminds us of it—as we chase after our internal and external goals. For some that chase is over, at least for the time being; they're happy with who they are, and maybe even happy with the man they've landed. But many of us still seem to be looking restlessly, hoping upon hope that with springtime's return our Adonis will be waiting for us just around the next bend, and that if he is, we might be someone he'd find equally compelling.

"I've had lovers I thought were 'perfect' for me at first, then they turned out not to be," one man wrote to me in an e-mail just a few days ago. "I've had lovers that I settled for, because I got tired of waiting, and that didn't work out so well, either . . . I think it's time I stopped focusing so much on them, and try to work out my own issues. I let myself go, put on some weight, and I need to figure out why then do something about it. Trust me, I don't think being in shape will solve all my self-esteem problems, but it might make my problems easier to solve. I don't think having a healthy outlook on life guarantees that I will find the man of my dreams, but it will damn sure make it easier to hold on to him when and if I find him. Whatever happens I just want to get to a place where I like myself again. Wish me luck!"

I do, man. It's something I wish for us all.

References

"10 Reasons Gays Chase Straights" (2003). *The Advocate,* August 19, pp. 49-52.
Alvear, Michael (2000). "The Man Who Made Gays Macho." *Salon,* April.
Alvear, Michael (2003). *Men Are Pigs But We Love Bacon: Not-So-Straight Answers from America's Most Outrageous Gay Sex Columnist.* New York: Kensington.
Alvear, Michael (2003). "Sex and Love and Men." *The Washington Blade,* July 11, p. 40.
Bergling, Tim (1998). "The Impossible Dream." *HERO,* p. 18.
Bergling, Tim (1999). "A&F Attraction." *HERO,* pp. 18-19.
Bergling, Tim (2001a). "I'll Be Watching You." *Instinct Magazine,* April, p. 31.
Bergling, Tim (2001b). *Sissyphobia: Gay Men and Effeminate Behavior.* Binghamton, NY: Harrington Park Press.
Bergling, Tim (2004). *Reeling in the Years: Gay Men's Perspectives on Age and Ageism.* Binghamton, NY: Harrington Park Press.
Bianchi, Tom (1991). *Out of the Studio.* New York: St. Martin's Press.
Bianchi, Tom (1995). *In Defense of Beauty.* New York: Crown.
Bianchi, Tom (2002/2004). *On the Couch,* Volumes 1 and 2. Berlin: Bruno Gmunder.
"Bitch Session" (2003a). *The Washington Blade,* October 31, p. E-3.
"Bitch Session" (2003b). *The Washington Blade,* December 5, p. E-3.
"Bitch Session" (2004a). *The Washington Blade,* February 6, p. E-3.
"Bitch Session" (2004b). *The Washington Blade,* April 16, p. E-3.
Bronski, Michael (1998). *The Pleasure Principle: Sex, Backlash, and the Struggle for Gay Freedom.* New York: St. Martin's.
Crea, Joel (2004). "New Study Finds Rampant Drug Use Among Gay Men." *The Washington Blade,* January 9, p. 1.
Hamer, Dean (2004). *The God Gene: How Faith Is Harwired into Our Genes.* New York: Doubleday.
Hamer, Dean and Peter Copeland (1999). *Living with Our Genes: Why They Matter More Than You Think.* New York: Anchor.
Harris, Daniel (1997). *The Rise and Fall of Gay Culture.* New York: Hyperion.
Lemon, Brendan (2003). "Letter from the Editor." *Out,* July, p. 19.
Lemon, Brendan (2004). "Letter from the Editor." *Out,* October, p. 31.
Perry, Joel (2004a). "Man to Man." *Instinct,* September, p. 92.
Perry, Joel (2004b). "Man to Man." *Instinct,* October, p. 94.

Rice, Christopher (2005). "Monogamy and Me." *The Advocate,* March 29, p. 72.
Signorile, Michelangelo (1997). *Life Outside.* New York: HarperCollins.
U.S. Drug Enforcement Administration (2004). "Anabolic Steroids: Hidden Dangers." Available online at www.deadiversion.usdoj.gov/pubs/brochures/steroids/hidden/index.html.
U.S. Office of National Drug Control Policy (2006). Steroid Fact Sheet. Available online at www.whitehousedrugpolicy.gov/drugfact/steroids/index.html.

Order a copy of this book with this form or online at:
http://www.haworthpress.com/store/product.asp?sku=5745

CHASING ADONIS
Gay Men and the Pursuit of Perfection

_____ in hardbound at $44.95 (ISBN-13: 978-1-56023-508-8; ISBN-10: 1-56023-508-X)

_____ in softbound at $16.95 (ISBN-13: 978-1-56023-509-5; ISBN-10: 1-56023-509-8)

278 pages • Includes illustrations

Or order online and use special offer code HEC25 in the shopping cart.

COST OF BOOKS_____	☐ **BILL ME LATER:** (Bill-me option is good on US/Canada/Mexico orders only; not good to jobbers, wholesalers, or subscription agencies.)
POSTAGE & HANDLING_____ (US: $4.00 for first book & $1.50 for each additional book) (Outside US: $5.00 for first book & $2.00 for each additional book)	☐ Check here if billing address is different from shipping address and attach purchase order and billing address information. Signature_____
SUBTOTAL_____	☐ **PAYMENT ENCLOSED:** $_____
IN CANADA: ADD 6% GST_____	☐ **PLEASE CHARGE TO MY CREDIT CARD.**
STATE TAX_____ (NJ, NY, OH, MN, CA, IL, IN, PA, & SD residents, *add appropriate local sales tax*)	☐ Visa ☐ MasterCard ☐ AmEx ☐ Discover ☐ Diner's Club ☐ Eurocard ☐ JCB Account #_____
FINAL TOTAL_____ (If paying in Canadian funds, convert using the current exchange rate, UNESCO coupons welcome)	Exp. Date_____ Signature_____

Prices in US dollars and subject to change without notice.

NAME_____
INSTITUTION_____
ADDRESS_____
CITY_____
STATE/ZIP_____
COUNTRY_____ COUNTY (NY residents only)_____
TEL_____ FAX_____
E-MAIL_____

May we use your e-mail address for confirmations and other types of information? ☐ Yes ☐ No
We appreciate receiving your e-mail address and fax number. Haworth would like to e-mail or fax special discount offers to you, as a preferred customer. **We will never share, rent, or exchange your e-mail address or fax number.** We regard such actions as an invasion of your privacy.

Order From Your Local Bookstore or Directly From
The Haworth Press, Inc.
10 Alice Street, Binghamton, New York 13904-1580 • USA
TELEPHONE: 1-800-HAWORTH (1-800-429-6784) / Outside US/Canada: (607) 722-5857
FAX: 1-800-895-0582 / Outside US/Canada: (607) 771-0012
E-mail to: orders@haworthpress.com

For orders outside US and Canada, you may wish to order through your local
sales representative, distributor, or bookseller.
For information, see http://haworthpress.com/distributors

(Discounts are available for individual orders in US and Canada only, not booksellers/distributors.)

PLEASE PHOTOCOPY THIS FORM FOR YOUR PERSONAL USE.
http://www.HaworthPress.com   BOF07